PAY AND ORGANIZATION DEVELOPMENT

7

LAWLER, Edward E. Pay and organization development. Addison-Wesley, 1981. 253p ill (Addison-Wesley series on organization development) bibl 80-28620. 7.50 pa ISBN 0-201-03990-7. CIP
Lawler's organizational behavior book examines the role that compensation systems play in organizational development. The systems approach, the conceptual material, and many of the examples used come from the research and consulting work of the author. The basic thesis is that the pay system used affects organizational effectiveness directly. Spefific pay plans such as gain sharing, skill-based pay, employee-determined pay, and flexible benefits are examined. Because pay accounts for from 40 to 70 percent of all costs it is a major expense to any organization. Over one half of employees are dissatisfied with their pay. How people are paid affects their absenteeism, productivity, and quality of work. Because pay systems are institutionalized, they are difficult to change. This is a major contribution to a neglected area of organizational behavior. Graduate and upper-division undergraduate levels.

PAY AND ORGANIZATION DEVELOPMENT

EDWARD E. LAWLER, III
*University of Southern California
and University of Michigan*

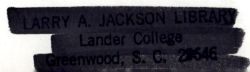

Addison-Wesley Publishing Company
Reading, Massachusetts • Menlo Park, California
London • Amsterdam • Don Mills, Ontario • Sydney

This book is in the Addison-Wesley series:

ORGANIZATION DEVELOPMENT

Editors:
Edgar H. Schein
Richard Beckhard

Library of Congress Cataloging in Publication Data

Lawler, Edward E
  Pay and organization development.

  (Addison-Wesley series on organization development)
  1. Compensation management.   2. Organizational change.
I. Title.
HF5549.5.C67L38   658.3'2   80-28620
ISBN 0-201-03990-7

ISBN 0-201-03990-7
ABCDEFGHIJ-DO-8987654321

To Patty for her support, love, and beauty

FOREWORD

It has been seven years since the Addison-Wesley series on organization development published the books by Roeber, Galbraith, and Steele, and it is almost twelve years since the series itself was launched in an effort to define the then-emerging field of organization development. Almost from its inception the series enjoyed a great success and helped to define what was then only a budding field of inquiry. Much has happened in the last twelve years. There are now dozens of textbooks and readers on OD; research results are beginning to accumulate on what kinds of OD approaches have what effects; educational programs on planned change and OD are growing; and there are regional, national, and even international associations of practitioners of planned change and OD. All of these trends suggest that this area of practice has taken hold and found an important niche for itself in the applied social sciences and that its intellectual underpinnings are increasingly solidifying.

One of the most important trends we have observed in the last five years is the connecting of the field of planned change and OD to the mainstream of organization theory, organizational psychology, and organizational sociology. Although the field has its roots primarily in these underlying disciplines, it is only in recent years that basic textbooks in "organization behavior" have begun routinely referring to organization development as an applied area that students and managers alike must be aware of.

The editors of this series have attempted to keep an open mind on the question of when the series has fulfilled its function and should be allowed to die. The series should be kept alive only as long as new areas of knowledge and practice central to organization development are emerging. During the last few years, several such areas have been defined, leading to the decision to continue the series.

On the applied side, it is clear that information is a basic nutrient for any kind of valid change process. Hence, a book on data gathering, surveys, and feedback methods is very timely. Nadler has done an especially important service in this area in focusing on the variety of methods which can be used in gathering information and feeding it back to clients. The book is eclectic in its approach, reflecting the fact that there are many ways to gather information, many kinds to be gathered, and many approaches to the feedback process to reflect the particular goals of the change program.

Team building and the appropriate use of groups continues to be a second key ingredient of most change programs. So far no single book in the field has dealt explicitly enough with this important process. Dyer's approach will help the manager to diagnose when to use and not use groups and, most important, how to carry out team building when that kind of intervention is appropriate.

One of the most important new developments in the area of planned change is the conceptualizing of how to work with large systems to initiate and sustain change over time. The key to this success is "transition management," a stage or process frequently referred to in change theories, but never explored systematically from both a theoretical and practical point of view. Beckhard and Harris present a model which will help the manager to think about this crucial area. In addition, they provide a set of diagnostic and action tools which will enable the change manager in large systems to get a concrete handle on transition management.

The area of organization design has grown in importance as organizations have become more complex. Davis and Lawrence provide a concise and definitive analysis of that particularly elusive organization design—the matrix organization—and elucidate clearly its forms, functions, and modes of operation.

Problems of organization design and organization development are especially important in the rapidly growing form of organization known as the "multinational." Heenan and Perlmutter have worked in a variety of such organizations and review some fascinating cases as well as provide relevant theory for how to think about the design and development of such vastly more complex systems.

As organizations become more complex, managers need help in diagnosing what is going on both internally and externally. Most OD books put a heavy emphasis on diagnosing, but few have provided workable schemes for the manager to think through the multiple diagnostic issues which face him or her. Kotter has presented a simple and workable model that can lead the manager through a systematic diagnostic process while revealing the inherent complexity of organizations and the multiple interdependencies that exist within them.

Human resource planning and career development has become an increasingly important element in the total planning of organization improvement programs. Schein's book provides a broad overview of this field from the points of view of the individual and the total life cycle, the interaction between the career and other aspects of life such as the family, and the manager attempting to design a total human resource planning and development system.

The study of human resources in organizations has revealed the variety of new life-styles and value patterns which employees of today display, forcing organizations to rethink carefully how they structure work and what they consider to be "normal" work patterns. Cohen and Gadon provide an excellent review of various alternate work patterns that have sprung up in the last decade and are revolutionizing the whole concept of a normal work week.

One of the most significant ways to develop organizations is to redesign the work itself. It has been widely recognized that a key to improving life in organizations is to find ways of making work meaningful and challenging. Hackman and Oldham have spent a decade developing ways of analyzing work situations and developing diagnostic tools and guidelines for work redesign, which are presented in concise form in their book for this series.

Finally, and most significantly, there is a growing connection between the "classical" problem of personnel—the reward and pay system—and the more recent structural and process interventions illustrated in the series. We are most fortunate to have been able to add the analysis of pay systems by Edward E. Lawler to the series. He is one of the real leaders in research and theory in this area, and his book adds a dimension to the series which is most important.

With the addition of the Lawler book we feel we have filled an important gap and now have a well rounded and well balanced series to introduce students and managers alike to the field of organization development.

Edgar H. Schein

PREFACE

My research interest in pay dates back to 1961. At that time I was a graduate student in Organizational Psychology at the University of California. Mason Haire and Lyman W. Porter, my major advisors, pointed out that pay was a very important area in which little research was being done. Recognizing the wisdom of their advice, I began a decade-long, basic-research program on the behavioral impact of pay. It was a productive and exciting period in my life.

During this period my work was influenced by my experiences at Berkeley and by a number of the outstanding colleagues whom I worked with in the Administrative Sciences Department of Yale University. This period of my research life came to an end with the publication in 1971 of my book *Pay and Organizational Effectiveness.* It summarized the behavioral research on pay and presented my theoretical views.

The next step in my research on pay seemed obvious to me. I needed to "test out" much of the basic research and theory I had been working on. Chris Argyris and others convinced me that the best way to advance my understanding of the role of pay in organizations was to actually implement and evaluate theory driven-pay systems. There was only one problem: I could find few organizations that were interested in change and innovation in the area of pay and reward systems. As a result, my research interest in pay was put aside and I started doing work on job design, information and control systems, and quality of work life. I then wrote a book on motivation. Slowly, however, things started to change. I began to get calls from organizations which had started organization development efforts by focusing on job enrichment, new plant designs, or team building. They found that their organization development efforts had raised important pay issues, and they were looking for "innovative" solutions to these problems.

Often I was called into organizations by the organization development people to help them convince the pay administration people that change was needed. On other occasions, I was invited by the compensation people to help them deal with the pressures the organization development people produced. Gradually, I found myself again doing pay research, but this time it was action research. This book is an account of what I have learned from that research.

Much of the work reported in this book was done while I was a program director at the Institute for Social Research of the University of Michigan. Like many before, I found it a very favorable place to do research. During my stay there I was blessed with bright and supportive colleagues and graduate students. At the risk of offending others, I would particularly like to mention Corty Cammann, Stan Seashore, G. Douglas Jenkins, Jack Drexler, David Nadler, Jeff Kane, R. J. Bullock, Phil Mirvis, and Mark Fichman. Finally, I was fortunate enough to have a fine support staff. Sue Campbell and Gary Herline provided able assistance for many years, and Carole Stone did an outstanding job of helping me prepare this book.

I was fortunate to receive financial support and intellectual guidance in my work from a diverse set of people outside the Institute for Social Research. Help in obtaining federal funding came from Richard Shore and Bob Foster. Ray Olsen, Mike Simmons, Myron Nunes, Franz Stone, Dick Kaufman, Selig Danzig, John Hillins, Gino Strippoli, Clyde Wills, Bob Stevenson, Lyman Randall, and a host of other
managers provided financial support and helped me work with their organizations.

Finally, helpful comments on an earlier version of this book were provided by J. R. Hackman, a special friend and person, Tom Patten, whose comments I valued but often did not heed, and Ed Schein.

Los Angeles, California   E. E. L. III
January 1981

CONTENTS

1
REASONS FOR PAY AND
ORGANIZATION DEVELOPMENT

A number of plants in the United States pay employees bonuses based on the performance of the plant. TRW, Dana, and Midland-Ross are among the corporations that have encouraged their plants to adopt performance bonus plans because they feel it can lead to the development of greater organizational effectiveness. In a number of other plants employees are paid based on the number of jobs they can do, rather than on the basis of the job they are doing. Furthermore, in some plants it is the employees who decide whether other employees have learned a job well enough to be paid more. Although it seems to cost more to pay people for skills than to pay them for the jobs they do, and although it seems risky to allow employees to determine each other's pay, there is evidence that these practices can increase organizational effectiveness.

The top executives of one medium-sized corporation meet annually to determine their bonuses. They are all familiar with each other's pay and performance so they feel it is only "natural" that they should meet as a group to decide how much of a bonus each of them should receive. When asked to evaluate this open approach to pay, they responded that they think it leads to better decision making and to greater organizational effectiveness.

As these examples illustrate, interesting innovation can take place in the ways people are paid for the work they perform. This innovation is part of a continuing search by organizations for better approaches to administering pay. Basic to this book and to the search for the right pay system is the belief that how people are paid has a direct impact on organizational effectiveness. Few doubt the validity of this belief, but widely divergent views exist about what the most effective system is. Beliefs, myths, opinions, and counteropinions abound in the literature on organizations concerning how much people should be paid and what methods should be used to pay them. Probably no other topic concerned with the management of work organizations is a subject of more debate, controversy, and misunderstanding. The reasons for this are not hard to identify. Pay is an important cost item for organizations. There has been little research on how it affects organizational effectiveness, and it is a highly emotional issue for many individuals. It is precisely because it is an emotional issue that generally accepted precise answers, based on rigid formulations and data, are so difficult to obtain.

The literature concerning the practice of organization development is strangely silent with respect to pay and its role in organization development efforts. Books, articles, and conferences on organization development often have little or nothing to say about what role, if any, pay should play in efforts to improve organizational effectiveness. At first glance, it seems hard to explain why such an important feature of organizations does not receive more attention. After all, pay has the potential to impact on organizational effectiveness and can play an important role in determining behavior. As such, it would seem to be a strong candidate for attention in most, if not all, organization development efforts.

There is no single explanation for why pay has been so frequently ignored in the field of organization development. It is the result of a number of circumstances. The major reason seems to be that part of the pay administration process is a highly technical one that requires considerable expertise, just like engineering, accounting, or marketing. Organization development practitioners rarely have this expertise and, as a result, can feel rather inadequate and have trouble holding their own in discussing pay issues with technical experts.

A second reason why pay is so frequently ignored in organization development efforts is structural in nature. In some organizations, responsibility for pay administration is not given to the personnel department. Even in those organizations which assign the prime responsibility for pay administration to the personnel department, organization development practitioners typically are in a different part of the department. As a result, organization development practitioners are often cut off from information and chances to influence pay policy and pay decisions. Often, their only contact with the individuals who have responsibility for the pay system occurs when the organization development practitioners come to the pay administrators to ask that a pay policy or practice be changed because it is interfering with one of their OD projects.

Finally, the value orientation of many organization development practitioners helps account for the low priority given pay. The organization development movement has always had a humanistic flavor. Pay and pay decisions emphasize the nonhumanistic aspects of work organizations. They are a critical part of the more materialistic reasons for people working, and at least partially relate to the satisfaction of the lower-level needs of individuals. The result is that many people who have gone into organization development because of its attention to humanistic values find discussions and work on pay to be counter to their basic interests and values.

Despite the existence of many "good" reasons for *not* becoming involved in pay and pay administration, in most cases it is a mistake for organization development not to be concerned with pay and its administration in organizations. There are a number of reasons why pay can and should play a vital role in most, if not all, organization development efforts. They stem from the nature of pay and its central role in organizations. It is worth reviewing the reasons briefly, since they serve both as a justification for the argument that pay should have an important role in organization development efforts, and as an introduction to pay and its impact on organizational effectiveness.

PAY CAN INFLUENCE ORGANIZATIONAL EFFECTIVENESS

As previously stated, pay can influence those behaviors which determine organizational effectiveness. How people are paid affects their absenteeism, productivity, and the quality of work they do (Lawler 1971). The strength of its influence is shown by a recent review of the research literature on productivity (Locke 1979). Four methods frequently used to improve productivity were compared. Pay incentives yielded the highest median increase: 30 percent; goal setting yielded 18 percent; job enrichment, 17 percent; and participation, only 0.5 percent. Given this, it is hardly surprising that companies like TRW are encouraging their plants to install bonus plans.

PAY IS AN IMPORTANT COST

In most organizations payroll costs are a significant portion of the organization's total cost of doing business. It is not uncommon, for example, to find that in manufacturing organizations, payroll costs run as high as 40 percent, and that in service organizations, they run well over 70 percent. This means that pay administration is an issue that is considered by top management, as well as accounting, financial, and production managers. In short, it is an issue that is considered by virtually all of the crucial decision makers in most organizations. This means that any effort that affects pay is likely to be taken seriously by the crucial decision makers in an organization. They recognize that it is a large investment, and that anything that can be done to improve the return they are getting on this investment can have a substantial impact on financial results. Because of this, programs that involve pay usually get high priority and are taken seriously.

PAY IS A PROBLEM

Study after study has shown that in most organizations 50 percent or more of the people in the organization are dissatisfied with their pay. There is also evidence that dissatisfaction with pay is increasing. In 1973, 48 percent of a representative national sample of people agreed that they received "good" pay and fringe benefits; by 1977, the percentage had declined to 34 percent (Quinn and Staines 1979). One implication of this is that pay is a hurt in most organizations, and is therefore an often expressed symptom when managers ask for organization development help.

When pay dissatisfaction is expressed, one approach is to point out that it is symptomatic of more serious underlying problems which must be dealt with first. This approach, however, is limited and risky since it is likely to be rejected, and to lead to the person who presents it losing credibility. Also, it is often wrong since there typically are both pay system problems *and* more serious underlying problems. An alternative, and a potentially effective strategy, is to accept the fact that people are dissatisfied with their pay, and to include needed changes in the pay system as part of an overall change strategy. In short, because pay is often a source of dissatisfaction and problems, it is an excellent entry point for an organization development effort. As will be discussed further in Chapter 12, pay can be both an entry point for an organization development effort and a factor that is considered in later efforts. In the case of the company mentioned earlier in which the executives met to decide each other's bonuses, it was clearly a factor that was dealt with later. This approach to administering pay seemed natural only because it followed several years of team development. Just the opposite is true in many plants that pay individuals for the skills they have. This approach to pay is useful in creating a climate of personal growth and in encouraging people to become broadly knowledgeable about how the organization operates.

PAY IS IMPORTANT TO INDIVIDUALS

Research on individual behavior in organizations has shown that pay is one of the most important job factors to people. Because it is important to most people, pay has the power to influence their membership behavior and their performance. As will be discussed further in Chapter 2, how important pay is, the reasons it is important, and how people respond to it vary considerably from person to person. Nevertheless, since most people are influenced by it, it is an important determinant of behavior.

PAY POLICY AND PAY PRACTICE ARE MALLEABLE

Although there are some constraints on how pay can be administered in most work organizations (legal and financial constraints exist), there are a number of options open to organizations. Because so many individuals are dissatisfied with their pay, organizations are often quite open to changing their pay systems. Some have even pointed out that in many organizations the only constant in pay administration is change. As will be discussed in more detail in Chapters 3 through 9,

options for change exist in both the mechanics of pay system administration and the process of pay administration. Falling into the mechanics area is an almost infinite array of different approaches to paying people. Literally thousands of different approaches to merit and
bonus pay exist along with a wide array of approaches to establishing
base pay and tying that to job worth. There are also numerous options
as to the form in which money can be paid to employees. These range
from hundreds of different kinds of benefits to strictly cash.

In regard to the process of pay administration, there are many
choices that need to be made about who is going to participate in decision making, and what kind of information is going to be communi-
cated. Current practice ranges from almost total secrecy and top-
down decision making through complete openness and decision
making at the production employee level. These radically different
approaches to the process of pay administration can have significant
effects on pay administration effectiveness, as well as on the overall
climate of the organization and its effectiveness.

It is precisely because both the mechanistic side and the process
side of pay have so many options that pay lends itself to organization
development efforts. The many complex decisions which need to be
made can only be made well if a good decision process is used, and decision processes are something that most organization development
practitioners know a great deal about. In addition, many of the decisions involve choices among pay systems that will affect, either directly or indirectly, such traditional organization development concerns as climate, group process, and employee development.

PAY SYSTEMS AND INSTITUTIONALIZATION

Pay systems in most organizations tend to be institutionalized through
written records, policies, and procedures. Because of this, they can be
difficult to change, which represents a problem in many organizational change efforts. On the other hand, once a pay system *is*
changed and institutionalized as a result of an organization development effort, it can represent a tremendous positive. One of the common issues in most organization development efforts is that of institutionalization. Time after time, programs which are based simply on

changes in managerial style or team development fade because of a lack of institutionalized structures and support for them (Walton 1975). Although this is a risk in pay system changes, the risk is often lower because of the formalized nature of most pay systems in organizations. Thus it would seem that organization development efforts that have pay as an important factor are particularly likely to be stable and long lasting in their impact if they produce positive results.

PAY AND SYSTEM-WIDE CHANGE

For better or worse, many organizations administer pay in a similar way across all their parts. This has an important implication for the potential impact of pay on a total organization. It means that an organization development effort that is tied in with a pay system change has a high probability of impacting on the total organization. This can be a particularly attractive feature when large organizations are being considered. Unfortunately, many of the traditional interventions that organization development specialists use impact on only small groups of employees. Pay system changes do not have this limitation; they can produce organization-wide change.

PAY IS VISIBLE AND TANGIBLE

Although some parts of most pay administration programs in organizations are secret, many parts of them are public and visible to everyone in the organization. In addition, because pay systems deal with a quantifiable hard substance—money—they have a certain reality to them. When a person's pay changes or when a pay policy changes in a way that results in a different set of pay rates in the organization, an individual can see, touch, and feel a real difference. Thus a change effort that is responsible for pay changes has a certain concreteness and reality to it that many organization development efforts lack. All too often, they end up dealing only with soft variables such as people's attitudes, interpersonal styles, and so on. As a result, the cynics and the doubters say they are not attacking anything important and they are not really making any difference. When pay system change takes place, this argument is hard to sustain.

PAY IS A SYSTEMIC FACTOR

Perhaps the single most important reason for focusing on pay in organization development efforts is its systemic nature. Throughout much of the remainder of this book, the focus will be on how pay relates to other aspects of organizations. Chapter 10 is totally devoted to considering what constitutes congruence between the pay system and other aspects of organizations. At this point, it is sufficient to say that pay systems in organizations are closely linked to the following major aspects of organizations: superior-subordinate relationships, job design, organizational structure, organizational climate, management training and development, information and control systems, performance appraisal, and management philosophy or style. In some cases, there is a link because input from these systems is needed in order to administer pay (e.g., performance appraisal and information and control systems). In other cases, the link is due to the influence another aspect has on how pay is administered (e.g., superior-subordinate relationships). In still other cases, there is a link because the condition of these factors strongly influences how pay should be and can be administered (e.g., organization and its structure).

Because pay is linked to many other factors, it is a potentially good place to begin a change effort, and it is a factor which must be considered in most change efforts. As will be discussed in more detail in Chapter 12, change efforts that begin with pay almost inevitably lead to a host of other issues when they are successful. Similarly, organization development efforts that begin in other areas almost always end up having strong implications for the pay system. Failure to deal with these implications can cause serious problems for the development effort.

REWARD SYSTEM INFLUENCE ON CHANGE EFFORTS

Reward systems can and often do have an influence on the effectiveness of organizational change efforts. When the impact of a change program on the reward system is not taken into account, the reward system can become an important impediment to individuals accepting the change. On the other hand, when the reward system is considered and made part of the change strategy, it can make a positive contribution to a change effort (see Chapter 12). It is precisely because of the systemic nature of organizations that almost any change effort has important implications for the reward system. If its implications are favorable in the eyes of individuals, then acceptance of the change can be high. On the other hand, if they are negative, strong resistance will occur.

The relationship between organizational change and rewards is clearly illustrated by the pay issues that are raised by job enrichment projects and management reorganizations. In job enrichment projects, job duties are redefined in a way that can lead to more meaningful jobs, increased pay, and better chances for promotion. As such, job enrichment may be sought by individuals. However, if the job changes that occur do not result in increased pay, or a skill-based pay system like the one mentioned at the beginning of this chapter, dissatisfaction may occur, and much of the positive effect of the job enrichment program negated. In the case of a reorganization, the pay system may play a big role in causing some people to oppose it. In almost all reorganizations, some people lose subordinates and responsibilities, and this may mean they should also be paid at a lower rate according to the organization's job evaluation system. Given this condition, they can be expected to resist the reorganization.

SUMMARY AND CONCLUSIONS

Despite the fact that pay is rarely considered in organization development efforts, a strong case can be made for including it. Among the factors that argue for its inclusion are: its importance as both a cost factor and a potential motivator of behavior, its systemic ties to important variables in the organization, its potential for impacting on the total organization, and its malleability with respect to both process and mechanics. Basic to an understanding of the impact of pay in organizations and to using it in organization development efforts is an understanding of how it influences individual behavior in organizations. Thus, in Chapter 2, we will consider what is known about the determinants of individual behavior in organizations.

In the remainder of the book, the focus will be on pointing out what options are available in the area of pay system practice and process, and on trying to point out when these options should be taken.

Because a sound system for determining total compensation is the basic building block of any pay system, we will begin our dicussion of pay and organization development by considering total compensation. Chapters 3 through 5 focus on the many process and mechanistic options that are available for determining the type and amount of total compensation that an individual receives.

As we have already seen, pay can be an important motivator of performance; however, in many instances it is not. The reason is simple: it is not administered in a way that clearly relates it to performance. There are many reasons why it is difficult to relate pay to performance and many approaches to accomplishing this. Because the issues involved in performance-based pay are so crucial, they will be dealt with in considerable detail in Chapters 6 through 9.

As has been stressed, the pay system is only one of the many systems that operates in an organization; thus it is important to consider how it interfaces with the other systems. Chapter 10 does this in a general way, while Chapters 11 and 12 consider the special issues involved in designing pay system change strategies in new and in established organizations. Chapter 13 concludes the book with a discussion of future trends in pay and organization development.

2
PAY AND BEHAVIOR IN ORGANIZATIONS

Organizations continually distribute rewards to their members, and among the most important are the financial rewards. Because they are important, they can have a significant, even dominant, effect on the attitudes and behaviors of employees. An understanding of the relationship between financial rewards and individual behavior is a crucial ingredient in understanding the role of pay in organizations. In this chapter, the research and theory on how rewards influence the attitudes and behaviors of individuals will be summarized, beginning with a look at what determines satisfaction. Next we will consider how satisfaction and reward practices influence membership behavior, and how rewards can affect motivation and performance. Finally, we will consider the effects of participation in decision making on decision quality and organizational change.

REWARD SYSTEMS AND SATISFACTION

A great deal of research has been done on what determines whether or not individuals are satisfied with the rewards they receive. This research has shown that satisfaction is a complex reaction to situations and is influenced by a number of factors. The research can be summarized in four conclusions:

1. *Satisfaction with a reward is a function of how much is received and how much the individual feels should be received.* Most theories of satisfaction stress that people's feelings of satisfaction are determined by a comparison between what they receive and what they feel they should receive or would like to receive (Locke 1976). As shown in Figure 2.1, three outcomes can result from this comparison: satisfaction, underreward, and overreward. When individuals receive less than they believe they should, they are dissatisfied; when they receive more than they believe they should, they tend to feel guilty and uncomfortable (Adams 1965).

Feelings of overreward seem to be easily reduced by individuals and are therefore very infrequent (surveys typically show less than 2 percent of employees in an organization feel overpaid). Feelings of overreward are usually reduced by individuals changing their perceptions of the situation so that they no longer feel overpaid. For example, they increase their perceptions of their worth and/or of the amount of pay others receive.

The same process of perceptual change does not seem to operate when people feel they are paid at too low a rate. That is, they do not adjust their perceptions so that they will be satisfied. Instead, they cling to their perceptions and to the feelings of dissatisfaction. Feelings of dissatisfaction can often be reduced only by an actual change in the objective situation—by higher pay or a new job (Lawler 1971). Thus, feelings of underpayment tend to be stable and difficult to eliminate, while feelings of overpayment are very transitory.

2. *People's feelings of satisfaction are influenced by comparisons with what happens to others.* A great deal of research has shown that people's feelings of satisfaction are very much influenced by what happens to others like themselves (Patchen 1961). People seem to compare what others do and what others receive with their own situations. These comparisons are made both inside and outside the organizations they work for, but are usually made with similar people. As a result of these comparisons, people reach conclusions about what rewards they should receive. When the overall comparison between their situations and those of others is favorable, people are satisfied. When the comparison is unfavorable, they are dissatisfied. Sometimes individuals differentiate between comparisons inside and comparisons outside the organization, such that they may be satisfied or dissatis-

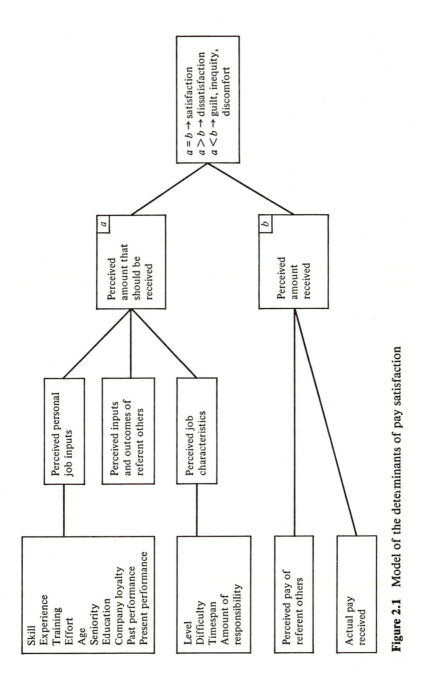

Figure 2.1 Model of the determinants of pay satisfaction

fied with their internal comparison and feel quite differently when it comes to their external comparisons. This is an important point since satisfaction with internal comparisons has different effects than satisfaction with external comparisons.

As shown in Figure 2.1, people consider such inputs as their education, training, seniority, job performance, and the nature of their jobs when they think about what their rewards should be. There are often substantial differences among people as to which inputs they think should be most important in determining their rewards. Typically, people believe that the inputs they excel in should be weighed most heavily (Lawler 1966). This, of course, means that it is very difficult to have everyone satisfied with their rewards, because people tend to make their comparisons based on what is most favorable to them.

Individuals also tend to rate their personal inputs higher than others rate them. It has often been noted, for example, that the average employee rates his or her job performance at the 80th percentile (Porter et al. 1975; Meyer 1975; Kane and Lawler 1979). Given this, and the fact that the average person cannot be rewarded at the 80th percentile (or for that matter, perform at the 80th percentile), it is not surprising that many individuals often are dissatisfied with their rewards. Still, it is possible for organizations to influence how satisfied employees are by altering the total amount of rewards they give and how those rewards are distributed. As will be discussed in Chapters 3, 4, and 5, some distribution patterns clearly are seen as more equitable and satisfying because they are more closely related to the inputs of individuals and, therefore, to what people feel they should receive.

It is because individuals make comparisons with what others receive that people who receive less of a given reward often are more satisfied with the amount of the reward they receive than are those who receive more (Lawler 1971). For example, people who are highly paid in comparison to others doing the same job often are more satisfied than are individuals who receive more for a different job, but are poorly paid in comparison to others doing the same kind of job.

3. *People often misperceive the rewards of others.* Considerable evidence exists that people often incorrectly perceive not only the skills, capabilities, and performance of others, but also the rewards others receive (see Lawler 1972 for a review). In many respects it is not surprising that people often misperceive such an important part of the world as how others perform and what they are paid. It is important

to them and is an emotional issue with direct consequences for their self-esteem. Considerable research on perception shows that misperception is particularly likely to occur when an individual's emotions are involved. In addition, organizations often do not provide accurate information to individuals so that they can base their perceptions on it. In most companies, individual salaries, the results of salary surveys, and the results of performance appraisals are kept secret. In fact, some companies go so far as to fire individuals who talk about these matters (Lawler 1977). Is it any wonder that misperceptions often develop?

There is some evidence which suggests that the kind of perceptual errors people make in perceiving the rewards of others contribute to dissatisfaction (see Lawler 1972). For example, it has been shown that individuals tend to overestimate the pay of others doing similar jobs, thus making their own pay look worse, in comparison, than it actually is. As was mentioned, they also tend to underestimate the performance of others, thus rating their own performance quite highly and as warranting high rewards.

4. *Overall job satisfaction is influenced by how satisfied employees are with both the intrinsic and extrinsic rewards they receive from their jobs.* A number of writers have debated the issue of whether extrinsic rewards are more important than intrinsic rewards in determining job satisfaction. No study has yet been done that definitely establishes one as more important than the other. Most studies show that both are very important and have a substantial impact on overall satisfaction (Quinn and Staines 1979; Lawler 1971; Vroom 1964). Also, it seems quite clear that extrinsic and intrinsic rewards are not directly substitutable for each other because they satisfy somewhat different needs. To have all their needs satisfied, most individuals must receive both the intrinsic and the extrinsic rewards they desire and feel they deserve. This means, for example, that money will not make up for a boring, repetitive job, just as an interesting job will not make up for low pay.

REWARD SYSTEMS AND MEMBERSHIP BEHAVIOR

There is a great deal of evidence showing that the rewards an organization offers directly influence the decisions people make about whether to join an organization, when and if to quit, and whether or not to come to work on a given day (Mobley et al. 1979; Porter and Steers 1973; Steers and Rhodes 1978). All other things being equal, individuals tend to gravitate toward and remain in those organizations that give the most desirable rewards. As will be explained next, this behavior occurs because high reward levels lead to high satisfaction which in turn is associated with low turnover. As will be discussed in later chapters, this point has important implications for where organizations should position their total compensation levels with respect to the marketplace. Some companies (e.g., IBM) intentionally position themselves at the high end in order to attract the best people. Others are unwilling to incur this cost and, as a result, are not able to attract job applicants to the same degree.

Turnover

Many studies have found that turnover is strongly related to job satisfaction and to satisfaction with the extrinsic rewards a person receives (Porter and Steers 1973). Apparently this is true because individuals who are presently satisfied with their jobs expect to continue to be satisfied and, as a result, want to stay with the same organization.

The relationship between turnover and organizational effectiveness is not so simple. It is often assumed that the lower the turnover rate, the more effective the organization is likely to be. This is a valid generalization because turnover is expensive. Studies that have actually computed the cost of it have found that it can cost an organization five or more times an employee's monthly salary to replace him or her (Macy and Mirvis 1976). However, not all turnover is harmful to organizational effectiveness. Organizations can certainly afford to lose some individuals and, indeed, may profit from losing them, either because they are poor performers or because they are easy to replace. In addition, if replacement costs are low, as they may be in unskilled jobs, it can be more cost effective to keep wages low and suffer with high turnover. Thus, turnover is a matter of rate, who turns over, and replacement cost.

The objective should be to design a reward system that is very effective at retaining the most valuable employees. To do this, a reward system must distribute rewards in a way that will lead the more valuable employees to feel satisfied when they compare their rewards with those received by individuals performing similar jobs in other organizations. The emphasis here is on *external* comparisons because turnover means leaving an organization for a better situation elsewhere. One way to accomplish this is to reward everyone at a level that is above the reward levels in other organizations. However, this strategy has two drawbacks. In the case of some rewards, such as money, it is very costly. Also, it can cause feelings of intraorganizational inequity because the better performers are likely to feel inequitably treated when they are rewarded at the same level as poor performers in the same organization, even though they are fairly treated in terms of external comparisons. Faced with this situation, the better performers may not quit, but they are likely to be dissatisfied, complain, look for internal transfers, and mistrust the organization.

What then is the best solution? The answer lies in having competitive reward levels and in basing rewards on performance. This should encourage the beter performers to be satisfied and to stay with the organization. However, it is important to note that not only must the better performers receive *more* rewards than the poor performers, they must also receive *significantly more* rewards because they feel they deserve more (Porter and Lawler 1968). Just rewarding them slightly more may do little else than make the better and poorer performers *equally* dissatisfied.

In summary, managing turnover means managing anticipated satisfaction. This depends on effectively relating rewards to performances, a task that is often difficult, as will be discussed next. When this cannot be done, all an organization can do is try to reward individuals at an above-average level. In situations where turnover is costly, this should be a cost-effective strategy, even if it involves giving out expensive rewards.

Absenteeism

Research has shown that absenteeism and satisfaction are related, although the relationship is not as strong as the one between satisfaction and turnover. When the workplace is pleasant and satisfying, individuals come to work regularly; when it isn't, they don't.

One way to reduce absenteeism is to administer pay in ways that maximize satisfaction. Several studies have also shown that absenteeism can be reduced by tying pay bonuses and other rewards to attendance (Lawler 1977). This approach is costly, but sometimes less costly than absenteeism (Lawler and Hackman 1969). It is a particularly useful strategy in situations where both the work content and the working conditions are poor and do not lend themselves to meaningful improvements. In situations where work content or conditions can be improved, such improvements are often the most effective and cost efficient way to deal with absenteeism (Hackman and Oldham 1980). Reward system policies are only one of several ways to influence absenteeism, but they are potentially effective if an organization is willing to tie important rewards with coming to work. In many ways this is easier to do than tying rewards to performance, because attendance is more measurable and visible.

PAY SYSTEMS AND MOTIVATION

When certain specifiable conditions exist, reward systems have been demonstrated to motivate performance (Lawler 1971; Locke 1979; Vroom 1964). What are those conditions? Important rewards must be perceived to be tied in a timely fashion to effective performance. In short, organizations get the kind of behavior that leads to the rewards their employees value. This occurs because people have their own needs and mental maps of what the world is like. They use these maps to choose those behaviors that lead to outcomes that satisfy their needs. Therefore they are inherently neither motivated nor unmotivated to perform effectively; performance motivation depends on the situation, how it is perceived, and the needs of people.

Expectancy Theory

The approach that can best help us understand how people develop and act on their mental maps is called expectancy theory. While the theory is complex at first view, it is in fact made up of a series of fairly straightforward observations about behavior. (The theory is presented in more technical terms in Appendix A, while Appendix B explains how it can be used to measure motivation.) Three concepts serve as the key building blocks of the theory:

1. *Performance-Outcome Expectancy.* Every behavior has associated with it, in an individual's mind, certain outcomes (rewards or punishments). In other words, individuals believe or expect that if they behave in a certain way, they will get certain things. Examples of expectancies can easily be described. Individuals may have an expec-

tancy that if they produce ten units, they will receive their normal hourly rate, while if they produce fifteen units, they will receive their hourly pay rate plus a bonus. Similarly, individuals may believe that certain levels of performance will lead to approval or disapproval from members of their work group or their supervisor. Each performance level can be seen as leading to a number of different kinds of outcomes, and outcomes can differ in their types.

2. *Attractiveness.* Each outcome has an attractiveness to a specific individual. Outcomes have different attractivenesses for different individuals. This is true because outcome values result from individual needs and perceptions, which differ because they reflect other factors in an individual's life. For example, some individuals may value an opportunity for promotion or advancement because of their needs for achievement or power, while others may not want to be promoted and leave their current work group because of needs for affiliation with others. Similarly, a fringe benefit, such as a pension plan, may have great value for older workers but little value for young employees on their first job.

3. *Effort-Performance Expectancy.* Each behavior also has associated with it, in an individual's mind, a certain expectancy or probability of success. This expectancy represents the individual's perception of how hard it will be to achieve such behavior and the probability of his or her successful achievement of that behavior. For example, employees may have a strong expectancy (e.g., ninety-ten) that if they put forth the effort, they can produce ten units an hour, but that they only have a fifty-fifty chance of producing fifteen units an hour if they try.

Putting these concepts together, it is possible to make a basic statement about motivation. In general, an individual's motivation to attempt to behave in a certain way is greatest when:

1. The individual believes that the behavior will lead to certain outcomes (performance-outcome expectancy).

2. The individual feels that these outcomes are attractive.

3. The individual believes that performance at a desired level is possible (effort-performance expectancy).

Given a number of alternative levels of behavior (ten, fifteen, or twenty units of production per hour, for example), an individual will choose the level of performance which has the greatest motivational force associated with it, as indicated by a combination of the relevant expectancies, outcomes, and values. In other words, when faced with choices about behavior, an individual goes through a process of considering questions such as: "Can I perform at that level if I try?" "If I perform at that level, what will happen?" and "How do I feel about those things that will happen?" The individual then decides to behave in a way that seems to have the best chance of producing positive, desired outcomes.

Expectancy Theory Model

On the basis of these concepts, it is possible to construct a general model of behavior in organizational settings (see Figure 2.2). Working from left to right in the model, motivation is seen as the force on an individual to expend effort. Motivation leads to an observed level of effort by the individual. Effort alone, however, is not enough. Performance results from a combination of the effort that an individual puts forth *and* the level of that individual's ability. Ability in turn reflects the individual's skills, training, information, and talents. Effort thus combines with ability to produce a given level of performance. As a result of performance, the individual attains certain outcomes. The model indicates this relationship in a dotted line, reflecting the fact that sometimes people perform but do not get outcomes. As this process of performance-reward occurs, time after time, the actual events serve to provide information that influences an individual's perceptions (particularly expectancies) and thus influences motivation in the future. This is shown in the model by the line connecting the performance outcome link with motivation.

Outcomes, or rewards, fall into two major categories. First, the individual obtains outcomes from the environment. When individuals perform at a given level, they can receive positive or negative outcomes from supervisors, co-workers, the organization's reward system, or other sources. A second type of outcome occurs purely from the performance of the task itself (e.g., feelings of accomplishment, personal worth, achievement, etc.). In a sense, individuals give these rewards to themselves when they feel they are deserved (Hackman and Oldham 1980). The environment cannot give them or take them away directly; it can only make them possible.

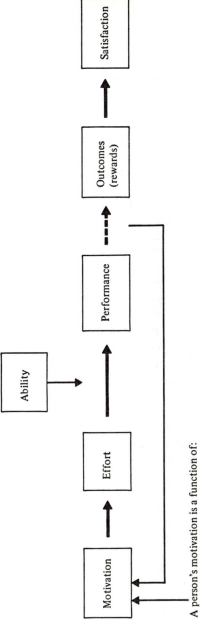

A person's motivation is a function of:

a. Effort-to-performance expectancies
b. Performance-to-outcome expectancies
c. Perceived attractiveness of outcomes

Figure 2.2   The expectancy theory model

The model also suggests that satisfaction is best thought of as a result of performance rather than as a cause of it. Strictly speaking, it does influence motivation in some ways. For instance, when it is perceived to come about as a result of performance, it can increase motivation because it strengthens people's beliefs about the consequences of performance. Also, it can lead to a decrease in the importance of certain outcomes, and as a result, decrease the motivation for those performances which are seen to lead to whatever reward becomes less important.

In many ways, the expectancy model is a deceptively simple statement of the conditions that must exist if rewards are to motivate performance. It is deceptive in the sense that it suggests all an organization has to do is actually relate pay and other frequently valued rewards to obtainable levels of performance. Not only is this *not* the only thing an organization has to do, but it is a very difficult task to accomplish (Tosi, House, and Dunnette 1972; Whyte 1955). As will be discussed further in Chapters 6 through 8, tying rewards to performance requires a good measure of performance, the ability to identify which rewards are important to particular individuals, and the ability to control the amount of rewards an individual receives. None of these things is easy to accomplish in most organizational settings—a fact that has led some to conclude that it is not worth trying to relate pay rewards to performance (Meyer 1975).

In addition to tying important rewards to performance, organizations must do so in a manner that will lead employees to believe the relationship exists. Just how infrequently this is done is highlighted by the results of a national survey of randomly selected, employed individuals. Only 27.2 percent of those surveyed said they were likely to get a bonus or pay increase if they did their job well (Quinn and Staines 1979), a rather startling figure for a society in which most employees are said to be on one form or another of merit pay.

In order for employees to believe that a performance-based pay relationship exists, the connection between performance and rewards must be visible, and a climate of trust and credibility must exist in the organization. The reason why visibility is necessary should be obvious; the importance of trust may be less so. The belief that performance will lead to rewards is essentially a prediction about the future. For individuals to make this kind of prediction they have to trust the system that is promising them the rewards. Unfortunately, it is not always clear how a climate of trust in the reward system can be established. However, as will be discussed in later chapters, research suggests that a high level of openness and the use of participation can contribute to trust in the pay system.

Another complexity in tying important rewards to performance stems from the differences in why rewards are important to individuals. There is nothing inherently valuable about many of the things that people seek in organizations. They are important only because they lead to other things or because of their symbolic value. A particular kind of desk or office, for example, is often seen as a reward because it is indicative of power and status. Pay is important because it leads to other things that are attractive, such as food, job security, and status. If money were to stop leading to some or all of these things, it would decrease in importance (Vroom 1964). Because pay typically leads to other rewards, it can satisfy many needs and be important to individuals for quite different reasons. This is one reason why pay is important to most people, even though it may be important to them for different reasons (Lawler 1971). It also means that in order to understand how an individual will respond to a particular pay action, it is important to understand both *how* important pay is to the individual and *why* it is important. Finally, because it leads to such rewards as status, pay can remain important when the material needs of individuals are satisfied. This is an important point because it refutes the often-made statement to the effect that once people's basic needs are satisfied pay is unimportant to them.

Importance of Rewards

Historically, one of the most frequently and hotly debated topics in organizational behavior concerns how important different rewards are to employees. One group of writers believes money is the most important, while another group thinks interesting work is of utmost importance (*Work In America* 1973). Both groups, of course, are able to find examples to support their points of view, because for some people money *is* most important, and for others, job content is most important. This confusion is compounded by the fact that some studies have found pay to be rated first in importance, while others have found it to be rated much lower (Lawler 1971). These differences seem to be accounted for by a variety of factors, including how the question is worded (e.g., *high* pay is rated lower than *fair* pay) and the characteristics of the people who are asked (e.g., their organization level and pay level).

People differ substantially, and in meaningful ways, in regard to what is important to them. Some groups, because of their background and present situations, value extrinsic rewards more than other groups. For example, one summary of the research on pay gave the following description of a person who is likely to value pay highly: "The employee is a male, young (probably in his twenties); he has low self-assurance and high neuroticism; he comes from a small town or farm background; he belongs to few clubs and social groups; he owns his own home or aspires to own it; and he probably is a Republican and a Protestant" (Lawler 1971). On the other hand, people with different personal and background characteristics typically value an interesting job more highly.

Also, the research on the importance of different rewards quite clearly shows that the amount of reward a person receives strongly influences the importance attached to it (Alderfer 1969). In the case of extrinsic rewards, for example, those individuals who receive a small amount of the reward typically value it the most. It also appears that the importance individuals attach to rewards shifts as they acquire and lose quantities of different rewards. Some evidence suggests that minimal amounts of the rewards that are required to maintain a person's physical well-being and security are needed before other rewards can become very important (cf. Cofer and Appley 1964; Wahba and Birdwell 1976).

Overall, the reward systems of organizations seem to have more influence on motivation than they have on the importance attached to specific rewards (Lawler 1971). Both motivation and importance can be influenced by the amount of rewards that organizations provide, and they are obviously related to each other since reward value influences motivation. But motivation seems to be much more susceptible to influence because expectancies are directly affected by how rewards are distributed. The importance of rewards, on the other hand, is strongly influenced by things that are beyond the control of organizations, such as family background and economic climate, as well as satisfaction.

PAY SYSTEMS AND PARTICIPATION

A considerable amount of research has been done on the effects of participation in decision making (see Vroom and Yetton 1973; Locke and Schweiger 1979). This research suggests that, under certain conditions, participation can lead to both better decision making and to more commitment in implementing these decisions. It also suggests: it is more time consuming to make decisions participatively; not everyone favors participative decision making; and people do not favor participative decision making with respect to certain decisions as much as they do to others. Table 2.1 presents the results of one study which observed how much influence a relatively well educated sample of the American work force thought they should have, and do have, over different workplace decisions (Renwick and Lawler 1978). Particularly relevant for our purposes are the data on pay decisions. It suggests that, in comparison to other areas of decision making, people do not want a great deal of influence, but they do want a great deal more than they presently have.

Very little of the research on participation has involved reward system decisions. Thus, the desirability of using participative decision making for reward system decisions is not clearly established. In fact, there is some reason to believe it is not a good idea. Some researchers have suggested that when an individual's self-interest is involved, he or she cannot be trusted to participate in decisions (Vroom and Yetton 1973). Clearly, when a pay plan is being designed, an individual's self-

Table 2.1
Average Response to Influence Questions (N = 2,300)*

| | Influence | | |
	Actually Have	Should Have	Difference (Should – Actual)
How to do own work	5.7	6.2	.5
Schedule own work	5.3	5.9	.6
Giving pay raises	2.1	3.8	1.7
Hiring people	2.6	3.7	1.1
Firing people	2.5	3.6	1.1
Promoting people	2.3	3.5	1.2
Making organizational policy	3.0	4.5	1.5

*On a scale of 1 to 7, 1 = no say, 7 = a great deal of say.

interest is involved; thus, caution is warranted with respect to decision quality. Quite the opposite is true with respect to acceptance of the decision. If anything, the fact that self-interest is involved would seem to make it more likely that whatever decision is made will be strongly supported since it will most likely fit with people's self-interests. Those studies that have looked at the effects of participation on pay decisions suggest that employees want it, and that it can produce high quality decisions and high acceptance of those decisions even though self-interest is involved (Lawler 1977). Apparently, under the right conditions, participation in pay decisions can lead to widely accepted decisions and to technically sound decisions.

As will be discussed further in Chapters 4 and 7, there is reason to believe that participation should occur more often than it typically does. In most organizations, reward systems are designed, implemented, and administered in a top-down authoritative manner. As a result, the acceptance level of reward systems is often low, and the design of the system often fails to take into account important information about the preferences and desires of those who fall under the system. Under certain conditions, participation in reward system decisions is an approach which will produce better understanding of the system, a better system, and a high commitment to implement it. Therefore, it is an approach that warrants consideration when an organization development effort is being undertaken. As will be discussed further in Chapters 10 through 12, how useful it is depends on a number of situational factors, as well as on whether pay system change will lag or lead other changes, and whether pay will be used to motivate particular approaches to implementing the change.

PAY AND ORGANIZATIONAL CHANGE

Pay systems can either facilitate or inhibit organizational change, although they should not automatically be assumed or counted on to do either. The expectancy theory model just presented can be helpful in understanding when pay systems will facilitate and when they will hinder change. According to the model, when they are perceived to reward change, they will encourage it, and when they are seen to punish change, they will discourage it. Individuals in organizations often perceive that they will be worse off under a new pay system than the old one, or that a major corporate reorganization will threaten their existing pay level. As a result, they resist the change. Under these conditions, it is hardly surprising that the pay system result is resistance to change; the model clearly predicts this. However, as will be discussed further in Chapter 12, the pay system does not have to be an impediment to change—it can be a stimulant. For example, when individuals are offered bonuses for successfully and rapidly implementing organizational changes, it can speed change; and when individuals perceive that a change will lead to a better pay system, change is encouraged.

SUMMARY AND CONCLUSIONS

Our review of the research on pay has shown that it can have an important influence on attitudes and behavior. The major relationships are as follows:

1. Satisfaction with rewards, such as pay, is a function of how much is received, how much others are perceived to receive, and perceptions of what should be received.

2. Satisfaction with rewards can influence overall job satisfaction as well as absenteeism, recruitment, and turnover.

3. Rewards will motivate whatever behavior is seen to lead to their reception if, and only if, they are important to the individual.

4. Under certain conditions, participation in pay decisions can lead to better decisions and to higher commitment to decisions.

5. Depending on how it is treated, the pay system can either be a positive or a negative force in organizational change efforts.

3
DETERMINING TOTAL COMPENSATION: STRATEGIC ISSUES

The financial rewards that employees receive from their organizations can, and typically do, come in a wide array of forms. Probably the most visible forms are cash compensation and such fringe benefits as vacation pay, health insurance, retirement pay, and life insurance. Some organizations, however, go far beyond such typical fringe benefits. For example, dental insurance is gaining in popularity, as are legal insurance, vision insurance, and supplementary unemployment insurance. When combined, the cash and fringe benefits that an individual receives from an organization constitute his or her total compensation.

The amount of an individual's total compensation is important for several reasons. From the organization's point of view, it is a major cost. Depending upon the type of organization, it may range from 10 percent of the organization's total operating costs to well over 50 percent. In addition to being a critical cost factor, the total compensation awarded an individual can have an important influence on his or her behavior. As was pointed out in Chapter 2, the total rewards an individual receives, when compared with what the individual feels he or she should receive, determine satisfaction. In turn, satisfaction strongly determines turnover and, to a lesser extent, absenteeism and tardiness. Thus the amount of an individual's total compensation can have an important impact on the individual's behavior with respect to organizational membership. It does not, however, directly affect the individual's motivation to perform. As will be discussed further in Chapters 6 through 9, motivation is a function of the degree to which pay is tied to performance and is only indirectly influenced by how much an individual receives in total compensaton.

From an individual's point of view, total compensation is an important determinant of lifestyle and of the kind of activities that one can engage in off the job. In addition, it can be an important determinant of social status and esteem in our society. To many people, compensation is more than just a given amount of money and benefits that can buy a certain set of goods and services; it means social respectability, power, and influence.

Determining what is an "appropriate" compensation level for an individual is an extremely important, difficult, and value-laden issue, as is determining the appropriate "mix" of benefits and cash compensation. Both of these issues involve sophisticated technologies and are fields of expertise in their own right. Salary surveys, for instance, are a critical factor in determining how an organization's pay levels compare to the outside world. Conducting an adequate salary survey requires a considerable amount of skill and the ability to use some fairly sophisticated survey and data analysis technologies.

The pay systems of most organizations rely on salary surveys and job evaluation plans to determine how different jobs should be paid within the organization, and how salaries in the organization compare to the outside market. It is hard to argue with this basic approach since it fits well with the model of satisfaction presented earlier (see Figure 2.1). There, it was pointed out that pay comparisons and job characteristics are crucial determinants of what individuals feel they should be paid. It seems only logical that any organization's pay system should be strongly influenced by these factors.

There are literally hundreds of different approaches to doing job evaluations and salary surveys. A full understanding of these is appropriately the subject of a book in its own right. In this chapter, no attempt will be made to review the strengths and weaknesses of the various technologies that are available to determine total compensation levels and compensation mixes. A number of excellent reviews of this material are available, and the reader can best obtain this information from them (see Henderson 1979; Patten 1977; Nash and Carroll 1975; Belcher 1974). Organization development practitioners who wish to deal with pay should review this material since they need a general knowledge of it if they are to be effective in influencing pay systems. It is the thesis of this book, however, that those interested in organization development should primarily concern themselves with the strategic and process issues that are involved in pay systems, since this is where their unique expertise can best be utilized.

At first glance, the strategic and process issues involved in determining total compensation may not seem to be as important as the technological ones. However, there is reason to believe that quite the opposite may be true. There are a number of reasonably good approaches to doing salary surveys and job evaluations available, and any one of a number of approaches can do an adequate job if the critical strategic and process issues are handled correctly. Unfortunately, they are often handled very poorly; and, as a result, systems which are mechanically and technically adequate fail to produce the desired employee behavior and reasonable compensation costs for organizations. In this chapter, we will focus on the strategic issues which are involved, while in the next chapter, we will focus on the process issues. In Chapter 5, some of the more innovative approaches to total compensation will be considered in more detail.

There are a number of strategic issues that are involved in establishing and managing a total compensation system. Nine of these issues will be identified, and alternative approaches considered.

DEVELOPMENT OF A COMPENSATION PHILOSOPHY

Many, but certainly not all, organizations develop a compensation philosophy. Having a compensation philosophy is not an absolute prerequisite to having an effective pay system but, in many cases, it can be a significant aid. Thus, an important strategic decision is whether to develop a compensation philosophy and, if the decision is made to develop one, what to include in it. In general, the best decision seems to be to develop one.

Having a well-developed compensation philosophy certainly does not guarantee an effective compensation system. However, it can help to articulate the purpose of the compensation system and give the people involved in the day-to-day administration of the system an anchor to which they can tie their decisions and practices. The latter is particularly important since it is very easy to lose sight of the purposes of a pay system when thousands of pay decisions have to be made day-to-day. A well-developed philosophy can also provide an important stability to the compensation practices of an organization. In turn, this can give the system the integrity and credibility that is so necessary if it is to be effective. For example, it is particularly difficult to get employees to accept the fact that their pay is based on their performance when this is not a consistently articulated matter of basic compensation philosophy. Another example of the advantages of well-developed philosophy is provided by what often happens in times of high inflation. Salaries typically do not keep up with inflation because organizations usually tie the amount of pay increases to changes in the compensation market rather than to inflation. This approach is always difficult for organizations to explain and justify, but it is easier when they have had a consistent well-articulated policy of meeting the market rather than meeting inflation. No generally accepted list exists of what should be included in an organization's compensation philosophy statement; however, the following list represents ten major issues that can, and in most cases should, be included:

1. *Goals of a Compensation System.* Pay systems should have a purpose. They represent a major expense and, as such, should produce some benefits. Possible benefits range from motivating performance to reinforcing a particular type of organizational climate.

2. *Communication Policy.* All organizations have communication policies concerning their pay systems. Careful thought needs to be given to them since they have a significant impact on the effectiveness of a compensation system.

3. *Decision-Making Approach to the Compensation Issue.* Pay decisions can be made in a number of different ways in organizations. As will be discussed throughout this book, it makes a difference how they are made, and this area needs to be part of any compensation philosophy.

4. *Desired Market Position.* The determination of whether an organization intends to be a high, low, or average payer needs to be made, and it needs to be made as part of an overall strategic business plan that looks at what the organization is trying to accomplish and how it intends to accomplish it. In some cases, it probably makes sense for organizations to be high payers; in others, it does not. In any case, what is needed is a clear-cut statement of what is supposed to be accomplished and the role of compensation levels in accomplishing it. A good example of what can be said in this area is provided by IBM. For years they have stated that they intend to employ the best available people by being the highest paying firm in their industry. In contrast, another computer firm states that it wants to attract and retain qualified people by paying wages that compete with those paid by all others in their industry, except IBM.

5. *Centralization and Decentralization in Compensation Policy Formation and Administration.* Large multi-location, multi-business organizations face some very interesting issues in the area of centralization and decentralization. As will be discussed later, there are a multitude of possible strategies, but whichever one is chosen, it helps if a clearly stated philosophy exists.

6. *Desired Mix Between Benefits and Cash.* Organizations vary widely in how they allocate their compensation costs between cash and benefits. There is no right answer, except that it often helps if an organization makes its strategy known.

7. *Role of Performance-Based Pay.* In the government, performance-based pay traditionally has not existed, while in industry it is often claimed to exist. It is important that its existence be part of the compensation philosophy if it is to have its desired effect.

8. *Performance Appraisal.* As will be discussed further in Chapter 8, most organizations do performance appraisal, but it often is unclear why they do them and what they are supposed to consist of. This confusion can be lessened if it is dealt with effectively in a compensation philosophy.

9. *Fit of Compensation System with Management Philosophy of an Organization.* Compensation systems can help reinforce and operationalize the overall management philosophy of an organization. For example, by rewarding performance, compensation systems can help build a motivating work climate. They are particularly likely to reinforce and complement the desired management philosophy when their relationship is clearly stated.

10. *Approach to Change in Compensation Policy and Practice.* Good compensation systems are always changing. This change can be managed in a number of different ways. It may be done through a participative process or through a top-down approach. A clear statement of philosophy can help whichever one is used to be more effective.

PROCESS VERSUS MECHANICS

An early strategic issue that should be faced when compensation decisions are being considered is the relative weight to be put on the process issues and the mechanistic issues involved. All too often, the major weight seems to go into the development of the correct mechanic for administering pay. The assumption seems to be made that if the right technology can be developed, the right answers will be found. The problem with this assumption is there are no objectively right answers to what an individual should be paid. People's reactions to their pay and their perceptions of what is fair are subjective. As a result, there is no such thing as an objectively right pay that will be accepted by everyone. Unfortunately, what is perceived to be right by one individual often is not perceived to be right by others. Hence, pay determination involves differing perceptions, values, and conflict.

Precisely because there is no objectively right pay level for people, factors like communication policy and participation in the design and administration of pay systems can have an important impact on people's perceptions of their pay and their behavioral reactions to the pay system. Considerable attention should be given to deciding how these issues will be handled when pay systems are being designed, implemented, and administered. There are a number of interesting alternatives in this area that deserve consideration. However, before any of these innovative alternatives can be considered, the organization needs to come to the decision that they are important, and to the realization that the answer to developing an effective pay system cannot be found solely in the latest, most sophisticated approach to job evaluation, salary surveys, or any other salary administration technique. They need to accept that it can only be found by dealing appropriately with the process issues involved in compensation in conjunction with having an appropriate set of procedures, methods, and practices.

PAYING THE JOB VERSUS PAYING THE PERSON

Almost all job evaluation systems are keyed to determining the total compensation levels for jobs. They typically use a scoring system to assign points to all the jobs in an organization. Points are usually based on such things as working conditions and the amount of responsibility the job involves. These points are then converted into pay scales. Characteristics of the person are used to make small adjustments in what an individual is paid. In many cases, this is a reasonable approach, but not always. In fact, many times it can be dysfunctional for the organization in several respects. It can lead to further bureaucratization of the organization, and it can decrease people's motivation to acquire new skills and abilities. For example, evaluation systems that measure amount of responsibility rather than the skills an individual has, often encourage individuals to seek management jobs, even though they lack skills in this area. For them it is often the only way they can advance to higher paying, more prestigious positions. Similarly, these systems can encourage individuals to try to acquire more subordinates and more resources, even though they do not need these in order to do their job effectively. This comes about because job evaluation systems are often based on the size of people's budgets and the number of people who report to them. Job evaluation systems are also a frequent cause of individuals resisting reorganization efforts, since reorganizations often result in some jobs being evaluated at a lower level.

The obvious alternative to basing total compensation levels on the job a person does is to base it on the skills and abilities the person has. This can have two potentially positive effects. It can lead to increased rewards for highly skilled individuals and for individuals who acquire new skills, even though they are not promoted. It can also help tie compensation levels more closely to the value the person has to the organization, rather than to the value of the person's job.

No one has suggested that person-based job evaluation systems should totally replace job-content-based evaluation systems. On the contrary, there is reason to believe that person-based systems are limited in their applicability. Nevertheless, they are proving to be useful in certain situations, and the decision to encourage them and allow them where appropriate is a key strategic issue in the design of compensation systems.

One place in organizations where person-based evaluation systems are clearly appropriate is in those staff groups where technical expertise, rather than managerial responsibility, is critical. The so-called technical ladders of some organizations recognize this fact. Unfortunately, the technical ladders are often only offered to research and development employees and are not offered to other technical specialists in the organization (e.g., accountants, organization development specialists, and lawyers). In addition they do not extend high enough in total compensation to allow for meaningful career advancement unless the technical specialist enters management. Clearly, if these systems are to work, the organization needs to make the decision that high total compensation is possible through technical expertise.

Until recently, the idea of paying for the person rather than the job has not been implemented with production-level employees. However, in an attempt to improve traditional job evaluation plans, some organizations have introduced skill-based evaluation pay plans at this level. In these plans, people are paid according to what they *can* do, rather than what they actually do. Most of these plans pay individuals according to the number of jobs in the organization they can perform, and do not take into account the job the individuals are actually performing at a given time. This has the effect of focusing on the individual rather than the job, and it encourages individuals to learn new skills. At present, the skill evaluation approach has enjoyed limited acceptance. Proctor and Gamble, General Foods, and TRW are among the organizations that have tried it in their plants. A detailed discussion of this approach will be presented in Chapter 5. At this point, it is sufficient to note that it seems to be practical to pay for skills, and that this approach is different in many important ways from traditional job evaluation plans.

MEANS-END RELATIONSHIP

Because compensation is such an important aspect of work organizations, the compensation system is an important part of their very fabric. It is so connected with other issues in the organization that it can become the dominant tool in the management and control of organizational behavior. There is nothing wrong with this since compensation should be an important part of the way an organization is managed. However, a means-end displacement can take place such that decisions in the organization get made in order to help the compensation system work effectively, rather than the reverse. Another way of saying this is that an effective compensation system becomes the end state that is sought by some, rather than organizational effectiveness.

There are a number of symptoms that appear in organizations when the compensation system has become an end rather than a means. Typical symptoms include: (1) someone not being moved to a job, even if it makes sense on a number of criteria, because the move cannot be fit within the compensation system (often because the individual's present salary is too high); (2) reorganizations that are abandoned because of the impact they would have on the compensation system; (3) paying salaries that are way above or way below market, simply because the job evaluation system indicates that this is appropriate; and (4) designing job structures and job descriptions such that they will fit into an appropriate category in the job evaluation system, rather than because they make sense from a motivational or some other perspective.

Other symptoms of displacement include such things as the total number of points the job evaluation system yields becoming a status symbol in the organization, and the inability of an organization to respond to its external environment because it requires a change in the pay system or pay policy (Galbraith and Nathanson 1978). The latter can occur when an organization moves into a new industry and finds that its compensation policies do not fit the industry. Rather than adopting new policies, some organizations stick to their traditional approaches, only to find themselves noncompetitive. This seems to be particularly likely to happen when conservative companies (e.g., utilities) try to enter growth-oriented areas (e.g., oil exploration). Rather than adopt aggressive performance-based pay plans, they use their same old system in order to maintain consistency.

There is no magic formula for preventing the pay system from becoming an end rather than a means. There is a strategic approach that can help, however. It involves the flexibility of the compensation system and its permanency. A means-end displacement is particularly likely to occur when a compensation system has been in place for a long period of time, and individuals have a particularly strong interest in seeing it maintained as it is. This suggests that at a strategic level, fairly frequent changes, adaptations, and updatings of the compensation system are needed, and that it should always be treated as a system that is open to change. It also suggests that as a matter of basic corporate philosophy the pay system should be identified as a tool that is supposed to produce certain outcomes. It should go on to point out that the pay system will be evaluated regularly on the degree to which it produces these outcomes (Lawler 1971). It should emphasize that the outcomes are things such as attraction, retention, and effective performance, rather than such pay system goals as internal equity and well-developed policies and procedures. Finally, it should stress that it needs to fit the environment in which the organization operates.

INTERNAL VERSUS EXTERNAL EQUITY

In any compensation system, individuals can compare their pay to people both inside and outside the organization. Similarly, an organization can place primary emphasis on its internal or external pay relationships; which it chooses is a key issue in any organization's compensation strategy and one that needs to be considered very carefully because it can influence turnover and job satisfaction.

In most cases, it makes sense to focus on external pay comparisons as the major criteria for determining total compensation levels. Both internal and external inequity have serious consequences for the organization. However, the consequences of external equity (e.g., turnover and absenteeism) are the most severe for the organization and are the ones that deserve primary attention. In practice, internal inequity often gets more than its fair share of attention because of its immediacy in the organization. Nevertheless, requests for internal transfers to better paying jobs are less painful than external transfers (turnover), and complaining is more tolerable than either overpaying people with respect to the external market, or losing them to higher paying jobs elsewhere.

Striving for *both* internal and external equity can create another kind of problem in the organization. It can lead to individuals being vastly overpaid in terms of the external market, simply because their internal job evaluation demands that they be paid comparably with highly paid people inside the organization. In this case, extra costs are incurred in order to maintain the system internally. Strategically, unless there is some particular need for internal equity to be exceptionally high, it would seem to be advisable for organizations to emphasize external pay comparisons.

SURVEYING THE RIGHT MARKETS

Establishing external equity demands good market data. The problem is that organizations often do not spend enough time determining what constitutes the correct market data for the many different types of jobs they have. The key is to gather market data on those jobs that the individuals whose jobs are being evaluated might move to. This is no simple task because people tend to make very different comparisons and have very different mobility opportunities. Depending upon the individuals and their level in the organization, it might be one of a very small number of jobs in a local community, or it might be a large number of jobs located all over the country, or even the world. The former is particularly likely to be true for lower skilled jobs, while the latter is likely to be true for management and technical specialist jobs.

One thing is certain: in most organizations there is no single set of organizations that can be surveyed that will constitute an appropriate market for all the jobs in the organization. What is typically needed is a set of surveys covering the range of jobs which exist. This suggests that, as a strategy, organizations should use a wide range of surveys and should be open to individuals bringing in survey data that are relevant to their particular technical specialty. It also suggests that they may want to make the survey data they collect public within the organization so that such data can be understood and challenged. In other words, the suggestion is that the salary survey process be "demystified" and made subject to participation, due process, and open communication. The negative consequences of surveying the wrong market are obvious. In some cases, it can lead to overcompensation and, in others, it can lead to undercompensation and a resultant loss of people who are needed. Open discussion of the surveying process can help prevent this from happening. It may also help to dis-abuse some individuals of the view that "all those other companies are paying a lot more."

CENTRALIZATION VERSUS DECENTRALIZATION

The compensation system, like most aspects of large organizations, can be designed, implemented, and administered on either a cen-tralized or decentralized basis. Neither a centralized nor a decen-tralized approach to compensation is always the right one. However, there is reason to believe that more often than is optimal, organiza-tions opt for a highly centralized approach to compensation adminis-tration. Centralized systems typically have standardized pay rates, standardized job evaluation systems, and standardized policies and procedures that cover the entire organization. The presumed advan-tages of this are ease of transfer of people from one part of the organi-zation to another, internal equity, effective cost control, and a tidy consistency across the organization.

A centralized approach to compensation administration is usually quite appropriate in small organizations, and in large ones that are in a single business and in a single centralized location. Its advantages, however, are considerably less obvious in large organizations which operate in multiple businesses and multiple locations. In fact, a num-ber of examples exist where this approach is highly dysfunctional in large complex organizations. It is dysfunctional because it effectively takes away the local autonomy that is needed to fit the compensation to the local market and to the kind of business that the organizations find themselves in.

An example of the kind of dysfunction that can appear is pro-vided by a large regulated gas company that decided to go into the coal business. Rather than develop new compensation practices, it simply put into place the same pay rates, fringe benefit package, and pay policies that it had used in the regulated industry. This turned out to be a grievous mistake because of the totally different pay practices in the coal industry. The organization ended up considerably overpaying its coal employees. Another organization decided to go into the oil ex-ploration business and found itself unable to compete for engineers because it lacked any incentive pay provisions in its pay policy. They were not common in its previous industry, but they are quite common in petroleum exploration. Finally, the organization ended up changing its corporate pay policy to allow for this since it found that it simply could not operate in the oil business without this change in philosophy.

A centralized pay philosophy also has severe implications for the amount of employee participation that is possible at different locations in an organization. As will be discussed in the next chapter, it can mean that people will not have as much information about the pay system and will not feel as committed to making it operate because they have not had a hand in developing it.

Another way of describing the choice between a centralized and a decentralized approach is to say that it is a choice between a differentiated approach to compensation systems which allows parts of an organization to design a system that fits the business they are in, and an internally consistent one that treats everybody in the organization the same way. The choice between these two approaches is an important one for organizations, and one that is not to be taken lightly. Each one has its unique advantages and disadvantages. As will be discussed further in Chapter 10, the effectiveness of the different approaches is determined by the environment in which the organization operates and by the business strategy of the organization. For example, the decentralized, differentiated approach seems to be advisable in large organizations that are in multiple businesses and that operate in multiple locations.

ROLE OF PERFORMANCE IN
DETERMINING TOTAL COMPENSATION

Performance does not have to play a role in determining an individual's total compensation. In many organizations it in fact plays a very minor role. This comes about either because performance is not used to determine pay changes or because the only thing that is determined by performance is an individual's raise and the variance between the best and the worst performer is so small as to be insignificant. The result is that performance has a minimal impact on total compensation. Much more important is seniority.

In some cases, not relating pay to performance is best, but it eliminates pay as a motivator and can lead to a number of severe problems. Most important of these is the underpayment of outstanding performers and the overpayment of poor performers. This comes about because poor performers and good performers are paid about the same. This puts poor performers in a relatively favorable situation because if they were paid according to performance they would receive a much lower pay; and, indeed, they are probably paid more than they could receive in the outside market. In the case of good performers, just the opposite is true. They are paid less than what is perceived to be fair by them since they feel that their high performance warrants high pay. In addition, they are also likely to be paid less than the outside market is willing to pay. The result is predictable: turnover of the good performers. The poor performer, of course, is hardly motivated to leave and is likely to be locked into the organization permanently because of his or her relatively high level of compensation.

Not paying for performance can also have an impact on who is attracted to the organization. There is some reason to believe that individuals who are highly motivated toward achievement and accomplishment tend to stay away from those organizations that do not reward performance. For them, it is a comparative disadvantage to be in a system that does not reward achievement and accomplishment. Overall, then, it appears that whether performance has a key impact on total compensation is a very important strategic issue in organizations.

COMPENSATION MIX

Organizations vary widely in the percentage of their total compensation costs that are allocated to cash and fringe benefits. Some organizations operate strictly on a cash basis, while others have more than 40 percent of their total compensation costs in benefits. Unfortunately, no matter what is done with respect to benefits, it is often less than optimal for a number of people. There are large individual differences in people's preferences for benefits and cash. Some people prefer cash while others prefer benefits. Among those who prefer benefits, important differences also tend to exist as to what benefits are preferred. One approach to solving this problem, cafeteria compensation, will be discussed in Chapter 5. It gives individuals a choice in how they receive their compensation. In the absence of the ability to give people choices, organizations that have high benefit costs often end up spending money that is not appreciated by the recipients. Thus, they end up spending more than organizations with low benefit costs, but they may not end up getting a good return on their additional expenditures. It is also difficult to vary benefits according to performance. As a result, money which might be used to motivate good performance is lost as far as this purpose is concerned. All this suggests that, in most situations, it is better to put money into cash than into benefits. Still, a situational analysis is required before the decision to emphasize cash should be made. Such things as the nature of the work force, tax laws, and the existence of a unionized work force can tip the scales in favor of an emphasis on benefits. For example, in a situation where the white-collar work force is relatively homogeneous, and where the production workers have a union contract that is heavy with benefits, it often makes sense to provide a strong benefit package in those areas where the tax laws encourage it. In this situation, the benefits are likely to be appreciated by most and may have more value than their taxable cash equivalents.

SUMMARY AND CONCLUSIONS

The compensation system of any organization is composed of many strategic decisions. In this chapter we have reviewed nine of them and have examined some of the options that are available with respect to each of them. In the discussion of each, it was pointed out that in no case is there a simple approach that will work for all organizations. Each organization needs to design its own compensation system to fit its own situation. This same point will be stressed in later chapters as we discuss some of the strategic decision alternatives in more detail. It will also be stressed in the next chapter, which focuses on process issues.

4
DETERMINING TOTAL COMPENSATION: PROCESS ISSUES

Two key process issues are involved in pay administration. The first, communication, involves a number of complex decisions about what to communicate and how to communicate to the members of the organization. The second, decision making, involves determining what type of decision process will be used in designing and administering pay systems. In this chapter, we will first consider the issues involved in developing a communication strategy, and second, those issues involved in decision making. Although these issues will be discussed in separate parts of the chapter, they are closely related, and constant reference will be made to how they affect each other.

COMMUNICATION

Secrecy about pay rates seems to be an accepted practice in most private sector business organizations and in many public sector organizations. Whether they have high or low pay rates, good or bad job evaluation systems, individual or group bonus plans, bonuses or salary increases, secrecy is a matter of policy in most organizations. Some organizations even go beyond keeping actual pay rates secret and decree that their entire pay plans are to be kept secret. Notable exceptions exist, however. Because of government regulations, publicly held corporations are required to make the compensation of their top executives public, the federal government makes pay rates public, and unions negotiate open pay rates.

In some companies, secrecy policies are taken very seriously, as the following newsnote from the February 18, 1975, issue of *The Wall Street Journal* illustrates:

> *Money Talks:* Jeannette Corporation illegally prohibited employees from discussing wage rates among themselves, an NLRB Judge rules. He orders reinstatement of a secretary who was fired for talking about her pay and tells the company to permit such conversations among employees.

The actions of the Jeannette Corporation also illustrate just how serious some organizations are about pay secrecy. Given the strong feelings that exist on the matter, one might conclude that substantial evidence exists which shows the advantages of pay secrecy. Evidence showing the advantages of secrecy, however, is not easy to come by. Indeed, research data which will be reviewed later suggests that secrecy may reduce organizational effectiveness and the quality of work life. Still, most managers seem to assume that people should not know what their co-workers are earning.

Reasons for Secrecy

Most managers, when asked why they favor secrecy, argue that everyone is more satisfied (the people who do and do not receive pay raises) when their pay is secret. They also point out that most individuals prefer secret pay. The following letter from the president of one company shows how he justifies secrecy in his organization.

> Memorandum to: Lois Jones
>
> Certain selected employees of this company have been chosen for a salary increase effective February 1, 1975. I am pleased to advise you that a salary increase in the amount of $600 has been approved for you beginning February 1, 1975.
>
> This salary increase should not be discussed with other employees simply because some of our employees have received no salary increase at all.

What most managers do not point out is that secrecy also gives pay administrators more freedom in administering pay, because they do not have to explain their actions. What is more, it can make their existence more "comfortable" because it makes it more difficult for a subordinate to effectively confront them about a perceived inequity. After all, a subordinate who is not supposed to know what other employees earn can hardly complain about being paid less than a peer. Finally, some managers argue that they favor openness, but only in situations in which pay rates are defensible. They usually go on to point out that, in their organization, it would take years to put the house in order so that pay rates would be defensible.

In most organizations that practice secrecy, there is no great demand by employees that pay rates be made public. In fact, quite the contrary seems to be true. In a number of surveys done as part of my research on pay, employees were asked whether or not they favor pay secrecy. In most cases, at least 80 percent were opposed to public pay at the individual level. On the other hand, they favored pay ranges and policies being made public. Table 4.1 shows the results from one company in which 1,205 managers were asked their opinions about secrecy.

The one exception to employees favoring secrecy is situations where pay is already public. Here my surveys show that a majority favor this practice. Apparently, once it is tried, it turns out to be less painful than was first feared. It is also worth noting that unions frequently demand that pay be made public; as a result, pay is public at nonmanagement levels in most unionized organizations. This often leads to the very highest and the very lowest paid members of corporations having something in common: public pay.

Table 4.1
Attitudes Toward Communicating Pay Information

Item	Individuals Agreeing (%)
Each individual's salary should be communicated to all employees	8.1
Having more information on pay levels would help me know where I stand	55.1
Persons should be told the ranking of their salary within their pay grade	85.7
Salary information should be more confidential	18.5
Staff members should be told the range of merit pay in their pay grade	93.2

Effects of Secrecy

There is some evidence that shows that making pay public can lead to a higher quality of work life, greater organizational effectiveness, and a more positive work climate (Steele 1975). This is true because openness can help clear up the kinds of misperceptions that occur when secrecy exists, and because openness generates pressure for a credible, trustworthy, and equitable pay system.

The earlier discussion of pay satisfaction stressed that it is strongly influenced by social comparisons. Obviously, secrecy has a strong impact on the kinds of comparisons that individuals can and do make. There is no evidence that secrecy eliminates pay comparisons, but there is evidence that when pay secrecy exists, people base their comparisons on inaccurate information, innuendo, and hearsay. If pay secrecy leads employees to estimate the pay of others correctly, then pay satisfaction should be roughly the same with secrecy or without. But, if secrecy causes people to overestimate the pay of others, pay satisfaction should be lower with secrecy.

The question of whether secrecy leads to high, low, or accurate comparisons has been researched extensively at the management level (see Lawler 1972; Milkovich and Anderson 1972). The results show that secrecy tends to lead people to overestimate the pay of individuals at the same levels as themselves in the organization (the most important comparison group). Furthermore, it shows that the greater the overestimation, the greater the dissatisfaction. The research evidence also shows that individuals tend to overestimate the pay of people below them and to underestimate the pay of individuals above them. These findings suggest that pay secrecy may do more to cause pay dissatisfaction than to reduce it, because it encourages misperceptions that lead individuals to believe that their pay compares less favorably to the pay of others than it actually does.

There is reason to believe that secrecy also can reduce motivation. As was stressed earlier, motivation with respect to pay depends on the rather delicate perception that performance will lead to a pay increase. This perception requires a belief in the organization and a trust in its future behavior. Secrecy does not contribute to trust. Openness does because it allows people to test the validity of an organization's statements, and it communicates to employees that the organization has nothing to hide (Steele 1975). In fact, with openness it is quite possible that more individuals would favor the idea of merit pay. One study

(Beer and Gery 1968) found that employees who had accurate information about the pay rates in their company were more favorable to the idea of merit pay than were those who had little information. This finding is hardly surprising. It seems logical that employees would be more willing to accept the risk of a merit system if they had clear evidence that the organization could be trusted to distribute pay fairly. With pay secrecy, it is difficult to see how this trust can be established.

Making pay information public does not automatically establish the belief that pay is based on performance or ensure that people will get accurate performance feedback. All public pay information can do is clarify those situations where pay is actually based on merit. This can be helpful in those situations where this fact might not otherwise be obvious because relative salaries are not accurately known. This was true in one organization that I studied. It had a merit-based plan and pay secrecy. At the beginning of the study, data showed that the employees saw only a moderate relationship between pay and performance. Data collected after the company became more open about pay showed a significant increase in the employees' perceptions of the degree to which pay and performance were related (Lawler 1971). The crucial factor in making this change to openness successful was that pay was actually tied to performance. Making pay rates public where pay is not tied to performance will only serve to emphasize this more dramatically, and thereby further reduce the power of pay to motivate effective performance.

The general tendency of managers to overestimate the pay of managers around them helps explain why managers may not see a relationship between pay and performance, even when a relationship exists. For example, in one organization I studied, the average raise given was 6 percent, but most managers believed that it was 8 percent; further, the larger a manager's raise was, the larger the manager believed other people's raises were (Lawler 1972). These misperceptions had the effect of wiping out much of the motivational force of the differential reward system that was actually operating. Most managers believed that they were getting less than the average raise. This was a serious problem for the high performers because they believed that they were doing well and yet receiving average or below average rewards. This was ironic because their pay did reflect their performances. Even though pay was actually tied to performance, these managers were not motivated because they could not see the connection.

There is another way in which pay secrecy may affect motivation. Several studies have shown that accurate feedback about performance is a strong stimulus to good performance (Nadler 1977; Vroom 1964). People work better when they know how well they are doing in relation to some meaningful standard. For a manager, pay is one of the most meaningful pieces of feedback information—high pay means good performance, and low pay is a signal of poor performance. The research already discussed shows that when managers do not really know what other managers earn, they cannot correctly evaluate their pay and the feedback implications of it. Because they tend to overestimate the total compensation and raises of subordinates and peers, the majority of managers consider their pay low; in effect, they receive negative feedback. Moreover, although this feedback suggests that they should change their work behavior, it does not tell them what types of changes to make. When managers are not doing their jobs well, negative feedback may be what they need if it is combined with clear guidance about how they can improve their performance. But it is doubtful that it is what is needed by managers who are performing effectively.

In addition to clarifying the relationship between pay and performance, openness has another important effect. It forces decision makers to defend their salary practices. Secrecy makes it difficult for people to obtain the kind of factual information they need to question their salary, to understand the raise they have received, and to determine the validity of what supervisors say about the relative size of the raise. With secrecy, the most individuals can say is that they feel they deserve more money. Without secrecy, the individuals who want to confront their boss can say specifically that, "X makes Y amount of money, so why don't I?" Potentially, this is desirable for both organizational effectiveness and quality of work life. It gives individuals the opportunity to find out how they are being dealt with by the organization, and it can motivate the superior and the organization to do a better job of administering pay and giving performance feedback.

There is one potential problem with openness that deserves mention. It may lead superiors to decide to pay everyone the same amount so that they will not have to explain or justify pay differences. This does not have to happen. There are organizations that practice openness and base pay on performance (an example of this was given in

Chapter 1). As will be discussed further in later chapters, organizations need a good performance appraisal process and a defensible pay decision process in order to make public performance-based pay work. If they have these, they can break away from the kind of closed-loop mentality that argues that pay should be kept secret because the rates are not defensible while, at the same time, encouraging nondefensible decision making by keeping pay secret.

Moving to More Open Pay

There is one final question that arises whenever greater openness about pay is discussed: How much information about pay should be made public? In other words, should everyone's salary be made public, or only pay ranges and distributions? The answer depends on the situation. If the organization has always had strict pay secrecy, it is foolish to try to move to complete pay openness overnight. The kind of open system that was cited in the first chapter (the managers who know and set each other's pay) is too much. As a beginning, most organizations I have worked with release some information on how pay is determined, on pay ranges, and on median salaries for various jobs. Some organizations also release their salary survey information and give individuals the chance to review their survey procedures. Most individuals do want at least this much information to be made public. Next, the organizations give out information about the size of raises and about who is getting them. Finally, they move to openness about the total compensation levels of specific individuals.

Despite some individuals' fears about the negative consequences of providing more pay information, in my experience, it usually is a positive. Clearly not every organization is ready for, or should have, public individual pay rates—many organizations that I work with stop short of this. But, in my experience, most can tolerate and gain by making pay ranges and other salary administration information public. The organizations I have worked with, in which this has been done, have found that after an initial flurry of interest it becomes an accepted fact of organizational life which, in many cases, increases people's feelings about the fairness of the pay system.

Finally, it is important to note that high levels of pay openness are particularly desirable when the whole organization is managed in an open style and is characterized by a high level of trust among supervisors, subordinates, and peers. As will be discussed in Chapter 10, the pay system must fit the climate of the organization. Authoritarian and democratic organizations require different pay systems. The latter can easily tolerate openness about pay, the basing of pay on performance, and, as will be discussed next, employee participation in pay decision making. It is much less clear that high levels of openness and participation can exist in an authoritarian organization.

DECISION MAKING

A number of difficult, complex decisions need to be made about compensation system policy and practice in organizations. Decisions need to be made about system design, about where individuals should fall in the pay system, and about what the salaries of individuals should be. In other words, decisions need to be made about how big the pie will be, what procedure will be used to divide it up, and what size piece each person will get. None or all of these decisions can be made on a participative basis. Although compensation decisions are typically made by top management, there is evidence to suggest that sometimes it may be best to have them made by the individuals who are directly affected by them. In Chapter 7, we will look at decision making concerning paying for performance and the effects of making these decisions participatively. In the present chapter, the focus will be on decisions concerning the design, implementation, and administration of total compensation plans.

The rationale for having employees participate in the design and administration of pay systems is shown in Figure 4.1. It shows that when participation takes place, people have more information about the system and greater feelings of responsibility, commitment, and control. As a result, they trust the system more, have more favorable perceptions of the plan, and the system is more effective in producing the desired behavior. It also shows that, in some cases, it leads to higher quality decisions. This is likely to occur only where individuals have information that is important—they almost always do when their pay is involved—and where the conditions are right for them to share that information and behave responsibly even though their self-interest is involved. Unfortunately, no exact mapping exists to show

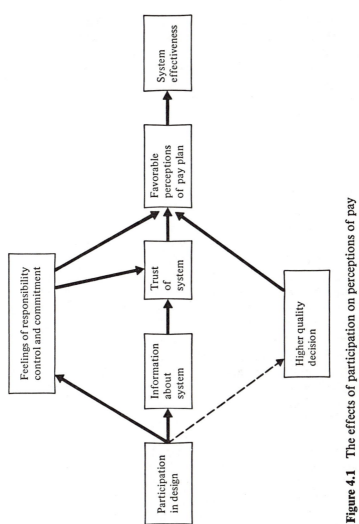

Figure 4.1 The effects of participation on perceptions of pay

when participative decision making should be used to make pay decisions. Evidence is also lacking on when the different approaches to participative decision making should be used (e.g., task forces and team decisions). Unfortunately, very little research has focused on employee participation in pay decisions. Still, it is possible to reach some conclusions about when participation can, and should, be used in the design of compensation systems and in the day-to-day administration of them. We will first consider design decisions and then administration decisions.

Participation in System Design

A study by Lawler and Jenkins (1976) illustrates what can be done in the area of base-pay system design. In this study, employees were asked to design a pay system for their organization, a small manufacturing plant in Ohio. Installation of the plan was made conditional upon the approval of top management. The design work was done by a committee of workers and managers who did considerable research on different kinds of job evaluation plans and gathered salary survey data. They ended up developing a plan that had public information and gave control of salaries to work groups. This plan was accepted by top management and put into effect.

The results of the new pay program were an 8 percent increase in the organization's salary costs and a significant realignment of employees' salaries. A survey of the company six months after the new system went into effect also showed significant improvements in turnover, job satisfaction, and satisfaction with pay and its administration. Table 4.2 shows some of the attitude results from this study (Lawler and Jenkins 1976).

Why did things improve? The workers seemed to feel better about their pay because the additional information they received gave them a clearer, more accurate picture of how it compared with others' pay. Furthermore, participation led to feelings of ownership of the plan and produced a plan where the actual pay decisions were made by peers. These factors led to a belief that the plan was fair and trustworthy. It also seemed that the new pay rates were more in line with the workers' perceptions of what was fair, so that pay satisfaction would have increased somewhat even if the employees had not de-

Table 4.2

Before and After Attitudes of Employees Participating
in Change Study (N = 58)

	Prechange, % positive	Postchange, % positive	Difference	Statistical Significance
Job satisfaction	44.4	72.2	27.8	.05
Pay satisfaction	7.1	37.5	30.4	.001
Trust in management	30.2	45.3	15.1	.05
Trust in co-workers	35.7	32.1	−3.6	—
Pay administration satisfaction	12.7	54.5	41.8	.001
Intention to turn over	40.0	70.9	30.9	.01
Job involvement	48.2	64.3	16.1	—

veloped commitment to the plan. This is not surprising. What constitutes fair pay exists only in the mind of the person who perceives the situation. In this particular organization, the plan allowed the people with the relevant feelings to control the pay rates. In this case, employee participation thus led to more understanding and commitment *and* to better decisions.

It remains to be seen whether having employees participate in pay system design, as they did in the Lawler and Jenkins study, will consistently produce favorable results. There is reason to believe that it can be a useful approach if the time is spent to educate the participants both in the economic realities of the business and in administration practices. Unfortunately, at the present time, few examples of this kind of participation exist. Thus it is difficult to reach firm conclusions about when it will work and how it should be implemented. More examples exist of workers' participating in day-to-day pay administration decisions.

Participation in Pay Administration Decisions

In a few organizations, nonmanagement employees participate quite extensively in pay administration decisions that affect their peers and, in some cases, affect themselves. For example, in Donnelly Mirrors and other organizations, employees play an important role in the job evaluation committees that determine the pay rates for each job. They are full-voting members of the job evaluation committee which determines where jobs should be placed in the pay structure. According to reports from both employees and management, as well as survey data, this seems to work very well. The employees make responsible decisions and pay satisfaction is high.

Similar findings are suggested by data collected by Jenkins and myself at the General Foods Topeka plant. There, pay rates are based on the skills of the employees, and other employees openly decide when the skill has been acquired. In this situation, pay satisfaction is high and turnover is practically nonexistent. A similar pattern of decision making seems to be operating effectively in many other new plants, although there is little published evidence to support this view (Lawler 1977). Indeed, some organizations, most notably Proctor and Gamble, have tried to prevent any information from being disseminated about their new plants (they view knowledge about how to run new plants as a competitive advantage), many of which are reported to effectively utilize peer decision making.

It is interesting to contrast the situation in plants, such as Topeka and those of Proctor and Gamble, with the way pay is handled for managers in most organizations and for most employees in nonunion companies. The process is almost completely different. In most organizations, pay rates are set by supervisors or higher management, and peers have little influence on these rates. Also, pay rates are kept secret, as are the results of salary surveys, so that the individual has little information about what others are paid. Given such a system, it is hardly surprising that employees often do not have any commitment to the pay plan and do not trust company statements that say they are fairly paid.

The major reason why most organizations do not involve employees in decisions affecting their pay and that of their peers is clear: organizations do not believe that employees can be trusted to make these decisions in a responsible manner. Despite the widespread "common sense" view that employees cannot be trusted to participate in pay decision making, there is evidence that they can. When given the chance, employees in the study by Lawler and Jenkins (1976) gave themselves only an 8 percent raise. This did not come about because they were highly paid already; rather, it came about because they decided to behave responsibly and set their wages at the 50th percentile of their labor market. There is other evidence of workers behaving responsibly when asked to set wages. Lawler and Hackman (1969), for example, noted that employees asked for a very small bonus in their study of janitorial service employees. Gillespie (1948) has reported on a study where workers were allowed to participate in setting rates:

> When a new job was to be quoted, the job description was sent to the shop and the men got together and worked out methods, times, and prices; the result went back via the foreman to the sales department in order that a quotation could be sent. I was surprised and horrified at this unplanned, nonspecialized, and dishonesty-provoking procedure and set out to improve organization and method. As I went deeper into the study of department economics I found:
>
> a. The group's estimates were intelligent.
>
> b. The estimates were honest and enabled the men, working consistently at good speed, to earn a figure *less than that common to similar shops on organized piecework.*
>
> c. The overhead costs were lower than they would have been if the shop was run on modern lines.

Perhaps the most interesting case of workers setting their own pay has occurred at the small Friedman-Jacobs Company. According to news reports ("Arthur Freidman's Outrage" 1975), Friedman decided to allow employees to set their own wages, make their own hours, and take their vacations whenever they felt like it. Apparently, this rather radical approach has worked well for Mr. Friedman.

> "It was about a month before anyone asked for a raise," recalls Stan Robinson, 55, the payroll clerk. "And when they did, they asked Art first. But he refused to listen and told them to just tell me what they wanted. I kept going back to him to make sure it was all right, but he wouldn't even talk about it. I finally figured out he was serious."

"It was something that I wanted to do," explains Friedman. "I always said that if you give people what they want, you get what you want. You have to be willing to lose, to stick your neck out. I finally decided that the time had come to practice what I preached."

Soon the path to Stan Robinson's desk was heavily traveled. Friedman's wife, Merle, was one of the first; she figured that her contribution was worth $1 an hour more. Some asked for $50 more a week, some $60. Delivery truck driver, Charles Ryan, was more ambitious; he demanded a $100 raise.

In most companies, Ryan would have been laughed out of the office. His work had not been particularly distinguished. His truck usually left in the morning and returned at five o'clock in the afternoon religiously, just in time for him to punch out. He dragged around the shop, complained constantly, and was almost always late for work. Things changed.

"He had been resentful about his prior pay," explains Friedman. "The raise made him a fabulous employee. He started showing up early in the morning and would be back by three o'clock, asking what else had to be done."

Instead of the all-out raid on the company offer that some businessmen might expect, the fifteen employees of the Friedman-Jacobs Company displayed astonishing restraint and maturity. The wages they demanded were just slightly higher than the scale of the Retail Clerks union to which they all belonged (at Friedman's insistence). Some did not even take a raise. One serviceman who was receiving considerably less than his co-workers was asked why he did not insist on equal pay. "I don't want to work that hard," was the obvious answer.

Thus, it seems that when employees are given the responsibility for decisions about something important like pay, they often behave responsibly. This is, of course, in contrast to the kinds of demands employees make when they are placed in an adversary relationship, such as most union-management negotiations. Here, large demands are the norm. The crucial difference seems to be that in negotiations, the workers are *bargaining* for salaries, not *setting* salaries.

Of course, having employees set their own wages will not work in all situations. For example, small organization size is helpful. In small organizations there is a better chance for employees to see a relationship between their behavior and the success of the organization. They quickly realize that if they take too much pay, the organization will not be able to function. Type of business also may be another important factor in determining how successful employee control of pay will be. Consumer businesses, like the appliance business that Friedman is in, probably are relatively amenable to this approach. All employees are usually aware that the firm operates on the margin between selling price, which is known to all, and the cost of goods, which is also known. Because most employees meet customers, they realize that higher prices mean less business, so they are aware that sales costs (translate salaries) can only be so high or the company will go out of business. It also seems to be important that salaries be public if they are to be self-set. Public pay allows group pressure to be used against anyone whose pay is too high and who is harming the business and jeopardizing the pay of all.

Despite the success of the Friedman-Jacobs Company, having employees participate in decisions affecting their peers' pay is probably a more broadly applicable idea than is having individuals set their own pay. The self-interests of individuals are less involved; thus, fewer supportive conditions need to be present. In the case of individual pay determination, it is important that general pay information be open, that the decision take place in a group that uses a good decision process, and that a technically adequate pay system exist. Without these conditions, it is virtually impossible to make pay decisions that are accepted as equitable.

A Perspective on Participation in Pay Decisions

A great deal more research is needed on what kind of participation in pay decisions is appropriate. The issue is complicated because the appropriateness of participation needs to be determined for making a number of different pay decisions. The situation is complicated by the fact that a number of organizational conditions can affect the appropriateness of any kind of participation. Furthermore, there are different levels of participation. These range from consultation to full participation, in which employees make the final decision (Tannenbaum and Schmidt 1958; Vroom and Yetton 1973).

In the study by Jenkins and myself (1976) and in the Lawler and Hackman study (1969), the employees were asked to make all the base-pay system design decisions, but were told that their recommendations with respect to amount of pay were subject to veto by top management. This approach seemed to work well. The employees made recommendations that management considered realistic. It is quite possible, however, that research will show this approach cannot be used in many situations, and that the type of participation that is appropriate depends on a number of situational factors, as well as on the type of decision to be made.

For example, in unionized situations, a different approach is clearly needed, but there are possibilities for participation in total compensation decisions nevertheless. Decisions concerned with the type of pay system and the relative pay of individuals can be made jointly by the union and management outside of the normal adversary relationship. At present this rarely happens. Unions do play an important role in assuring that external equity exists because they try to get similar pay for their members in different organizations. They also act as appeal agents for individuals who feel inequitably treated. However, only a few unions participate in joint union-management job evaluation committees. This would seem to be an area where more unions could play an important role. Unions also could do more to influence the kinds of pay systems organizations use (e.g., bargain for skill-based pay).

It seems likely that participation can most easily be employed in designing the base-pay system. Although individuals clearly have vested interests here, there is basic agreement in most organizations about the guiding principles that should be used; for example, that pay should be based on seniority, job level, and performance. It seems to be much more difficult to take a participative approach to deciding how much will be given out in wages or how much each individual will receive. In most situations, the employees have a great deal of self-interest at stake in such decisions, and this can and often will influence their decision making. In most organizations, therefore, management probably will, for the foreseeable future, determine just how much money will be spent.

Decisions about how individuals will be treated within an established pay structure are different from decisions about how much money will be spent. As was mentioned earlier, in the Topeka plant and in other plants around the world, this decision is made by peers, and this approach seems to be working reasonably well despite a few problems. Probably the most important of these próblems is the difficulty peer groups have in refusing a pay raise request when there are no limits on how many individuals can get raises for good performance ratings. This is a particular problem where there are no objective standards for job performance.

Some organizations have tried to handle the tendency of groups to approve too many raises by giving the group a total sum to allocate among its members. This prevents the group from deciding that everyone is doing well and deserves the maximum increase the organization can offer. But this total sum approach does not prevent the group from deciding to give everyone the same raise. This often is not functional for the reasons noted previously, and yet it seems to be a frequent outcome because individuals have trouble talking about each other's performances. This seems to be particularly true when there are no agreed-on standards. Another problem with this approach is that it is consistent with traditional approaches to control and does nothing to build trust and responsible decision making. A second approach, which I have used frequently, is to establish agreed-on standards before pay decisions are made. This seems to work best when these standards are developed by the work groups which will use them and when they include objective tests and other quantitative measures. For example, skill-based plans work best when they include objective tests of skill acquisitions.

Finally, it is important to stress that peer pressure can be very effective in preventing runaway pay levels. Runaway pay is always a danger when participation is used because, as was mentioned in Chapter 2, overpayment is only temporarily aversive. People adapt rather quickly to higher pay levels and begin to see them as equitable. The combination of peer pressure and the initial aversiveness of overpayment, however, seems to be sufficient to prevent participation from leading to a pay giveaway. The key is to develop group and organization norms which support responsible behavior. Without them, participation in pay decisions does not make sense. Positive norms are not easy to develop but they are likely to come about when people feel they have a stake in the organization, when people feel they are trusted, and when they are included in the information flow of the organization.

SUMMARY AND CONCLUSIONS

In summary, data are accumulating to support the thinking represented in Figure 4.1. Participation in pay decision making, in some situations, does seem to increase pay satisfaction and motivation. It has this effect because it increases trust and commitment, improves decision quality, and assures that employees will have accurate information about how pay is administered. It also seems to help assure that pay will actually be allocated in ways that fit employees' perceptions of equity, and this leads to pay satisfaction.

5
NEW APPROACHES TO TOTAL COMPENSATION

The charge is often made that major innovations in personnel administration are few and far between. Furthermore, it is noted that even when innovations are suggested, adoption and dissemination are painfully slow. Although this charge can be made in most areas, it seems to apply to the area of compensation particularly well. In many respects, it is not surprising that innovations in compensation practice are rare. The field is a mature one and the costs associated with unsuccessful innovation are great. Possibly because the risks are so great, the innovation which takes place tends to concentrate on making small improvements in already existing technologies (e.g., adding to or reducing the number of factors in a job evaluation system, improving a fringe benefit, or adding a new one like dental insurance). Against this background of low innovation, four "new" approaches stand out. None of them represent radical changes, although each of them, in its own way, takes an old problem or practice and casts it in a new light. They all have been around for a few years and there is some evidence that under the right conditions they can work. Thus, although they are different, they are not completely untried or unproven.

The remainder of this chapter will be devoted to reviewing each of them in the hope that the discussion of their strengths, weaknesses, and applicability under different circumstances will lead to their further adoption and development. The oldest of the new approaches, the all-salaried work force, will be discussed first. Skill-based job evaluation systems will be discussed next. Finally, two approaches (cafeteria or flexible benefits and lump sum salary increases) to allowing individuals to determine parts of their compensation packages will be considered.

THE ALL-SALARIED WORK FORCE

Most organizations distinguish between their management and non-management employees in terms of the fringe benefits provided and whether employees are paid on an hourly or salaried basis. As a rule, hourly employees punch time clocks, lose pay when they are late, and have little, if any, sick leave or personal leave. Salaried employees, on the other hand, do not punch time clocks, do not lose pay if they are a little late, and have well-developed, often generous, leave programs. The idea of putting all employees on salary seems to be slowly growing in popularity. It is not a new idea in the sense of only recently being thought of and implemented. Some organizations have used it for decades (e.g., IBM). It is a new idea, however, as far as most organizations are concerned since they typically have not tried or, in some cases, even heard of the all-salaried approach. Given that the all-salary idea has been around since at least the 1930s, this is dramatic testimony to the slowness with which innovations in compensation practice are adopted.

The presumed advantages of the all-salaried approach include increases in both organizational effectiveness and the quality of work life (Hulme and Bevan 1975). The all-salaried work force is supposed to increase organizational effectiveness by reducing administrative costs and producing more committed and loyal employees. It is supposed to increase the quality of work life of employees because it gives them more flexibility and treats them as mature and responsible adults.

There is some evidence that workers do prefer to be on salary. Typical of these data are the results of a survey I did with G. D. Jenkins in a New England factory. Such a plan was strongly favored by 55 percent of the work force but it was opposed by about 30 percent of the employees. A company president, in commenting on his own experiences, has pointed out one reason why employees do not like salary pay plans: "We took the right not to work away from our people by putting them on salary. When they chose to go hunting or fishing or drinking instead of coming to work, it didn't make sense to them to be paid for not working. They felt a little guilty, so they didn't enjoy the day off. They couldn't understand how the company could stay in business that way—which is a helluva good perception" (Sheridan 1975).

All-salary plans are also sometimes opposed by some employees because they feel other employees will take advantage of it (i.e., be absent more) and, as a result, they will have to do more work. Overall, however, most employees do prefer a salary plan to an hourly plan because it accords them more mature treatment and eliminates an inequity that is experienced when some, but not all, employees are on salary. In addition, when it grants the same fringe benefits and perquisites as those given to managers and white collar employees, it often means improved benefits. Thus it probably does represent an improvement in the quality of work life for most people.

The United Auto Workers (UAW) has raised the issue of all-salary plans with the big three auto manufacturers in past negotiations, and it has been implemented in one UAW contract (Kinetic Dispersion). Still, there has been little widespread union support for the idea. Some unions see all-salary plans as a strategy to prevent unionization (for example, at Boston Edison); in fact, all-salary plans have been implemented mostly by nonunion companies. IBM, for example, went to an all-salary plan in the 1950s, as did Gillette. Still, because most workers seem to prefer salary plans, there is good reason for unions to make them a negotiable issue.

There is no solid evidence to indicate that an all-salary pay plan contributes to organizational effectiveness. Although it is frequently argued that such a plan produces increased commitment to the organization, there is nothing but secondary evidence to support this claim. Typical of the kind of statements that are made is the following one by Frank Pluta of Kinetic Dispersion Corporation: "I don't think the men work any harder as a result, but there are some benefits to the company. There is a sense of loyalty. And the men come up with ideas to help keep things going a little better. There is an easy kind of relationship between the workers and supervisors. I can't say there has been a measurable gain in productivity, but the employees will help you to innovate, especially in a time of shortages" (Sheridan 1975).

This statement probably represents a valid assessment of how most employees react to all-salary plans. Still, it would be useful to have some solid data showing what benefits come about when employees are placed on salary plans. The major place where benefits are likely to show up is in turnover. To the extent that it makes working for a particular organization more attractive (something it should do since it is a desired approach), it should help to reduce turnover, and this can contribute to organizational effectiveness.

Critics of the all-salary idea argue that there is a real danger that it will lead to increased absenteeism and tardiness. They argue that when time clocks disappear and the threat of lost pay decreases, employees may think they have been granted a license to cheat the company. The counterargument to this is that workers will be less motivated to cheat because the company has trusted them (besides, who says you cannot cheat on a time clock?). Just because a time clock is not present does not mean that management cannot be concerned when people do not come to work or show up late. Management has not given up its right to notice and dismiss individuals who do not show up on time or are frequently absent. White-collar workers show up even though they are not on time clocks, and there is little reason to believe they are more responsible than hourly employees.

Unfortunately, there is little firm evidence as to whether or not all-salary plans lead to higher absenteeism and tardiness rates. A number of companies (e.g., Gillette and Dow Chemical) have been quoted as saying that when they moved to an all-salary plan, absenteeism either went down or stayed the same (see Hulme and Bevan 1975). Others report that all-salary plans have led to a slight increase in absenteeism. There simply is not adequate evidence to indicate what the most common effect is. A good guess is that the effect depends very much on such other factors as the style of management, the nature of the job, and the attention given to absenteeism.

If the all-salary pay plan is the only thing management does to get employees involved in their work and to communicate to them that they are expected to be responsible, it probably will not decrease absenteeism and tardiness. Although such a plan gives workers a message that they are trusted, it has to compete with a lot of other messages that say they are not. This message is often a difficult one to get across and cannot stand a lot of competition, particularly when the desired behavior (coming to work) has to compete with other attractive alternatives (such as recreation and shopping). If, however, an all-salary plan is combined with more challenging jobs, greater decision-making latitude, and other changes in the reward system, it can be a useful base on which to build a better relationship between the organization and the individual. This in turn could reduce absenteeism. If all-salary pay is to help reduce absenteeism and tardiness, supervisors must take an active role in dealing with them. Rules must be made and enforced, and the few that abuse the privilege must be disciplined. As will be discussed later, this discipline does not have to come from the supervisor; it can come from the work groups, but it must come.

In summary, the all-salary pay system appears to be a promising approach that can increase both the quality of work life and organizational effectiveness. However, it is not likely to be universally accepted; nor should it be; since it is not likely to be universally effective. It is likely to be effective only if it is part of an overall management strategy and organization design that emphasizes employee participation, meaningful work, and mature treatment of employees. More will be said about this point in Chapters 10, 11, and 12, where the role of compensation in organizations and organizational change efforts will be discussed.

SKILL-BASED JOB EVALUATION SYSTEMS

The idea of paying the person and not the job is a common one in many professional organizations (e.g., universities, law offices, and research and development labs). However, it has not been used for lower level jobs in most organizations. Its recent application to production and service jobs in some companies is therefore potentially important. It represents a fundamentally different approach to determining total compensation in these situations—one which seems to be applicable in a variety of situations and which fits with a more participative approach to management. Perhaps its greatest strength is that it communicates to the employee a concern for the development of his or her skills. This is in notable contrast to traditional job evaluation plans, which tend to communicate a concern for job descriptions, job evaluation, and market comparisons.

The plan at the Topeka plant of General Foods provides a good example of how a skill evaluation pay plan works. It is based on a starting rate given to new employees upon first entering the plant. After entry, employees are advanced one pay grade for each job they learn. Jobs can be learned in any sequence and all jobs earn equal amounts of additional pay. When all the jobs in the plant are mastered, the top or plant rate is obtained. Employees are given encouragement and support to learn new jobs, but it usually takes a minimum of two years for an employee to learn all the jobs. The members of an individual's work team decide when a job has been mastered. After individuals have learned all the jobs, they continue to rotate among the same jobs, but the only opportunity they have for additional pay lies in acquiring a specialty rate which is given to an individual who has gained expertise in a skilled trade, such as pipe fitting. In one plant which has a skill-based plan like the Topeka one, employees are also given the opportunity to learn about the economics of the business. When they can pass a test based on it, they receive additional pay, just as if they have mastered a new maintenance or production skill.

Analysis of the Topeka plant reports that the pay plan seems to be successfully contributing to both organizational effectiveness and a high quality of work life (Lawler 1978; Walton 1972, 1975). Organizational effectiveness seems to have come about because of the flexibility of the work force, the broader perspective of the work force on how the plant operates, and the low level of turnover. A high quality of work life seems to have been achieved because the plan reinforces a spirit of personal growth and development and produces wage rates that are perceived to be equitable. The latter point is supported by the data collected by Jenkins and myself. Several years after the plant opened we compared the attitudes toward pay of the Topeka employees with those of employees in other similar plants that did not have skill-based pay plans; the result was some rather dramatic differences. The Topeka plant had much higher levels of pay satisfaction, and the employees generally felt their pay was well and fairly administered. The plant also showed very low absenteeism and turnover rates. In this one case, a skill-based pay plan did seem to have contributed to both organizational effectiveness and a high quality of work life.

Despite their high degree of promise, skill-based pay plans are not without their problems. Even under such plans, for example, individuals run up against the top end of a pay range because they have learned all the jobs there are to learn. There is nowhere to go financially unless some type of bonus or other performance-based system is used. This "topping-out" effect may be a substantial problem as a plant matures and many people reach the top pay rate. Depending on the complexity of the plant or work situation, this may take anywhere from a few months to a few years. It may also become a more serious problem if a highly trained work force is developed whose skills cannot be used fully by the organization. So far, this does not seem to have become a problem in any of the skill-based plans. It has apparently been negated by the selective use of promotion and by the fact that not all employees want to learn all jobs. At Topeka, for example, some employees stopped learning jobs after they mastered five or fewer of them.

These plans also require a tremendous investment in training. This investment can take many costly forms, ranging from formal classroom education to having inexperienced individuals doing jobs to add to their skills. In order to control training costs in some complex production facilities, employees are limited to learning jobs in their immediate work area. That way no one employee is likely to ever learn all the jobs in the plant. This is done to limit the amount of training that has to be done and to be sure that individuals will be performing a job they know well. My interviews in several plants indicate that as long as there is a variety of jobs to be learned in the work area, the effectiveness of the skill-based approach is not harmed by this approach.

The desire of employees to learn new jobs can also cause problems if it is not managed well. Since the pay system rewards individuals for learning new jobs, it can lead to situations where an employee wants to move on to a new job as soon as he or she has mastered the previous one. If people are moved as soon as they learn a job, an organization can rapidly find itself in the position of having most tasks being performed by individuals who are just learning how to do them. The impact of this on organizational effectiveness can be quite negative.

Three approaches have been successfully used to see that most tasks are assigned to individuals who know how to perform them. The first is to specify a performance period for each task. Individuals are required to perform the job for a certain period of time *after* they have mastered the job. The second is to install an individual performance pay plan in combination with the skill-based plan. This has the effect of evaluating and rewarding individuals for learning the job and continuing to perform it well. The third approach is to install a plant level performance pay system. As will be discussed further in later chapters, this increases the motivation of people to see that the organization is functioning effectively and makes it less likely that individuals will end up performing jobs they cannot perform well. In essence, it creates a countervailing force to the one created by the skill-based system.

Another problem that has arisen with skill-based pay plans is setting pay rates. Most pay plans set pay rates in terms of the rates paid for similar jobs in the same community. This is difficult with skill-based plans, however, because the emphasis is on individuals, not on jobs. Because each organization has its own unique configuration of jobs that individuals learn, it is unlikely that individuals with similar skills can be found elsewhere. The situation is further complicated by the fact that an organization that has a skill-based plan is likely to be the only one in the community with such a plan. My interviews at the Topeka plant indicated that the employees had no clearly developed idea of whose pay their pay should be compared with. They did feel that their pay should be higher than that of people who did only one of the jobs they did, but beyond that, many had no clear position. A few did compare their pay to that of foremen in other plants because they felt they had as much responsibility as they, and, in some cases, more skills. Although the lack of community pay comparisons makes setting pay rates more difficult, it can help to reduce turnover because it tends to create situations in which individuals have no options that are nearly as attractive in terms of pay level and skill utilization.

Like the all-salary pay plan idea, skill-based plans are not likely to be effective in all situations. It is interesting to note that most of the plants where skill-based plans have been used successfully are essentially process production plants (for example, chemicals or bulk food). This seems to be a production technology where it is particularly advantageous to use skill evaluation plans. With process production, there is a definite advantage to having employees know a number of jobs and understand the total plant as a system. The latter is particularly important in process plants because jobs are so highly interrelated.

The type of production technology may also moderate the desire of employees to have a skill-based plan. As part of the experiment in worker participation in pay system design that was mentioned in the previous chapter, workers were asked to vote on whether or not they wanted a skill-based plan (Lawler and Jenkins 1976). They voted it down, giving as one reason that they were skilled machinists who wanted to learn their own jobs better. There might have been some advantages to the company if the machinists had wanted to learn other jobs—it would have created a more flexible work force. The advantages would have been limited though because of the nature of the workflow. The company manufactures products in a way that creates fairly independent jobs. The employees finally decided in favor of a system that would pay individuals more as they became more skilled at operating a single machine.

Overall, skill-based plans appear to be a promising approach to administering rewards in a way that will provide a high quality of work life and contribute to organizational effectiveness. They seem to be particularly appropriate in process production plants, in situations where skill acquisition and personal growth should be emphasized, and, as will be discussed further in Chapter 10, in situations where they fit the overall management style of the organization.

LUMP SUM SALARY INCREASES

Most organizations provide no flexibility for an employee as to when pay raises are received. Although many organizations speak in terms of annual salary increases, all but a few organizations give raises by adjusting the regular paychecks of employees. For example, if employees are paid weekly, their weekly paycheck is increased to reflect the amount of their annual salary increase. Similar changes are made for employees paid on a biweekly or monthly basis. This approach allows employees absolutely no flexibility with respect to when they receive their raises. They have to wait a full year to get the full amount of their annual increase. This approach often has the effect of perceptually burying a raise so that it is hardly visible to the recipient. Once the annual raise is divided up among regular paychecks and the tax deductions are made, very little change appears in an employee's take-home pay.

Recognizing these problems, a few organizations (e.g., Aetna, B. F. Goodrich, Timex, and Westinghouse) have started lump sum increase programs that are aimed at making salary increases more flexible and visible and, at the same time, communicating to their employees that they are willing to do innovative things in the area of pay administration. Under a lump sum increase program, employees are given the opportunity to decide when they will receive their annual increase. Just about any option is available, including receiving it *all* in one lump sum at the beginning of the year. Employees can also choose to have the increases folded into their regular paychecks, as has been done in the past. The following quote from a publication of an insurance company that has installed such a plan illustrates the philosophy behind it:

> The Lump Sum Increase Program (LSIP) is a payment option offering you the flexibility to tailor part of your total compensation to your specific needs. Under this program you can elect to receive all or part of any salary increase—whether merit, promotional, or a special adjustment—in the form of one lump sum payment (less a small discount for payment in advance). By making the full amount of your increase available as soon as it is effective, LSIP allows you to plan realistically for large expenditures without using retail credit plans having high interest rates.

Each year employees can make new choices. They are not bound by any of their past choices, and each year they have the opportunity to allocate not only the current year's raise but also the raises from some of the years since the program began. The number of raises that can be taken as a lump sum varies from two in some companies to all past raises in others. In some cases this can give individuals a considerable amount of flexibility in when they receive a significant portion of their total compensation.

In most plans, the money that is advanced to employees is treated as a loan. This means that if an employee quits before the end of the year, the portion of the increase which has not yet been earned has to be paid back. Also, because the money is advanced to individuals before they earn it, in some plans they are charged interest to offset the cash flow problem such payments cause the company.

Unfortunately, there is no research evidence on how effective the lump sum program is. All that can be reported so far is that most employees who are subject to it seem to be enthusiastic about it. Most employees, for example, seem to opt for a lump sum when they have the chance. One article estimates that from 40 to 95 percent of the employees in firms offering the plans have chosen a lump sum payment (Smith 1979). Lower acceptance rates seem to come when the money is treated as a loan and interest is charged. Employee acceptance of the idea is not surprising since it costs individuals very little and gives them the opportunity to shape their income to fit their unique needs and desires. In short, a lump sum program represents one way in which employees are treated more as individuals by the organizations that employ them and, as such, it improves the quality of work life.

There are some reasons to believe lump sum increases can also contribute to organizational effectiveness. For one thing, the costs involved to an organization are minimal. The administration of a lump sum increase plan does involve some extra costs because it requires extra bookkeeping and record keeping. There are also some situations where money is lost because employees quit and do not pay back the advances they receive. However, organizations need not lose interest income on the cash they advance since they can charge interest on it. Most organizations that have tried the plan so far have charged relatively low interest rates. These organizations realize that they might be able to invest their cash more profitably but they feel, nevertheless, that the lump sum program is worthwhile. One organization even decided to charge no interest.

What are the advantages to an organization that provides a lump sum increase plan? The major positive outcome should be that it makes working for the organization more attractive. All other things being equal, organizations that give employees choices about when they will receive their pay increases should have a competitive advantage in attracting and retaining employees. Like other practices that make organizations more attractive, the lump sum plan can pay off in a number of ways—better selection ratios, lower turnover, and lower absenteeism. These, in turn, can result in lower personnel costs and a more talented group of employees.

Giving lump sum increases also increases the visibility of the amount of a salary increase. A large raise tends to come across clearly as a large amount of money, and a small raise comes across as just what it is—a small increase. Increasing the saliency of the amount of a raise may or may not be functional for an organization; it depends on how well pay is administered by the organization. If pay is administered in an arbitrary and nonperformance-based manner, then it is hardly functional to highlight the size of an increase. On the other hand, if an organization does a good job of administering pay, then increasing the saliency of raises can be functional. When increases are based on performance, the lump sum approach has the potential of making pay a more effective motivator because pay will be more clearly tied to performance. If pay increases are equitably distributed, lump sum increases can make this clear, thereby increasing pay satisfaction and reducing the tendency of individuals to look for other jobs. On the other hand, if pay increases are inequitably distributed, lump sum increases can highlight this.

In summary, the lump sum increase approach is usually seen as an attractive benefit by employees, and it can magnify both the positive and the negative aspects of a pay plan. It can help an organization if pay increases are well administered, and it can hurt if pay increases are poorly administered. Therefore, it is a tool to be used only when an organization has a reasonable, well-functioning salary increase plan.

CAFETERIA BENEFIT PROGRAMS

The typical fringe benefit program provides equal amounts of such benefits as life insurance and health insurance to all organization members who are at similar levels in the organization. Typically, there is one fringe benefit package for hourly employees, one for salaried employees, and a third for the top levels of management. This approach emphasizes the differences between levels of the organization but fails to emphasize the significant differences among people who are at the same level. It also fails to give individuals any choice in the mixture of benefits and cash they will receive. For decades, research has clearly shown that the perceived value of benefits to employees varies widely from employee to employee (Nealey 1963). Such things as age, marital status, and number of children influence which benefits a person prefers. For example, young unmarried men prefer more time off the job whereas young married men prefer less time off. Likewise, older employees prefer greater retirement benefits while younger employees prefer more cash.

These findings are hardly surprising; people in different life situations have different needs. The fact that many people do not get the fringe benefits they want has some interesting implications for the effectiveness of fringe benefit programs. Essentially, it means that most fringe benefit programs fail to get a good return on the dollars they cost. These programs end up costing more than they buy; therefore, they do not contribute fully either to employee satisfaction or to employee desires to work for the organization. What organizations are doing is taking something of value (money), converting it to something of less value (benefits), and then trying to use this commodity in order to attract and retain employees.

One way to increase the perceived value of fringe benefits is simply to increase everyone's coverage on all benefits so that everyone has an ample amount of each benefit. Although this would contribute to improving the quality of work life, it is very costly. A less costly alternative is a cafeteria style or flexible benefits pay plan. This kind of plan involves telling employees just how much the organization is willing to spend on their total pay package and giving them the opportunity to spend this money as they wish. They can choose to take it all in cash or they can choose to take some cash and use the rest to buy the benefits they want. Although it has not been done, the cafeteria plan could contain a lump sum feature so that not only would employees have a choice of how much cash they would receive, they would have a choice of when they would receive it. A flexible benefits plan makes it clear to employees just how much the organization is spending to compensate them, and it assures that the money will be spent only on the benefits the employees want. Such a program can increase an employee's perception of the value of the pay package and this, in turn, can increase pay satisfaction. From the point of view of quality of work life, the cafeteria style plan clearly seems superior to the traditional pay and benefit approach. As might be expected, a survey in one company that has a flexible benefit program found a very high level of satisfaction with the plan and with the overall level of benefit coverage.

Although there is little supportive evidence, it seems likely that a cafeteria style plan can contribute to organizational effectiveness. It involves no additional direct compensation costs and it has the potential to decrease absenteeism and turnover and allow the organization to attract a more competent work force. Since individuals receive the benefits they want rather than the benefits someone else thinks they want, working for the organization becomes more attractive.

There are some practical problems with the cafeteria approach but they are far from insurmountable. Some managers feel that if employees are given the chance to choose their own pay and benefit package they will be irresponsible and choose only cash. If illness or other problems occur, the employees will not be protected and they may blame the organization. This concern can be dealt with on three levels. First, the research evidence indicates that most people will behave responsibly, given the choice (Lawler and Levin 1968; Nealey 1963; Schlachtmeyer and Bogart 1979). Second, it is not clear that employers should intervene if people take all cash. Controlling the kind of benefit package an employee selects is a form of control that places the employee in a dependent and passive position. Such control is also in direct opposition to providing a work life that allows freedom of choice. In addition, people may choose not to take health care coverage, but who is to say they are not covered by the spouse's policy? Finally, if an organization wants to be sure everyone has certain minimum amounts of coverage, it can simply give everyone a minimum benefit package and then allow employees to supplement it according to their needs.

Probably the most serious practical problem with the cafeteria approach stems from the fact that the cost and availability of many benefits, such as insurance plans, are based on the number of people who are covered by them. It is therefore difficult to price a benefit plan and to determine its availability in advance so that an employee can make an intelligent decision about participating in it. This is not likely to be a serious problem in large companies because a minimum number of participants usually can be guaranteed. Smaller companies may have to try to negotiate special agreements with insurance companies and others who underwrite aspects of the benefit package or they may simply have to take some risks when the plan first goes into effect. After some experience with the plan, however, an organization should be able to judge in advance the number of employees who will select different benefits, and thus be able to price them accordingly.

Up until the 1978 Revision of the Tax Code, there was also a tax liability problem with cafeteria compensation. Prior to 1978, the IRS indicated that if individuals took cash instead of benefits, those individuals who took the benefits might be liable for taxes on their previously tax-exempt benefits. This now seems to have been ruled out and, as a result, one obstacle to the spread of these plans has been eliminated. Finally, there are likely to be some additional administrative costs associated with flexible benefit plans. These may be rather heavy during start-up but, assuming computerization is adopted, should not continue to be heavy.

Despite the practical problems with cafeteria style plans, three organizations—the Systems Group of TRW Corporation, the Educational Testing Service, and American Can—have put them into effect. The largest and first plan is the one at TRW (Fragner 1978). It started with a series of surveys designed to estimate how many people would choose different benefit options. The plan, as it was finally put into practice in the fall of 1974, is far from a full cafeteria plan. It allows for a limited number of choices and requires everyone to take minimum levels of the important benefits. (The ETS and American Can plans allow for only slightly more choice). The TRW plan does, however, put all of the approximately 12,000 employees in the organization on the plan. It allows individuals to change their benefits plan every year and gives employees choices among significantly different benefits. Interestingly over 80 percent of the employees took advantage of this opportunity and changed their benefit packages when the plan first went into effect. At the present time, for example, the employees can choose among four hospital plans. It should be noted that the plan is supported by an extensive computer software program; and that its introduction was preceded by several years of developmental work.

The TRW project represents an important initial effort to make cafeteria compensation plans a reality. Unfortunately, little research has been reported on the effects of the TRW plan or, for that matter, on any cafeteria plan. My interviews at TRW indicate a high level of satisfaction with the plan and a belief on the part of management that it has aided in attracting and retaining skilled workers. One article on the American Can plan reports a survey showing that "more than 90 percent of American Can's salaried employees have had a positive reaction." Unfortunately, this is the only evaluation of the plan which is offered and not much information is known on how the data was collected. It is thus impossible to say with any certainty whether any of the hoped-for benefits (e.g., lower turnover) of the plan have been realized.

Flexible benefits would seem to be potentially effective in most organizations. They do not seem as limited in their applicability as are some of the other "new" approaches. In addition, there are certain types of organizations where they are likely to work particularly well. For example, large organizations, organizations with good data processing capability, and organizations with well-educated work forces seem particularly well suited to flexible benefit programs. At present, more organizations are needed that are willing to try plans which allow high levels of flexibility (e.g., taking all cash). A true test of the concept requires a full-blown test. There appears to be some forces that are likely to lead to the development of more flexible benefit plans. These include: better tax treatment, inflation, the rising costs of benefits, the increase in dual career families and their tendency to produce dual benefits, and a more educated work force that can make decisions and prefers individual treatment. Unions could also provide some inpetus in encouraging more organizations to experiment in this area. So far, however, no union has tried to bargain for a cafeteria style plan, but there are reasons why they might begin to do so. First, these plans promise to make union members more satisfied; and second, unions are often in the position of having to bargain for benefits many of their members are not interested in. Cafeteria plans could eliminate this problem. Hopefully, more organizations will soon have full cafeteria plans in operation. Only if this happens will we be able to fully assess the degree to which they can contribute to organizational effectiveness and to the quality of work life.

SUMMARY AND CONCLUSIONS

Table 5.1 provides an overview of the four new approaches and lists the advantages and disadvantages of each. A major advantage of most of them is increased satisfaction and job attractiveness. Although this may not have an immediate direct impact on profit or organizational effectiveness, it is still a significant advantage since it can reduce absenteeism, turnover, and tardiness. These, in turn, have significant impacts on profits and organizational effectiveness.

Also shown in the summary are some of the situational factors that favor each of the new approaches. The importance of these situational factors cannot be emphasized too strongly. The potential advantages of these practices can be realized only if they are installed in a situation that is favorable to them.

Table 5.1
Summary of New Practices

	Major Advantages	Major Disadvantages	Favorable Situational Factors
All-salary:	Climate of trust; increased satisfaction and job attraction	Possible higher costs and absenteeism	Supervisors who will deal with absenteeism problems; a participative climate; an involved, responsible work force; well-designed jobs
Skill-based evaluation:	More flexible and skilled work force; increased satisfaction; climate of growth	Cost of training; higher salaries	Employees who want to develop themselves; jobs that are interdependent
Lump-sum salary increases:	Increased pay satisfaction; greater visibility of pay increases	Cost of administration	Fair pay rates; pay related to performance
Cafeteria benefits:	Increased pay satisfaction; greater attraction	Cost of administration	Well-educated, heterogeneous work force; large organization; good data processing

Two situational factors, the management style of the organization and the condition of the present pay system, must be considered carefully. Figure 5.1 shows how management style and pay fairness affect the applicability of the four pay practices. It assumes that an effort is being made to use pay as a motivator and, therefore, a clear visible relationship between pay and performance is desired. Basically, it suggests that most of the new practices belong in organizations having a participative management style. In most cases, these practices have been implemented after a participative management style has been adopted, but a few organizations have experimented with using changes in pay administration practices as a way of moving the

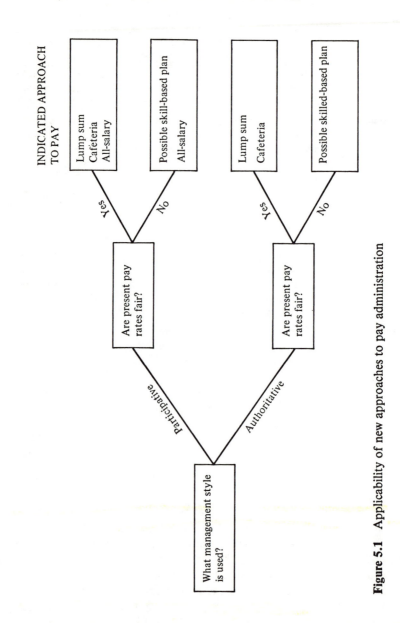

Figure 5.1 Applicability of new approaches to pay administration

organization toward a more participative management style. As will be discussed further in Chapter 12, pay system changes have been used as an important change lever in a larger change program. It is also apparent that most of these practices are applicable only when a good basic pay structure is in place. All-salary plans and cafeteria benefit programs are not substitutes for a good basic salary system that sets fair salaries. They can, however, often lead to significant advantages when a good basic salary plan is in place.

6
PERFORMANCE-BASED PAY: STRATEGIC ISSUES

The idea of basing pay on performance is so well accepted in many organizations that it may seem it is universally accepted. Nothing could be further from the truth. Most unionized and most civil service employees in the United States are not on merit pay systems. Instead of being paid for their performance, they are simply paid a job rate which is the same for all employees holding the same job. Some job rate systems also include a progression feature which automatically increases employees' pay during the first few years they are on the job so that not everyone is paid the same. It used to be safe to state that the job rate type of system almost never existed in the private sector and almost always existed in the public. Some recent changes, however, have made this association too simplistic. A major change in the federal civil service pay system has put the top 90,000 government managers on a merit pay system that pays bonuses, while, at the same time, some companies have moved toward civil service type systems.

At this point the reader may be wondering who is right, the civil service for moving toward performance-based pay, or the companies that are moving away from it. Before we can answer this question we need to look at the strategic issues which are involved in performance pay. But first, it is worth taking a moment to briefly review the reasons for basing pay on performance.

ADVANTAGES OF PERFORMANCE-BASED PAY

The most important reason for basing pay on performance is undoubtedly the potential it has for motivating effective performance. As was pointed out in Chapter 2, people are motivated to behave in those ways that they perceive are rewarded.

The second reason for basing pay on performance has to do with its potential influence on membership behavior. There is reason to believe that different kinds of people are attracted to organizations that base pay on performance. Specifically, the more entrepreneurial, achievement-oriented individuals seem to be attracted to those organizations where rewards are based on competency and performance. Since most organizations desire this type of individual, it makes sense for them to try to relate pay to performance.

Another aspect of the attraction/membership issue in organizations also argues for tying pay to performance. Since good performers expect, and indeed require, more pay in order to be as satisfied as are lower performers, it follows that in order to retain good performers, they must be paid more than poorer performers. Failure to do this is likley to lead to a situation in an organization where the poorer performers are retained by the system and the good performers leave because they know they will receive better rewards elsewhere. The only exception to this is in organizations that simply pay everybody above the market as a matter of company policy (e.g., IBM and Hewlett-Packard). In this situation the good performers probably will stay, although they will feel internal inequity. Poor performers are certain to stay since they cannot obtain as good pay on the outside as they are getting with the organization. The problem with this is that they are being overpaid compared to what is needed to retain them and, as a result, the organization is not using its salary dollars in a cost-effective manner.

Finally, there is evidence that individuals are more satisfied with their pay when they perceive it to be based on their performance. Higher pay satisfaction can in turn lead to lower turnover rates. It is not entirely clear why individuals are more satisfied with their pay when they feel it is related to their performance. It probably stems from the commonly accepted belief or norm that pay should be based on performance since this leads to individuals being paid in proportion to their inputs (see Lawler 1971).

Despite the obvious advantages of pay based on performance and the lip service most organizations give to the idea, it is not at all clear that it is effectively implemented in most organizations that state they have performance-based pay systems. In fact, a considerable amount of evidence argues that the principle of paying for performance is often honored more in the breach than in the reality (Lawler 1971). There are, of course, many reasons why paying for performance is difficult to accomplish and why it may not be appropriate. This point leads us directly to a discussion of the strategic issues involved in this type of pay system. As was true when we discussed total compensation, the emphasis here will not be on the mechanics of any particular performance-based pay system. Rather, it will be on broad strategic decisions that need to be made in setting up such a system in an organization. These often are the critical decisions in determining how effective any performance-based pay system will be.

LEVEL OF AGGREGATION

A key issue in establishing a performance-based pay plan is the level or levels of aggregation at which performance will be measured. Possible alternatives include the individual level, the work group level, the department or plant level, and the total organization level. In addition, there is the option of creating a plan which combines two or more of these payout levels. For example, a bonus pool may be determined based on company performance but distributed to individuals based on their individual performance. The Lincoln Electric Plan is an example of a very successful plan which does just this (Lincoln 1951; Zager 1978).

The decisions concerning which level or levels of aggregation to use in setting up a plan are critical because of the strong influence the aggregation level has on the motivational impact of the plan. Two things happen from a motivational point of view as more and more people are aggregated for the purpose of measuring performance and determining pay. First, individual performance is further and further removed from the actual amount of reward. As a result, the perceived connection between pay and performance is usually lessened. Second, up to a point, the degree to which the plan motivates cooperation and joint effort is usually increased dramatically. When payouts are based on group or plant level performance, it becomes very much in the self-interest of individuals to work together to see that the total organization functions effectively. Often larger and larger aggregation levels also allow for more objective measurement of performance. As will be discussed later, this has some very definite advantages in performance-based pay systems. In some situations, particularly unionized ones, pay based on larger aggregation levels is the only approach to performance-based pay acceptable to the work force. Recently, for example, some unions have accepted plant level bonus or gain sharing plans (see Chapter 9) despite their strong historical opposition to piece rate and merit salary increase plans.

There is no easy prescription for how to make the decision about what aggregation level or levels to use. It requires a careful study of the situational factors in each organization. Such things as the climate in the organization, the size of the organization, the technology which is used, and the sophistication of the performance measurement system all need to be analyzed. Table 6.1 summarizes how these factors influence the favorability of using individual versus larger aggregation levels. As can be seen from the table, individual plans make the most

Table 6.1
Factors Influencing Aggregation Level

	Favors Individual	*Favors Group, Plant, Department, or Total Organization*
Technology	Low complexity; individual tasks that are not interdependent	High complexity; interdependent tasks
Trust	Good superior-subordinate relationships; high trust of supervisor	Good trust of organization; good communication about organizational work objectives and performance
Size	Large; individual lost in larger system	Small; individual can influence and relate to group and/or plant events
Information system	Good measures at individual level	Measures only at group or plant level
Union status	Nonunion	Union or nonunion

sense when the technology creates low interdependence, trust is high, large systems are involved, good measures exist at the individual level, and a nonunion status exists. As also shown in the table, a different set of conditions favor the use of group, plant level, or department plans.

Not covered in Table 6.1, but clearly relevant, is the issue of how to choose among the different levels of aggregation that are above the individual; that is, how to choose among group, plant, department, and total organizational plans. The same factors are relevant here and the same kind of diagnostic procedure is needed. For example, in choosing between a group and a plant level plan, one of the key issues is the interdependence between the groups and, of course, the kind of information system data that is available. In many organizations, groups need to cooperate in order to produce a product; as a result, the only viable choice is a plant level plan. As far as the performance information system is concerned, this also may drive the choice toward a plant level plan. In many cases, the plan needs to be based on objective performance, and it is only at the plant level that reasonably reliable and valid performance data can be obtained.

Certain conditions favor the development of a combination plan; that is, one which uses measures at multiple levels. The most commonly used combination plans involve generating a bonus pool at the group or plant level and then allocating them on an individual basis. This type of plan seems to fit best when most conditions favor the higher level of aggregation, but certain conditions (specifically a climate of trust, good individual performance measurement, and good superior-subordinate relations) make an individual plan possible. When these conditions exist, it is reasonable to have superiors make judgments about individuals and to divide pay up among individuals based upon these judgments of performance. This kind of plan has the obvious advantage of combining the motivation for cooperation and interdependence that is inherent in group or plant level plans with the individual performance motivation that comes from singling individuals out for performance-based pay.

A good example of this type of plan is the one used by TRW for its top management group. Their bonuses are determined by total corporate performance and by their individual performance. This plan seems to work well because there is a high level of trust present and because the different business units in TRW are not highly interdependent. Often, however, this is a difficult type of plan to make work effectively because it needs performance measurement at several different levels and is rather complicated to administer.

HOW MANY PERFORMANCE-BASED PAY PLANS?

Many organizations, particularly large ones, require more than one performance-based pay plan. The most common approach is to have different pay plans for individuals at different levels in the organization. For example, in some organizations, top management has one plan, middle management has another, while lower management and production employees have yet another plan. This approach often makes sense in large diverse organizations; however, careful consideration needs to be given before it is adopted. It has the danger of splitting the organization into hierarchical groups that are not appropriate for the needs of the business. At the plant level, for instance, it is often not functional to have some people at the plant on a bonus system and not others, particularly if the plant is one where high interdependence exists. What is needed is an overall plan that covers everybody in the plant, not a plan that divides the plant on the basis of level of management or some other convenient criterion. In many ways, deciding how many different plans to have rests on the extent to which a need for cooperation and a sense of mutual interdependence exists across horizontal levels.

Less common, but gaining in popularity, is the idea of slicing organizations vertically into performance units, each of which have their own performance-based pay plan. Some organizations have established multiple plant level bonus systems (e.g., Dana, TRW, General Electric, Borg-Warner, Midland-Ross, and De Soto Chemical). This approach makes particularly good sense in situations where little interdependence exists between the plants and where performance is measurable and controllable at the plant level. It fits particularly well when plants and/or divisions are treated as profit centers. When these conditions exist, the only limit to the number of different bonus plans that can, and should, exist within an organization is the number of independent plants and/or divisions that the organization has. In TRW, for example, there are performance bonus plans that cover the middle levels of management in each of the business groups and, where appropriate, there are plant level plans below them. This gives the corporation bonus plans at three levels (a corporate plan, multiple group level plans, and multiple plant level plans). All the plans cover several organizational levels.

In addition to creating multiple pay plans based on vertical and/or horizontal slices of the organization, it is possible to have multiple plans based on their time span of payout. As will be discussed later, pay plans differ widely in the time span of performance they cover and, therefore, in the frequency with which they pay out. In those situations where there are both short- and long-term performance goals for individuals, it often makes sense to have multiple plans—one or more of which pays out based on short-term performance indicators and one or more of which pays out based on long-term performance indicators.

Overall, there is no easy way to determine how many performance-based pay plans should exist in an organization. What is needed is a diagnostic look at the overall organization with an eye toward identifying performance units in the organization that have clearly measurable performance results. Once these performance units have been identified, it then becomes possible to divide up an organization for the purposes of performance-based pay.

One way to identify performance units is to start with individuals at the bottom of the organization and work up through the hierarchy until a level is reached at which (1) peformance is clearly measurable in relatively objective terms, (2) no important interdependencies which affect that individual's work fall into parallel parts of the organization, and (3) the individual controls most of the factors that influence his or her performance results. At this point, a performance-based pay system should be considered—be it the individual, group, or even divisional level. The process should then take place again until an appropriate horizontal level is reached that again meets the criteria of measurement, interdependence, and influence. Here a second bonus system can be established to cover the person at that level and those down to the level of the first plan. If an appropriate level is not reached before the top of the organization is reached, and the organization is larger than a thousand employees, the idea of performance-based pay should be abandoned until the organizational structure is changed to allow for better performance measurement.

In large organizations, this process may have to be repeated several times in order to reach the top of the organization. Similarly, it probably will have to be replicated at each horizontal level many times. That is, individuals at the bottom of the organization will have to be selected from multiple plants, multiple departments, and so on in order to identify all the strategic performance areas in the organization. Ideally, it should be done for each nonmanagement individual in the organization in order to be sure that everyone has their pay based on an appropriate performance indicator.

SALARY VERSUS BONUS

The next strategic issue involves the choice of adopting a salary increase plan, a bonus plan, or a plan that combines both of these. Probably the majority of merit pay plans in the United States use salary increases rather than bonuses, although bonuses do seem to be growing in popularity.

Recently, a few companies have experimented with combination plans. Parts of AT&T, for example, have installed a performance-based pay plan that gives regular salary increases (up to a control point set at market value) to all satisfactory performers. Bonuses are given only to the top performing individuals.

Both salary increase and bonus plans have their advantages and disadvantages, but from a performance/motivation point of view, it is clear that bonuses are preferable. They offer the possibility of substantial time period to time period swings in pay, thus tying more money directly to performance. The problem with salary increases is they often become an annuity since organizations are unwilling to cut pay; as a result, pay reflects not recent performance, but a long history of performance and other factors. This means that even dramatic increases or decreases in performance have only a marginal impact on pay, and the motivational impact of the pay is minimal.

There is an additional problem with salary increases. Most salary increases reflect changes in both the market and merit. In periods of high inflation and large pay market movement, much of the increase may be simply an adjustment for changes in market conditions. The percentage of a salary increase that is merit, therefore, is masked and not obvious to the individual. From a motivational point of view, of course, this is highly undesirable since it fails to reinforce the connection between pay and performance. In the case of some bonus systems, market movement is normally handled by a base pay increase and the bonus payment is based strictly on performance. This, in turn, gives clarity to how much of the pay movement reflects merit and how much reflects market changes. In a few organizations, this is also done with respect to salary increases. An individual is told how much of his or her salary increase reflects market movement and how much of it is related to merit. This approach can help to clarify the situation, but it also is rather discouraging since so much of most salary increases reflect market movement and so little reflect performance. Often, the effect is to make it all too clear to the individual that there is really not much merit in most salary increase plans.

SIZE OF MERIT PAY

Unfortunately, there is no magic formula to tell how big a merit payment is required in order to have an effect on an individual's motivation. What research there is suggests that it varies substantially from individual to individual and also as a function of some organizational conditions. For example, in situations where pay is public, a small amount of merit pay can have quite an impact. In situations where secrecy exists, this often is not true because much of the recognition value of merit pay is lost.

The total compensation level of the individual is another factor which has a strong influence on the amount of merit pay that is needed in order to have an impact on motivation. It is clear that as individuals earn more, the amount of merit pay they receive also needs to go up in absolute dollar terms (Hinrichs 1969). There is some evidence, however, that when total compensation is high that it can drop as a percentage of total compensation.

Perhaps the best summary of how one should think about the necessary size of the merit pay package is to say that the potential should exist for an individual to receive a noticeable increment in his or her pay. There are two key terms here—one is *noticeable increment,* the other is *potential.* In thinking about the size of a merit pay award, we are talking about a perceptual phenomenon. It is crucial that individuals see it as representing a noticeable change in their pay status. A good rule of thumb here is that at least a 3 percent change is needed in order for the individual to "notice a difference." As far as potential is concerned, it is critical that individuals feel they personally can receive a noticeable change in their own pay.

Individuals form their perception of what is possible in this area based on public statements by organizations and on their own past history in dealing with the system. At the beginning, public statements are all they have to deal with, but after a period of time, history gives them a reality base for determining what, in fact, is possible in the area of merit awards. Perhaps the best rule of thumb for organizations to operate with is that unless, on a regular basis, performance-based pay awards average at least 3 percent of base salary, then the program probably is not worth its administrative time. In times of high inflation, this number probably needs to be much higher. Of course, some individual awards should be much larger than 3 percent in order for individuals to feel that if they do particularly well, a large award is possible.

MEASURES OF PERFORMANCE

Choosing the criterion or criteria upon which to base a merit pay system is critical to the success of the plan. Since each situation is unique, it is difficult to state any general principles about what can be considered the best criteria. Nevertheless, it is important to consider the tradeoffs involved in choosing between an objective criterion and a subjective one. Most organizations rely upon subjective ratings to determine how much merit pay an individual receives. As will be discussed further in the next chapter, the nature of these ratings varies widely from situation to situation. Although always subjective, in some cases, ratings are much more valid than in others. Supervisors' ratings sometimes are also used to determine bonuses, both at the individual level and at the group and department level. For example, in one large company, the president rates the different divisions in order to determine the bonus pool for each division. In this particular case, the bonus system seems to work reasonably well because the president is seen as a high credibility, trustworthy individual. In many cases, however, performance-based pay plans that are determined by subjective ratings do not provide much motivational impact because the perception that performance will be validly assessed is not present.

One advantage of subjective measures is they are often easy to gather and do not require an expensive management information system in order to arrive at an appraisal. A second advantage is that, when done well, they can provide a relatively inclusive measure of all the behaviors a person needs to perform in order to do the job effectively. Objective measures often fail in this area because some things are simply very difficult to quantify and count.

Failure to include all the activities that are important for effective job performance can have disastrous results. Because pay is an effective motivator, those aspects of the job which are singled out for financial rewards tend to receive a disproportionate level of effort and attention on the part of the job performer. If these behaviors are not all that is necessary, the plan can backfire in ways that can seriously harm the organization. In fact, many plans have backfired in this area (for example, salespersons who have pushed sales at the expenses of long-term customer relations, profit margins and trade in prices, and city maintenance crews that have filled potholes without regard to whether they stay filled). The message is clear. Unless all important job behaviors can be included in a performance-based pay system, it is better not to have this type of system at all.

Clearly, the key to making subjectively based systems work is trust. Without a high level of trust, there is little chance that the subordinate will believe that pay is fairly based on performance. Figure 6.1 illustrates the relationship between trust and the objectivity of the performance measure. It indicates that even with the most objective system, some trust is required if the individual is to believe pay is based on performance. It also suggests that unless a high degree of trust exists, plans based on subjective criteria have little chance of succeeding.

FREQUENCY OF PAYOUT

Performance-based pay plans differ widely in the frequency with which they make payments. At one extreme, some piece rate plans pay out on an hourly basis; and at the other extreme, some executive incentive plans pay out after five- or ten-year periods. The choice of how frequently to pay out is an important one. Too short a time period can lead to individuals focusing their efforts on achieving short-term goals and ignoring the long-term needs of the organization.

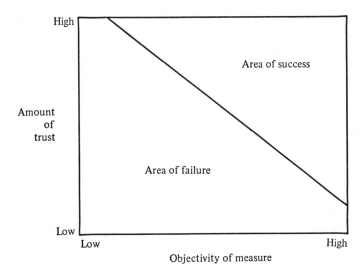

Figure 6.1   Relationship of trust and the objectivity of performance criteria to success of the program

Too long a payout period can cause the plan to lose its motivational value because of the very remote and distant connection between pay and performance. Organizations differ on whether or not they review the pay of individuals on a regular basis (usually once a year) or whether they leave it up to the individual manager to set the frequency. The latter approach allows the manager to give better performers more frequent and larger increases. This has an inherent appeal, but those organizations that have it often find it difficult to administer and manage. It also may cause the worst performers to have the fewest performance appraisals, a questionable practice.

Deciding what time period to use in a particular plan has to be very carefully related to the type of situation and to the type of people involved. As a general rule, the higher the management level in the organization, the longer the appropriate time period between payouts. There are two reasons for this. First, higher level managers are more accustomed to delayed rewards. Second, performance at higher levels of an organization typically demands more attention to long-term goals and often is only measurable after months, or even years, have elapsed. The concept of time span of discretion captures this point nicely (Jacques 1961, 1979). According to this concept, jobs and organizations vary tremendously in the time it takes for a person's performance to show up in effectiveness indicators. At the lowest level jobs in an organization it typically takes only a few moments, whereas at the top levels it takes years.

Because jobs in many organizations have different time spans of discretion, the pay plans that cover the top people should have very different frequencies of payout than those that cover the lower levels. In addition, the tasks that an individual performs in a given job often differ in their time span of discretion. Some have relatively short time spans and others have longer ones. Therefore, it makes sense to consider having different payout frequencies which are tied into the time span of discretion of particular tasks. In some instances, this can lead to some individuals being covered by multiple payout systems—one or more to cover the short-term goals they have to achieve and one or more to cover their long-term goals. A case can also be made for treating new employees differently from older employees. New employees are often on a steep growth curve and, as a result, expect more frequent pay increases. In addition, by delivering a pay action in close proximity to improved performance the organization can go a long way toward establishing a close link between pay and performance for the new employee.

Most organizations fall into the habit of awarding annual salary increases or bonuses. In many cases, it makes sense because it fits the business cycle and it fits people's expectations. This approach usually works satisfactorily for most employees, except new employees, some lower level employees, and top level employees. The exception is in times of high inflation; during this period, it seems nonresponsive and out of touch.

CHOOSING A PERFORMANCE-BASED PAY PLAN

Now that we have reviewed each of the key strategic choices that are involved in designing a performance-based pay system, we are ready to consider how the individual choices go together to form a total system. In the sections that follow, some different types of plans will be identified and then their effectiveness briefly considered. Finally, how organizational conditions influence the effectiveness of plans will be considered.

The choice among the many possible approaches to performance-based pay is a difficult one for three reasons. First, the possibilities are almost limitless since so many strategic decision options are available. Second, each type of plan has both strengths and weaknesses. Finally, the effectiveness and appropriateness of the plans is very much influenced by a number of organizational conditions.

Types of Plans

As is shown in Table 6.2, if we classify plans on just three of the factors we have discussed so far, we can identify a variety of plans, some of which have well-known names and some of which do not. The table gives the names of some of the better-known plans. This classification could easily be extended by adding more factors, and the result would be to identify hundreds of different types of plans.

Plan Effectiveness

Table 6.3 provides an effectiveness rating for seventeen types of plans based on four criteria. First, each plan was evaluated in terms of its effectiveness in creating the perception that pay is tied to performance. In general, this indicates the degree to which the approach ties pay to performance in a way that leads employees to believe that higher pay will follow good performance. Second, each plans was evaluated in

Table 6.2
Classification of Performance-Based Pay Plans

Level of Aggregation	Performance Measure	Reward Offered	
		Salary Increase	*Cash Bonus*
Individual	Productivity		Sales commission Piece rate
	Cost effectiveness		
	Superiors' ratings	Merit rating plan	
Group	Productivity		Group incentive
	Cost effectiveness		Improshare
	Superiors' ratings		
Organizational	Productivity	Productivity bargaining	
	Cost effectiveness		Rucker, Scanlon
	Profit		Profit sharing

Table 6.3
Ratings of Various Pay Incentive Plans*

		Tie Pay to Perfor-mance	Produce Negative Side Effects	Encourage Cooperation	Employee Acceptance
Salary Reward					
Individual plan	Productivity	4	1	1	4
	Cost effectiveness	3	1	1	4
	Superiors' rating	3	1	1	3
Group plan	Productivity	3	1	2	4
	Cost effectiveness	3	1	2	4
	Superiors' rating	2	1	2	3
Organizational plan	Productivity	2	1	3	4
	Cost effectiveness	2	1	2	4
Bonus					
Individual plan	Productivity	5	3	1	2
	Cost effectiveness	4	2	1	2
	Superiors' rating	4	2	1	2
Group plan	Productivity	4	1	3	3
	Cost effectiveness	3	1	3	3
	Superiors' rating	3	1	3	3
Organizational plan	Productivity	3	1	3	4
	Cost effectiveness	3	1	3	4
	Profit	2	1	3	3

*On a scale of 1 to 5, 1 = low and 5 = high.

terms of whether or not it resulted in the negative side effects that often are produced by performance-based pay plans. These include social ostracism of good performers, defensive behavior, and the giving of false data about performance. Third, each plan was evaluated in terms of the degree to which it encouraged cooperation among employees. Finally, employee acceptance of the plan was rated. The ratings range from 1 to 5; a 5 indicates that the plan is generally high on the factor and a 1 indicates it is low. The ratings were developed based on a review of the literature and on my experience with the different types of plans (see, for example, Lawler 1971).

A number of trends appear in the ratings. Looking only at the criterion of tying pay to performance, we see that individual plans tend to be rated highest; group plans are rated next; and organizational plans are rated lowest. This occurs because in group plans, to some extent, and in organizational plans, to a great extent, an individual's pay is not directly a function of his or her behavior. An individual's pay in these situations is influenced by the behavior of many others. In addition, when some types of performance measures (e.g., profits) are used, pay is influenced by external conditions which employees cannot control.

Bonus plans are generally rated higher than pay raise and salary increase plans. This is due to the fact that with bonus plans it is possible to substantially vary an individual's pay from time period to time period. With salary increase plans, this is very difficult since past raises tend to become an annuity.

Finally, note that approaches that use objective measures of performance are rated higher than those that use subjective measures. In general, objective measures enjoy higher credibility; that is, employees will often accept the validity of an objective measure, such as sales volume or units produced, when they will not accept a superior's rating. When pay is tied to objective measures, therefore, it is usually clearer to employees that pay is determined by performance. Objective measures are also often publicly measurable. When pay is tied to them, the relationship between performance and pay is much more visible than when it is tied to a subjective, nonverifiable measure, such as a supervisor's rating. Overall, the suggestion is that individually-based bonus plans that rely on objective measures produce the strongest perceived connection between pay and performance.

The ratings of the degree to which plans contribute to negative side effects reveal that most plans have little tendency to produce such effects. The notable exceptions here are individual bonus and incentive plans at the nonmanagement level. These plans often lead to situations in which social rejection and ostracism are tied to good performance, and in which employees present false performance data and restrict their production. These side effects are particularly likely to appear where trust is low and subjective productivity standards are used.

In terms of the third criterion—encouraging cooperation—the ratings are generally higher for group and organizational plans than for individual plans. Under group and organizational plans, it is generally to everyone's advantage that an individual work effectively, because all share in the financial fruits of higher performance. This is not true under an individual plan. As a result, good performance is much more likely to be supported and encouraged by others when group and organizational plans are used. If people feel they can benefit from another's good performance, they are much more likely to encourage and help other workers to perform well than if they cannot benefit and may be harmed.

The final criterion—employee acceptance—shows that, as noted earlier, most performance-based pay plans have only moderate acceptance. The least acceptable seems to be individual bonus plans. Their low acceptance, particularly among nonmanagement employees, seems to stem from their tendency to encourage competitive relationships between employees and from the difficulty in administering such plans fairly. They are often rife with conflict about the fairness of standards and the desire of management to raise the standards. A notable exception here are salespersons. They often prefer performance-based pay because they like being on their own and in control of their earnings. The low acceptance of individual bonus plans among production workers is shown by the negative attitudes of most unions toward them. However, some unions favor group and, particularly, organizational plans. They correctly recognize that these plans potentially allow employees to share in any gains in organizational effectiveness that they produce. This solves many equity problems before they arise. They also recognize that these plans can unify a work force instead of dividing it, as do many piece rate plans.

The ratings in Table 6.3 show a general tendency for employees to prefer merit salary increases to bonuses. The reason for this high acceptance of salary increase plans is obvious—a merit salary increase tends to become a permanent part of a person's pay, but a bonus does not. Unless the bonus potential is much larger than the raise potential, employees typically prefer raises. Finally, the ratings show a slight tendency for plans based on objective measures to be more preferable than those based on superiors' ratings. This stems from the preference for valid measures that individuals trust because they can control and influence them.

It should be clear from this short review that no one performance-based pay plan represents a panacea. Unfortunately, no one type is strong in all areas. It is therefore unlikely that any organization will ever be completely satisfied with the approach it chooses. Furthermore, some of the plans that make the greatest contributions to organizational effectiveness do not make the greatest contributions to quality of work life, and vice versa. Still, the situation is not completely hopeless. Some approaches contribute more than others to both a high quality of work life and organizational effectiveness. When all factors are taken into account, group and organizational bonus plans that are based on objective data, and individual level salary increase plans, rate high. It is interesting to note that many of the quality-of-work-life projects in Scandinavia also seem to have concluded that group plans are desirable. Many of the experiments there have involved installing group bonus plans as part of larger work redesign programs (see Linestad and Norstedt 1972). We also know that many of the approaches not mentioned in the table, such as stock option plans, across-the-board raises, and seniority increases, have no real effect on the performance/motivation of most employees because they do not relate pay to performance.

Perhaps the most important conclusion arising from the research on different performance-based pay plans is that the effectiveness of all pay plans varies according to a number of situational conditions. A plan that works well for one organization often is unsatisfactory for another for a whole series of reasons. Although it is tempting to say that a particular approach to pay administration is always best, it is wiser to consider the factors that determine which kind of plan is likely to be best in a given situation.

Factors Influencing the Effectiveness

We have already considered many of the organizational factors that influence the effectiveness of different types of performance-based pay plans. However, they are worth briefly reviewing because they play such a key role and are so frequently ignored.

One factor that must be considered when a pay plan is evaluated for a particular situation is the degree of cooperation that is needed among the individuals who are paid by the plan. When the jobs involved are basically independent of one another, it is reasonable to use an individual plan. Independent jobs include outside sales jobs and some kinds of production jobs. In these jobs, employees contribute independently to the effectiveness of the total group or organization. It is thus appropriate to implement an incentive plan that motivates these employees to maximize their individual productivity and to pay little attention to cooperative activities.

Many jobs, however, demand that work be done either successively (work that passes from one person to another, e.g., assembly operations) or coordinately (work that is a function of the joint effort of all employees, e.g., process production as is done in chemical plants). With successive jobs, and especially with coordinate jobs, individual incentive plans are usually inappropriate. For one thing, on these jobs it is often difficult to measure the contribution of any one individual and, therefore, to reward individuals differentially. Another problem with individual plans is that they typically do not reward cooperation, because cooperation is difficult to measure and to visibly relate to pay. Cooperation is essential on successive and coordinate jobs, however, and it is vital that the pay plan reward it. Thus group and organizational plans are best in situations where jobs are coordinate or successive.

A related issue is the degree to which inclusive objective performance measures or criteria can be created for individuals. For many jobs, it is quite difficult to establish criteria that are both quantitatively measurable and inclusive of all the important job behaviors. The solution to this problem often is to establish a group or organizational incentive plan. Inclusive criteria sometimes can be stated at the group and organizational levels even when they are not possible at the individual level.

There are many situations where objective measures do not exist for individual or even group performance. Often, this is because of a poorly developed organizational structure and information system and/or because the organization is undergoing a period of rapid change. One way of dealing with these situations is to measure performance on the basis of larger and larger groups until some objective measures can be found. Another way is to use subjective measures of performance at the individual or small group level. This is possible in some situations, but not in others. The key factor is the degree of superior-subordinate trust—the more subjective the measure, the higher the degree of trust needed, as was pointed out earlier. Without a high level of trust there is little chance that the subordinate will believe that pay is based on performance.

One further issue concerned with performance measurement that must be considered is whether the individuals under the plan will actually be able to influence the criteria on which they will be evaluated. All too often, the criteria used in pay plans are unrelated to the individual worker's efforts (e.g., profit sharing in a company like Sears). This can create low motivation and a poor quality of work life if payouts decrease or go away because of things beyond the control of most employees. For this reason, it is particularly risky to have a profit-sharing plan in a large corporation.

One final issue that needs to be considered in the implementation of performance-based pay plans is the preferences of the employees. All too often, these are ignored and, as a result, the performance plans are resisted. It was mentioned earlier that unions often oppose perfor-mance-based pay plans. This is true, but overall there is considerable evidence that employees favor the idea of relating pay to performance. For example, one study measured managers' attitudes about how pay should be determined. The results show that managers prefer to have their pay based on performance and that they believe performance should be the single most important determinant of their pay (Lawler 1966). The study also found a consistent tendency for a large gap to exist between how important managers felt performance was in deter-mining their pay and how important they felt it should be.

Studies among blue-collar workers to determine their preferences also show a strong preference for performance-based pay. However, the preference there does not seem to be quite as strong as it is at the managerial level. Illustrative of the studies of this topic is one by Fac-tory (1947), which reports that 59 percent of the workers sampled, who were not paid on an incentive basis, said they would like to work under such a system if it were fairly run. The results were even higher for those employees who had already worked under one. Nevertheless, it is possible that in certain situations employees will *not* favor the idea of a merit pay system and this needs to be taken into account. This re-sistance may take the form of specific union opposition to a plan, for example. More likely, however, employees will prefer a certain kind of plan because it fits their value system and their preferred manner of working. It is critical that these preferences weigh heavily in the selec-tion of a plan. If the employees enjoy working as a group and do not believe that individuals should be differentially rewarded, putting in an individual piece rate pay plan is simply asking for disaster.

SUMMARY AND CONCLUSIONS

It should be clear from the discussion so far that there are conditions under which organizations should not try to relate pay to performance. When the conditions for this are not right, installing a performance-based pay system runs the risk of being more dysfunctional than functional. We have already mentioned a number of conditions that must be present if rewards are to motivate performance, but it is worth summarizing them here: (1) important rewards can be given; (2) rewards can be varied depending on performance; (3) performance can be validly and inclusively measured; (4) information can be provided that makes clear how rewards are given; (5) trust is high; and (6) employees accept the performance-based pay system. If these conditions do not exist, it is usually better not to attempt to use pay as a motivator of performance.

Putting performance-based pay in situations where conditions are not right may only make the situation worse. It can contribute to superior-subordinate mistrust and the breakdown of communication. It can lead to subordinates presenting false data both about their past performance and what they can do. It can lead to individuals performing in ways that are dysfunctional for the overall goals of the organization. It can contribute to cynicism on the part of employees about how fair the organization is in dealing with them and how concerned it is for them. In short, it can cost the organization a considerable amount of money for which little positive effect is gotten in return.

It is precisely because of negative effects of merit pay that some organizations do not have performance-based pay systems for their lower level employees. They have found that performance is often difficult to measure there, and because of inflation and other factors, better performers can only be given slightly larger increases. They have thus concluded that merit salary increases are not worth the trouble (as will be noted in Chapter 13), particularly in a world where they have to be defended in court. Does this mean that the civil service is doing the wrong thing by installing a bonus system for top level managers? Maybe not. The situation is quite different there. In some cases, better performance measures are available and a significant bonus can be paid. It seems possible that the government's move toward performance-based pay and the move of some corporations away from it may be both correct. The moral of the story is that performance-based pay is not for everyone or every situation. Finally, it should be remembered that in situations where it is indicated a careful diagnosis is needed in order to determine what type of plan is appropriate.

7
PERFORMANCE-BASED PAY: PROCESS ISSUES

The process issues involved in setting up and running a performance-based pay system are very similar to those considered earlier in the discussion of total compensation (see Chapter 4). First, there is the issue of information dissemination and communication. Second, there is the issue of influence and participation in the design and administration of the plan. These will also be discussed in this chapter. It is important to again emphasize that how these issues are handled is at least as important in determining the success or failure of a performance-based pay system as are the strategic decisions that were discussed in Chapter 6. They are important because they influence the credibility of the reward system and the degree to which rewards are perceived to be related to performance. Despite their importance, in my experience, they often are given little consideration when organizations design and install new performance-based pay systems.

The importance of the process issues, as well as the lack of attention that is typically given to them, is illustrated by some data collected by Jack Drexler and myself. We were asked to assess a merit pay plan that had recently been installed in a large research and development lab. Communication concerning the plan was pretty much left up to the individual section managers. Some did an excellent job of explaining the plan and working on its installation; others did very little. When we surveyed the employees, their reactions varied widely depending on the process their section manager had used in putting the plan into effect. In some cases it was hard to believe that the employees were describing the same plan, since they had such different feelings about it. In retrospect, this is not surprising. Although they were subject to the same plan mechanics, employees in different sections actually were not paid by the same plan since the process approaches were so different.

COMMUNICATION

The issues involved in openly communicating how much performance-based pay is given out in organizations are very similar to the ones involved in communicating total compensation levels. Most organizations practice secrecy with respect to the size of performance-based payments, just as they practice secrecy with respect to total compensation levels. As a result, there is evidence that individuals overestimate the amount of the merit pay rewards received by other individuals, which makes their own merit pay rewards look smaller (Lawler 1972). The reasons given by management for keeping merit pay amounts and salary levels secret are similar. They argue that individuals do not want their pay to be made public and that it would be destructive to the self-esteems of individuals and to the climate of the organization if individuals found out that they received low merit payments.

Research on individuals' preferences with respect to making performance-based pay public partially supports the view that individuals do not want to have it completely in the open. As shown in Table 7.1, managers in one organization favored having everything made public about their performance-based bonus payments except the actual amount received by individuals. This finding is typical of those that have come out of other similar studies done in my research program. Overall, it appears that individuals want to know everything except who got what amount of money. This amount of information would represent a substantial increase over what individuals typically receive. Sometimes, they do not even know the average amount or the budgeted amount. Because the amount of the bonus payment or salary increase budget is kept totally secret, they almost never know the range or the distribution of rewards by areas, departments, or levels in the organization.

Table 7.1

Managers' Attitudes toward Communicating Bonus Information (N = 230)

	Agreement (%)
Range of bonus rewards should be public	57
Individual bonus rewards should be public	5
More information should be given about bonus plan	92
The size of the bonus fund should be public	60

Even though they may not make actual pay amounts known, most organizations do provide information to their employees on how their performance-based pay plans operate. However, some organizations do not provide even this information, and in many of those that do, the information is often so abstract and garbled that it is unintelligible. In some pay systems, individuals are essentially told: "If you perform in a way that is deemed effective, some mechanism will be used to see that you are rewarded. Unfortunately, we cannot tell you what kind of performance is effective or what the mechanism is." It is hard to understand how organizations can expect a pay system to motivate employees when the employees are not told how their performance-based pay systems operate. Motivation depends on a belief that pay and performance are related. In the absence of information about how they are related, most individuals cannot be expected to believe they are and to perform accordingly.

From a process point of view, it is hard to argue with the idea of letting individuals know how much is budgeted for merit pay and how it is distributed. This is precisely the kind of information individuals need in order to understand how they have been treated by the performance-based pay system, and to develop faith and trust in the fact that pay and performance are actually related. In the previous chapter it was stressed that, except under the most ideal circumstances, a high level of trust is needed in order for a performance-based pay system to work. In the absence of trust, there is a high likelihood that individuals will either not respond to the pay system or they will respond to it in a dysfunctional, counterproductive manner. That is, they will bargain for lower performance standards or they will cheat. As was stressed earlier, public information is not a guaranteed way to eliminate mistrust but it can help since, in itself, it is an act of unilateral trust by management. In effect, it says to employees that the management thinks enough of them to trust them with this important information.

It should go without saying that making information public about performance will not increase trust if the decisions are poor. In fact, it may decrease trust if the pay decisions reflect poor performance measurement or favoritism on the part of the decision makers. There is reason to believe, however, that when pay decisions are public, supervisors are less likely to make poor decisions. Making performance-based pay information more public can motivate supervisors to do a good job of making pay decisions. In the absence of at least this kind of information, it is difficult to hold supervisors accountable for how they deal with performance-based pay, and it is difficult for individuals to establish that the system is being administered in a performance-based manner.

What about the idea of making individual merit payments public? Is it necessary in order for a merit pay system to function effectively as a motivator? Is it desirable? Perhaps the best answer is that there certainly are advantages to it, but unless the individuals feel comfortable with it, it is not advisable.

The advantages of public performance-based pay amounts are several. First, it can be the final link in establishing the credibility of a performance-based pay system. It not only shows that pay varies, but it allows the individual to see exactly who got the highest performance payment. If this individual is one who is seen as a high performer, it can add the final link of credibility to the contention that pay and performance are related in the organization. Similarly, if a known poor performer receives a low payment, it can further reinforce the idea that pay and performance are actually related in the organization. Second, it can make the discussion between the supervisor and a subordinate much more meaningful in terms of what the individual needs to do in order to improve his or her performance. It can establish rather clearly who is a good role model as far as outstanding performance is concerned, because everyone knows who the supervisor has decided is the outstanding performer.

Perhaps the most important advantage of public performance-based pay lies in what it can lead to. Without it, it is very difficult for individuals to participate meaningfully in decisions about how payments based on performance should be distributed to their peers. With it, they can make meaningful inputs into the decision process. As will be discussed in the next section, however, this is something that is evolutionary in nature and should only be tried when individuals in work groups feel that they are ready to take on the challenge of making pay administration decisions.

It is interesting to compare the issues which are involved in making performance-based pay amounts public (whether bonuses or salary increases) with those involved in making total compensation levels public. In my experience, there is usually less opposition and more reason to making the former public. The reason for the lower level of opposition is not clear, except that perhaps people see total compensation more as a matter of personal privacy. The reasons why it is often more important to make performance-based pay public is much clearer. For pay to be a motivator, a pay-performance connection must be perceived to exist; with secrecy about how performance-based pay is handled, it is hard to see. Because total compensation is influenced by so many things other than performance, making information about it public often does little to clarify the pay-performance relationship in an organization.

PARTICIPATION IN SYSTEM DESIGN

As was emphasized in Chapter 1, a number of key decisions need to be made when pay systems are designed. These decisions are typically made by a process that is top-down and authoritative in nature. Little input is solicited from people who are actually going to be affected by the pay plan, and these people are given no direct say in the design process. As was stressed in Chapter 6, evidence is now accumulating that individuals will behave responsibly when given a chance to participate in the design of total compensation systems, and when they participate, a positive impact on the effectiveness of the plan can be seen. Similar evidence exists for the design of performance-based pay systems.

Two of the original studies on participation in performance-based pay system design provide clear evidence that participation can make a difference in the impact of the plan. In the first study, two work groups were observed. In one group, productivity was very high and had continued to go up for more than ten years (Cammann and Lawler 1973; Lawler and Cammann 1972). In the other group, productivity was low and had remained relatively stable for years. Both groups did the same kinds of jobs and both had similar pay incentive

plans. In the second study, identical incentive plans designed to motivate attendance were installed in a number of work groups (Lawler
and Hackman 1969; Scheflen, Lawler, and Hackman 1971). In some
groups, the plan was highly successful in reducing absenteeism, but in
others it was only moderately successful.

The reason the same bonus plans worked well in some groups and
not in others can be explained by looking at who was involved in designing the pay plans. In the attendance-bonus study, the one characteristic that distinguished the groups where the plan worked from
those where it did not was decision making. The plan was designed
and developed by the employee groups where it worked, but it was imposed on those groups where it was less effective. In the first study,
the group where the plan worked had a long history of participating in
decision-making, and they had actually voted on the plan when it was
put into effect years earlier. In the other group, no history of participation existed, and the plan had simply been designed by management
and imposed on the employees.

Recently, a number of additional studies in which employees have
participated in the design of their own bonus systems have been
launched as part of the Quality of Work Research Program of the Institute for Social Research. In three of these studies, joint employee-
management task forces were created in order to design plant level,
gain-sharing bonus systems. In one case, the company was unionized;
in the other two, it was not. In all three cases, the task forces were told
that whatever plan they developed would have to be approved by both
management and the employees. In all three cases, they successfully
designed and implemented a plan. In two of the three cases, the plans
seem to be working quite effectively. In the third case, it is not yet
clear whether the plan will prove to be successful. In all three cases,
however, the plans were accepted by the work force when they were
put into practice. Apparently, the design process was quite effective in
overcoming the resistance to change which is usually present when
major organizational changes are proposed. In two of the three cases,
there was an unfortunate history of bad employee-management relations, and considerable suspicion of management existed. It is the estimate of most individuals involved that without a participative design
process, acceptance by an overwhelming majority of the work force
would not have been possible.

From a technical point of view, there is every reason to believe that these participative plans were as well designed as they would have been if they had been designed by an outside "expert." It is still too early to mark any of these three cases as long-term successes, but it is not too early to say that the participative design process seems to have gone well and has contributed to successful implementation.

In four other studies in my research program, task forces of managers were asked to review the bonus systems that determined their pay and to redesign them. In all four of these studies, the review and design process went well. Important recommendations were developed by the task forces and changes were made in the plans. In only one case was implementation a significant problem. In that case, some of the recommendations simply were not acceptable to top management and, as a result, were never implemented. Interestingly, these recommendations primarily had to do with making more information about a bonus plan public. It turned out that top management valued and wanted to preserve the freedom which secrecy gave them (the freedom to make decisions for which they were not accountable). It is still too early to judge the relative success of any of these projects, but it is encouraging that they were able to go through a successful design effort. Overall, a substantial body of evidence is accumulating that indicates that employees can meaningfully participate in the design and redesign of their own performance-based pay system.

The success of participative design efforts raises the question of why participation makes a difference. In some situations, it may lead to the design of a better plan because it involves a high level of information exchange. However, in some of the studies this cannot account for the differences because similar plans produced different results. In these studies it must be because participation contributed to the amount of information employees had about what was occurring and to their feelings of control over and commitment to what was decided (Vroom 1964).

In summary, when employees participate in the design of a system, there are four possible reasons why they are more likely to believe that a pay-performance relationship exists: (1) they have more information about the plan, (2) they are committed to it, (3) they have control over what happens, and (4) they trust the system. This reasoning was summarized in Figure 4.1. This figure also shows that, under some conditions, participation leads to higher quality decisions which, in turn, lead to favorable pay perceptions.

Despite positive evidence that the participative design of performance-based pay systems can be very effective, it is clearly not appropriate in all situations. Among other things, it requires a broad commitment on the part of management to using participative management and a work force that is interested in participation. Since participation takes time, it tends to work best in situations that are not in need of a "quick fix." For example, it took from six months to a year for the employee task forces to design the plant level bonus systems which were mentioned earlier. An extensive period of education was needed before the groups could start work, and most of the important decisions were then checked with the rest of the work force before they were made.

There are two situations where participation is particularly appropriate. The first, which will be discussed further in Chapter 11, is in new plants where participation is a standard operating procedure for most important decisions. The second, which will be discussed in Chapter 12, is in change efforts that are using pay system change as a lever for an overall movement of the organization toward a more participative style of management. The key in both of these situations is that participative design of the pay system is congruent with an overall philosophy of participative management.

PARTICIPATION IN SYSTEM ADMINISTRATION

The logical extension of the practice of having individuals participate in the design of performance-based pay systems is to have them participate in the making of day-to-day pay decisions. Having peers decide each other's pay, however, is seen in many organizations as an extremely radical step. Even more radical is the idea of having individuals set their own pay. Nevertheless, both of these alternatives have been tried in organizations, and there are reports to indicate that the efforts have been successful.

Let us start with the idea of having a peer group process decide individuals' performance-based pay. Several new plants have successfully incorporated into their systems the idea of having nonmanagement peer groups decide the pay of employees. As was mentioned earlier in the chapter on determining total compensation, this assessment is based partially on performance, but primarily on skill acquisition. One new plant that is just starting up is converting this assessment into a clear performance-based assessment. There is no logical reason why a peer group process cannot be as effective in determining performance-based pay as it is in determining skill-based pay. The issues are essentially the same, and there is considerable evidence that peers are just as valid raters of performance as are superiors (Kane and Lawler 1978). If a peer group process works for one, it should logically work for the other. One piece of evidence showing it does work is provided by a report that says that the employees at Romac Corporation actually vote on the pay of individuals who are nominated for performance-based raises (*Wall Street Journal* 1979). According to the report, the process is "surprisingly effective" in producing pay decisions which are reasonable and fair.

At the executive level, there is a rather dramatic, and apparently successful, effort of the executives in one company, Graphic Controls, to use a peer group decision process for determining their bonus payments and their stock options (Dowling 1977). Although no formal assessment of this procedure has been made, the participants reported to the author that it works quite well for them. It is important to note that they began this process after several years of intensive team building and organization development work with their group. To them, the idea of determining pay on a peer group basis followed logically from a history of setting performance goals and discussing the performance of each division in a group setting. It seemed only logical that the follow-up on the goal setting should take place in the group setting just as the goal setting had. In fact, it would have been counternormative in this situation for performance-based pay to be a one over one decision process when so many other important decisions in the organization had become a group decision process.

Two reports exist of individuals determining their own performance-based pay. One report describes a bonus plan in a twenty-nine-person branch bank. The plan was tied to the amount of courteous behavior demonstrated by the employees. Individuals could receive up to a $20-a-month bonus if they increased the frequency of their courteous behavior. The interesting thing about this plan was that em-

ployees were asked to keep their own records of behavior and to post
the results at the end of each day on a public chart in the lunchroom.
A person who then met the standards which he or she had helped set
received a bonus. According to a report of the plan, courteous behavior increased dramatically, as did the operating results of the
branch. In six months, the branch moved steadily from eleventh to
first in new accounts. Today, the plan still continues to operate effectively.[1]

Perhaps the most extreme case of workers setting their own performance-based pay was cited in Chapter 4. It occurred at the
Friedman-Jacobs Company, a small appliance firm in Oakland, California. Friedman decided to allow his employees to set their own
wages based on their perception of their performance. This radical
approach apparently has worked well. Instead of an all-out raid on the
company coffers, the employees displayed responsible behavior. They
set their wages slightly higher than the scale of the union to which they
belonged and apparently find their pay quite satisfactory. When one
appliance serviceman who was receiving considerably less than his co-
workers was asked why he did not insist on equal pay, he replied, "I
don't want to work that hard."

Clearly, the idea of having individuals set their own performance-
based pay levels and the idea of having a peer group process decide
performance appraisal is not for every organization. It is a dramatic
break with traditional approaches to management and, therefore,
needs to be used carefully. However, because it is a dramatic break, it
is a potentially useful tool in organization development. As will be discussed further in later chapters, it can be a key follow-up to the participative design of pay systems and it can reinforce the general effort of
participative management. Stated another way, failure to include it in
a long-term movement toward participative management can put the
pay system out of synchronization with the way the rest of the organization is being managed.

Participation in performance-based pay decisions need not go as
far as having individuals set their own pay. As will be discussed in the
next chapter, there is a growing body of evidence which argues that a
great deal can be gained when performance appraisal is done on a

---

1.   Described by Carl Pitts, *The OD Practitioner,* Washington, D.C.: O.D.
Network, 1979.

more participative basis. Specifically, subordinates react better when they can contribute to how they are evaluated. The idea of having subordinates provide input during this performance appraisal can be implemented in many organizations today. It is not that radical a move.

SUMMARY AND CONCLUSIONS

It should be clear from the discussion in this chapter, and in the preceding chapter, that there are conditions under which organizations should not try to relate pay to performance. Regardless of the process used, when the conditions are not right, installing a performance-based pay system runs the risk of being more dysfunctional than functional. Gaming, counterproductive behavior, rigid bureaucratic behavior, and providing false data are just a few of the dysfunctional behaviors that can result. Given this list, it is hard to argue with the view that unless the conditions are right for it, an organization is likely to be better off without a performance-based pay system than with it.

When the conditions are right for a performance-based pay system, then our review of the process issues involved in establishing and administering one suggests that under some conditions organizations may benefit from using an open participative approach. This approach is particularly likely to be effective when the following conditions exist: (1) it is part of an overall participative approach to management, (2) it is favored by employees and managers, and (3) a climate of trust and joint problem solving is present. When these conditions exist, an open participative approach can be expected to produce good decisions which are accepted and which motivate.

8
PERFORMANCE APPRAISAL

At the heart of most salary increase plans, and many bonus plans, is a performance appraisal system that asks a supervisor to make a subjective judgment concerning a subordinate's job performance. A subjective judgment is asked for because, in most jobs, objective measurement simply is not possible for many reasons. These include the complexity of the measurement task, the changing environment, and the difficulty in defining individual jobs. The effectiveness and integrity of these performance-based pay systems depend upon the effectiveness of the performance appraisal process.

In addition to being used for pay administration purposes, performance appraisals may also be used (1) to counsel employees, (2) as a source of data for long-range personnel planning and development activities in an organization, (3) as a vehicle for giving motivating and corrective feedback to employees about their performance, (4) as a way of defining what performance is expected of a jobholder, and (5) as a basis for making promotion decisions. Recent surveys of company personnel practices show that more and more organizations have formal performance appraisal programs and that they are becoming more and more important (see, e.g., Lazer and Wickstrom 1977). Today most nonunion employees in large organizations are regularly appraised. Unionized employees are rarely appraised because few union contracts have "merit pay" provisions in them; thus, one of the most important reasons for doing appraisals is absent. Sometimes clerical and nonexempt employees are not appraised in organizations because they too are not on merit pay systems.

The performance appraisal practices of organizations vary widely. For example:

- Some organizations have appraisees write a narrative summary of their accomplishments for the year. This is then reviewed with whomever is making the appraisal.

- When President Carter wanted an evaluation of the White House staff, he asked that all employees be rated by their supervisors on a long list of traits such as "loyalty," "savvy," and the like. Many other organizations also use this trait-rating approach.

- Many research and development labs rank all their employees based on their overall job performance. The result is a listing of all employees, running from the best to the worst performer. In some organizations this list exceeds a thousand names.

- Recently, a number of organizations have adopted complex Management by Objectives (MBO) systems that include goal setting at all organizational levels and the evaluation of individuals against these goals.

Despite their importance and the many functions they are expected to serve, abundant evidence exists that many organizations do a poor job of appraising the performance of their employees if, in fact, they do it at all (Campbell et al. 1970). There is also evidence that appraisals can do more harm than good (Meyer et al. 1965). In the area of performance-based pay, for example, appraisals can contribute to cynicism and to the belief that pay and performance are not related, despite public statements and policies to the contrary. Although not a great deal is known about how to do performance appraisals effectively, there are clearly some rights and wrongs in carrying out the performance appraisal process (Landy and Farr 1980).

DOING EFFECTIVE APPRAISALS

Basic to carrying out an effective performance appraisal is the realization that its success is at least as much influenced by procedural and process issues as it is by the type of measurement recording form or system which is used. All too often, organizations place great emphasis on developing the right form and very little emphasis on looking at how the appraisal is actually carried out (Kane and Lawler 1979; Landy et al. 1978).

Performance appraisal is a subjective process that involves human judgments; as such, it is infinitely fallible and subject to many sources of invalidity. Many of these sources are involved in the appraisal process and must therefore be taken into account. It is crucial to remember that for the appraisal to accomplish most, if not all, of its objectives, it must have a favorable impact on the person whose performance is being appraised. As we shall see, process issues seem to be particularly important in determining how appraisees react to their performance being evaluated. Table 8.1 illustrates the complexity of the appraisal process by showing that performance appraisal can be broken up into three distinct periods: a preperformance period, a performance period, and a postperformance period. As is shown, each of these periods has a set of critical issues associated with it. Some of the key issues involve which types of measures will be used, while others involve process issues. In addition, appraisals are

Table 8.1
Critical Issues in Performance Appraisal Time Periods

Preperformance Period	Performance Period	Postperformance Period
1. Superior-subordinate agreement on goals or performance areas	1. Ongoing feedback 2. Changing environment	1. Evaluation of performance
2. Agreement on measures and performance period		2. Feedback
3. Agreement on use of rewards		3. Administration of rewards

done in individual and organizational situations that are either relatively favorable or relatively unfavorable to a positive outcome from the appraisal process. The remainder of this chapter will look separately at each of the three time periods involved in performance appraisal and then consider the key situational factors.

PREPERFORMANCE PERIOD

There are three critical events that may or may not take place during the preperformance period. Whether they take place and how they are handled can be crucial in determining the effectiveness of the performance appraisal. Figure 8.1 outlines the potential flow of these events. Basic to effective performance appraisal is an adequate definition of the appraisee's job. Probably the only case in which this is not necessary is when the job is so simple and so clearly defined that there can be no question about what behavior is appropriate. In most jobs, however, this is not true, and considerable confusion exists about what constitutes the job of the person who is to be evaluated. The job definition process can be either a joint or one-way one. Normally, the one-way process is top-down but it may also be a bottom-up, one-way process. It is generally accepted that the best process is a joint one because, at the end of it, both the superior and subordinate are more likely to feel that they have a good understanding of what constitutes the job, along with mutual agreement on and commitment to the definition of the job (Kerr 1976).

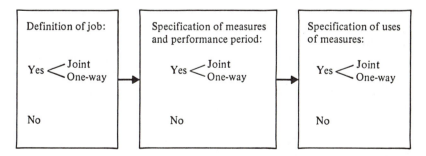

Figure 8.1   Critical events in the preperformance period

Following agreement on the definition of the job, there may or may not be agreement on the measures and the objectives upon which performance for the period is to be measured. There also may or may not be agreement on how long the performance period will be. Individuals are typically appraised on an annual cycle for administrative convenience, although some should be appraised more frequently than this, and others less frequently. As a general rule new employees and employees in lower level jobs should be appraised more often than once a year, and employees in higher level jobs should be appraised less often. The key here is how long it takes for performance results to become visible and how soon the individual can profit from feedback. In higher level jobs, performance results take longer to show up, and thus feedback and measurement need to wait longer. A few organizations have innovated in this area and have entered into long-term performance contracts with their top managers. These contracts often call for five-year performance periods and for large bonuses if certain performance levels are reached at that time.

Agreement on measures, objectives, and timing would seem to be critical to effective performance appraisal, except in the rare instances where these are self-evident. This is a key part of most MBO systems, and there are a number of reasons for believing that it can have positive effects. There is evidence that the setting of goals, by itself, can have a positive impact on performance (see Latham and Yukl 1975). All too often, superiors assume that performance goals are self-evident to subordinates. Unfortunately, at the end of the performance period, they often find that they did not agree on the same self-evident performance objectives and measures.

Just as with the job definition process, the definition of measures and objectives may be either joint or one-way. Although not absolutely necessary, it would seem that this specification process, like the definition process, is most likely to be successful when it is a joint mutual-influence process. One-way processes that are either appraiser or appraisee demonstrated run the danger of misunderstanding and failure to develop reasonable measures and objectives (McGregor 1957; Levinson 1970). Particularly in the area of objective setting, it seems to be crucial that both parties lend their expertise to the process (Kerr 1976). There is a real danger that if only one party lends its expertise, the objectives may be either unrealistically high or unrealistically low. Although it may seem that if subordinates set them they will be unrealistically low and if superiors set them they will be unrealistically high, there is some evidence that this is not necessarily so. In fact, it seems that subordinates often have a tendency to set unrealistically high goals, and it takes interaction with a supervisor to come up with more realistic goals (Lawler 1977).

Finally, there may or may not be agreement as to how the performance appraisal results will be used. In most cases, if agreements are reached they are usually at a very general level (e.g., as a basis for determining pay or an input into the promotion process). A strong case can be made that, wherever possible, greater specification than this is desirable. It would seem to be much more desirable to detail exactly what levels of performance lead to what amounts of pay and what levels of performance are needed to qualify for promotion. Although this may be an unreasonable or impossible task in many cases, if it can be done, it can do a lot to form clear expectations about the relationship between pay and performance. As is true with the other parts of the preperformance process, this specification may be arrived at in either a joint or one-way manner. In general, it is probably best done on the basis of a joint process. This is particularly likely to lead to mutual agreement, mutual understanding, and a perceived relationship between performance and rewards.

PERFORMANCE PERIOD

During the performance period, both the appraiser and appraisee form impressions of the appraisee's performance. Each, of course, gathers his or her own kind of data based on the very different perspectives they have on performance. In addition, other individuals gather data about the appraisee's performance. Because of the imperfect way people gather and process information, the information of all parties observing performance are, to some extent, invalid and biased. There is no way to guarantee that any observer will gather totally objective and valid data. In the case of the appraiser, for example, he or she often sees only a small percentage of the total behavior of the individual, and that which is seen is viewed through filters that are influenced by past behavior, expectations about future behavior, and interpersonal likes and dislikes.

Given the biases which are likely to be present in observing performance, it is particularly important that steps be taken to minimize their intrusion into the final judgment of the individual's performance. Several things can be done. First, as was mentioned in the previous chapter, objective information should be used wherever possible. This can be particularly useful where good management information systems exist and where the environment is relatively stable. In situations where change is rapidly occurring, information system data often has to be interpreted based on the changing situation. This causes subjectivity to increase dramatically. This is a particularly difficult problem for MBO systems, since objectives which are set at the beginning of a performance period can quickly become outdated in a rapidly changing work environment. The only way to solve this problem is to regularly update objectives. In some organizations this is handled through regularly scheduled review meetings.

Where objective data are not obtainable, it is particularly helpful if the supervisor tries to keep a written record of the specific behaviors that are observed. This can be a tremendous aid to the final superior-subordinate discussion. It can facilitate the discussion in focusing on performance and behavior, rather than on traits or general impressions. If the critical incidents are recorded, they can also be reviewed by the supervisor before a final judgment is reached. This can help to refresh the appraiser's memory about the accomplishments of the subordinate and overcome the common tendency of supervisors to rate subordinates based on their most recent performance. Rating on the basis of recent performance can lead to serious problems where individuals have performed particularly poorly during the last few months before their appraisal.

The same points which apply to the supervisor's behavior also apply to the subordinate's behavior. It can be very helpful if the subordinate keeps a record of his or her own behaviors, so that, at the end of the period, discussions will focus on specific behaviors rather than general global traits.

Perhaps the most important key to a successful final appraisal is having regular superior-subordinate discussions during the performance period. This can be critical in preventing unhappy surprises at the end of the performance period and in keeping the supryisor up to date on the subordinate's performance. All too often, this particular step is left out of the appraisal process because appraisal is viewed as a once a year event.

In summary, during the performance period, it is particularly critical that the supervisor record behavior in as objective a manner as possible and that the subordinate do the same. It is also critical that regular discussions take place between the superior and the subordinate about the subordinate's performance.

POSTPERFORMANCE PERIOD

Organizations differ widely in how they administer the performance appraisal process at the end of the performance period. As Figure 8.2 shows, a number of events potentially can take place during this period. In most organizations, many of these events do not take place; when they do take place, often it is in a very truncated and difficult-to-recognize form. One thing that is almost sure to take place is some sort of recording of the individual's performance. In the absence of this, it is hard to say that performance appraisal has really taken place at all. The best way to consider the postperformance period is to go step-by-step through the events that could potentially happen in an appraisal system.

Prescoring Discussion of Performance

In a few performance appraisal systems, a discussion between the superior and subordinate takes place before the individual's performance is actually scored or formally evaluated. The purpose of this session is to allow the individual to make inputs to the supervisor about how the subordinate sees his or her performance during the performance period. In many cases, this is a joint discussion in which the supervisor shares his or her reactions to the subordinate's performance, and the subordinate provides additional information. It can also be a one-way process, or it may not take place at all. Typically, it does not take place at all.

Some recent data collected by M. Mohrman and myself strongly support the view that a joint two-way discussion of performance prior to the performance appraisal can be an important aid in making the

Figure 8.2 Critical events in the postperformance period

appraisal an effective one. There are two reasons for this. The first has to do with information exchange. It is often true that the subordinate has information that the supervisor simply does not have and, as a result, when this information is supplied to the supervisor, the appraisal is a more accurate one. The second has to do with the perceived fairness of the appraisal on the part of the subordinate. In the absence of an opportunity to input to the supervisor, the subordinate cannot be sure whether the supervisor really has the information that he or she needs in order to make a fair and reasonable judgment of the subordinate's performance. The discussion can, of course, help to assure that the subordinate perceives that the supervisor has this necessary information.

Probably the major reasons why a discussion does not take place are time and comfort. It takes a considerable amount of time to go through a reasonable discussion of performance. Performance appraisals often seem to be left for the last moment and are done on a crash basis. Given this, it is often difficult to get supervisors to take time to talk to their subordinates in advance of their completing the appraisal form. A second and more important reason why this discussion does not take place has to do with the supervisor's discomfort with conducting it. It is very easy for the supervisor to feel that all that will happen is a sell job on the part of the subordinate, and that he or she will constantly be faced with disconfirming the subordinate's perceptions of his or her own performance. This is a risk, of course, but it can be reduced if reasonable performance goals or measures are agreed to in the beginning so that there is relatively little ambiguity about how well the subordinate has performed during the performance period. Some of the interpersonal discomfort also can be reduced by having the subordinate do a self-appraisal in written form before the meeting so that the supervisor can be prepared and have a written document to refer to.

Scoring Method

There are a number of different methods for recording and scoring the performance of an individual or group during a performance period. The traditional approach is to use either a single global rating of performance or a trait rating which rates individuals on such dimensions as reliability, dependability, attitude, quality of work, etc. In the last ten years, a number of other approaches have been tried. Probably the most common approach is to tie performance goals into an MBO system. In this system, individuals set goals during the preperformance period and are then scored on degree of goal accomplishment. Behaviorally anchored rating scales (bars) are a more recently developed approach (see Dunnette and Borman 1979; Schwab et al. 1975). These describe behavior in terms of the actual behavioral level capabilities of the individual (see Figure 8.3). Finally, there is the traditional approach of writing a narrative description of the individual's performance and potential.

A great deal of time has been spent on trying to develop the best possible forms for recording performance appraisal results. This is consistent with the often-made assumption that the problem is a mechanical scoring problem rather than a process problem. So far, looking at performance appraisal as a mechanical scoring problem has not yielded a great deal of progress. No one approach to recording and scoring performance has proven to be the answer (Kane and Lawler 1979). The most recent effort to improve scoring is the behaviorally anchored rating scale. There was some initial reason to believe that this approach would yield higher quality data and better scores. This has been questioned by several studies, though. It is now not at all apparent, in terms of the validity of the ratings produced, that it is better than a single global rating of overall performance (Kane and Lawler 1979).

The most important thing that has been learned about the effectiveness of the different approaches to rating concerns the usefulness of trait ratings and global ratings in the area of feedback to individuals. It seems clear that when individuals are told how they have been scored on a trait-rating approach or on a global-rating approach, they get little useful feedback and, in some cases, it can actually do more to harm their performance than to improve it (Meyer et al. 1964; Meyer 1975). Traits are so general that when individuals are told they are low on a trait they do not know how to change their behavior in order to improve and, as a result, they tend to become frustrated and defensive. This strongly suggests that feedback is best given in terms of behavioral incidents or the accomplishment of some agreed-to objectives.

Could be expected to exchange a blouse purchased in a distant town and to impress the customer so much that she would buy three dresses and three pairs of shoes.

Could be expected to smooth things over beautifully with an irate customer who returned a sweater with a hole in it and turn her into a satisfied customer.

Could be expected to be friendly and tactful and to agree to reline a coat for a customer who wants a new coat because the lining had worn out in "only" two years.

Could be expected to courteously exchange a pair of gloves that are too small.

Could be expected to handle the after-Christmas rush of refunds and exchanges in a reasonable manner.

Could be expected to make a refund for a sweater only if the customer insists.

Could be expected to be quite abrupt with customers who want to exchange merchandise for a different color or style.

Could be expected to tell a customer that a "six-week-old" order could not be changed, even though the merchandise had actually been ordered only two weeks previously.

Could be expected to tell a customer who tried to return a shirt bought in Hawaii that a store in the States had no use for a Hawaiian shirt.

Figure 8.3 Department manager job behavior rating scale for the dimension "handling customer complaints and making adjustments."

Table 8.2
Evaluation of Four Approaches to Measuring Performance

	Traditional Trait Rating	Single Global Rating	Behaviorally Anchored Ratings	Objectives-Oriented Evaluation
Acceptability to superior and subordinate	Poor	Moderate	Good	Good, except for work load
Counseling and development information	Poor	Poor	Moderate	Good, if it includes activities measures
Salary and reward administration	Poor	Moderate to good	Good	Moderate
Motivation based on goal setting	Poor	Poor	Poor	Poor
Clarify nature of job	Poor	Poor	Moderate to good	Good

Table 8.2 summarizes the strengths and weaknesses of the varying approaches to measuring performance. The most general conclusion it suggests is that the answer to doing good appraisals is not in the scoring method. It also suggests that trait ratings probably should not be used at all since they are not useful for either overall scoring purposes or for feedback purposes.

Uses of Appraisal Information

Once the appraisal has been completed, there are a number of things that can be done with the information. First of all, it can be fed back to the individual simply to let the individual know how he or she has done. Second, it can be used as a basis for such reward system decisions as promotion and pay actions. Third, it can be used as part of a counseling and career development program. Finally, it can be used as part of a corporate information system for manpower planning and career planning actions.

What happens to the information may make a tremendous difference in what happens during the appraisal. A number of individuals have pointed out that there is an inherent conflict between the feedback and counseling functions and reward system function (McGregor 1957; Meyer et al. 1965). Effective counseling of an individual requires open and valid exchange of information between the superior and the subordinate. Reward system allocation decisions require the supervisor to make an overall comparative judgment of the individual's performance versus the performance of other individuals. This can lead to individuals being defensive, withholding information, and being hesitant to talk about their shortcomings. This is often worsened by the fact that the average individual typically rates his or her performance much higher than does the appraiser. In my research, it has usually turned out that the average subordinate's self-rating is at about the 80th percentile. Although raters tend to rate highly, their rating is normally lower than the ratee's appraisal and, as a result, the superior and the subordinate find themselves in disagreement. In addition, when pay is on the agenda, individuals tend not to hear and remember much of what is said about things other than their pay. The pay decision therefore interferes with and, indeed, blocks good counseling. This has led some people to suggest that the different functions of the appraisal be separated so that they would not interfere with each other (Meyer et al. 1965).

There is no question that feedback and career counseling are easier to do when reward system issues are totally eliminated and rewards are not based on performance. This has a number of severe costs, however, if it means that no appraisal is done in conjunction with the pay action. First, much of the potential for extrinsic motivation is given up. Second, some organizations have found that interest in performance discussions declines substantially when they make no difference in terms of the rewards for the individual. Finally, my research has shown that when they are not related, it can lead to increased dissatisfaction with the pay system. The loss of motivation can be partially offset if the individual is part of a group- or plant-level bonus system. Nevertheless, it seems clear that organizations should think very carefully and very long before they decide to abandon the idea of basing pay and promotion on the outcomes of a performance appraisal, particularly since it is something most employees seem to want.

In many situations, the most effective way to handle the problem of a conflict between counseling and reward systems is to hold separate sessions in which these issues are handled. It seems advisable to first hold a session in which performance is discussed and evaluated. At this meeting the subordinate's inputs are solicited and accepted, and performance feedback is given. Relatively soon after this discussion, the pay issue needs to be dealt with. At this meeting, salary or bonus ratios are discussed and related to the performance appraisal. At a different time, career counseling and individual development are discussed. In essence, the distinction is one between reward system decisions which are past-oriented, and counseling and development discussions which are future-oriented.

Some organizations try to handle this pay discussion by separating it as much as six months from the appraisal discussion. This undoubtedly serves the purpose of clearly distinguishing one from the other. However, it runs the risk of separating performance measurement too far away from a key discussion which needs to tie in to it—that is, reward action.

Final Feedback About Rewards

Regardless of how the pay decision is related to the appraisal discussion and decision, it is important that the final pay action be discussed with the subordinate. In many organizations, the final reward system decisions are not made by the supervisor at the time of the initial performance appraisal discussion. The supervisor must make a recommendation to the next level of management which, in turn, reviews it and considers its impact on such things as the budget and what is going on in other parts of the organization. This often results in a lag of at least several weeks between the completion of the appraisal itself and final word on what the pay action will be. In some instances, the supervisor fails to get back to the individual to let the individual know what his or her actual pay change will be as a result of the performance. In others, a great emphasis is placed upon the supervisor communicating directly with the subordinate about the final pay action, so that the individual does not find out what his or her new pay rate will be by noticing a slight change or a large change in the next paycheck.

Although there is no research to directly support it, it seems that at the very least the supervisor should get back to the subordinate and discuss with him or her how the final salary action was determined. This seems to be particularly critical if the organization is going to try to tie pay to performance and use pay as a motivator. In the absence of this kind of closing of the loop, a situation can develop where individuals think they are getting a pay raise based on a favorable or unfavorable performance appraisal and end up getting something else. This can lead them to seriously mistrust the relationship between the appraisal and the pay increase, unless it is carefully explained to them why these two are at variance.

Appeal Process

Once the complete appraisal/reward process has been completed, a few organizations provide individuals the opportunity to appeal any decisions which affect them. This gives them the chance to have their cases heard by someone other than their supervisor if they feel strongly that they have been unfairly treated. In some organizations this appeal is made to the personnel department, in others to higher management. From an effectiveness point of view it is crucial that the individuals feel that they will get a fair hearing and that they will not be harmed for appealing.

Given the potential benefits to an organization of having an effective appeal process it is surprising how few have them. In an era when individuals can go to court to challenge appraisal decisions, it seems particularly prudent for organizations to provide individuals an internal hearing that might prevent a court case from developing. In addition, an appeal process can help motivate managers to do a good appraisal and it can help assure the credibility of the whole reward system. Finally, even if it does none of these it may correct errors which would lead to people being incorrectly paid and promoted such that they would quit or be underutilized.

SITUATIONAL FACTORS

The success of a performance appraisal is partially determined by a number of situational factors. The four factors that will be reviewed have the power to make it difficult to do a good appraisal unless they are favorable to one. Before an appraisal is done, therefore, their condition needs to be reviewed and a decision made as to whether they can prevent an effective appraisal from being done. If they can, then consideration needs to be given to changing them or to not doing the appraisal.

Recent research on job enrichment has demonstrated the importance of job design in influencing behavior. Jobs having such characteristics as high task identity and feedback have been shown to increase intrinsic motivation (Hackman and Oldham 1980). Although it is rarely emphasized in literature, there is reason to believe that jobs which are "enriched" make performance appraisal easier. The reason for this is twofold. First, relatively enriched jobs usually mean that the individual is responsible for a whole piece of work, and that his or her performance stands out because it is visible in an end product. Second, if the job provides ongoing intrinsic performance feedback to the individual, then the individual is in a much better position to assess his or her own performance and should be much less surprised by the performance feedback received during the performance appraisal process. This leads to the interesting point that jobs that are particularly well designed from an intrinsic motivation point of view are also likely to lend themselves to the use of performance-based rewards and, therefore, to be optimal for extrinsic motivation. Support for this conclusion is present in the data recently collected by M. Mohrman and myself. We found that when jobs were well specified, had high task identity, provided autonomy, and provided feedback, the reactions to performance appraisal were favorable.

A second factor that seems to influence the effectiveness of a performance appraisal is the overall climate of the organization. Organizations that are characterized by climates of mistrust, threat, defensiveness, low support, and poor communication are very difficult ones in which to do performance appraisal effectively. The very essence of performance appraisal is the open exchange of information between superiors and subordinates. If this is not the norm in the organization, performance appraisal is extremely difficult to do effectively.

The nature of the superior-subordinate relationship is a third crucial influence on the effectiveness of the appraisal process. If the history has been one of defensiveness, poor communication, and punitive behavior, it is unreasonable to expect the exchange of valid information and an effective performance appraisal. The suggestion, then, is that in the absence of reasonable superior-subordinate relationships, it is probably better not to do performance appraisal at all.

Finally, it takes substantial interpersonal and cognitive skills on the part of *both* the superior and the subordinate in order for performance appraisal to be done well. For the superior, it takes the ability to define goals and jobs, listen empathetically, and communicate ideas and feelings effectively. For the subordinate, it takes the ability to define goals, receive feedback, and communicate aspirations, hopes, and feelings to a superordinate figure. There is no reason to believe that most superiors or subordinates naturally come to the performance appraisal situation with these skills. In the absence of training and experience in carrying out effective performance appraisals, there is every reason to believe that the appraisal will not go well.

Table 8.3 summarizes the kinds of situational factors which favor an effective performance appraisal process. They are not factors that frequently exist in an organization; thus, it is not surprising that performance appraisals go astray and prove to be either valueless or harmful.

PERFORMANCE APPRAISAL IN PERSPECTIVE

Should all employees be part of a formal appraisal system? Probably not, but there is good reason to believe that most should be. If the decision is made to use a merit pay system which is based on perfor-

Table 8.3
Factors Favoring Effective Performance Appraisal

Situational Factor	Characteristics
Job design	Enriched jobs with high task identity, autonomy, and feedback
Organizational climate	High level of trust, security, openness, and concern for personal growth
Superior-subordinate relationship	Constructive, frequent communication
Skill level of superior and subordinate	High in listening and communicating

mance appraisal results, then it follows that appraisal must be done and done very well. Even if performance appraisal results are not used for merit pay purposes, there is good reason to believe that appraisals should be done. The functions that appraisals perform (e.g., goal setting and feedback) are important and needed in any organization. If these functions are not done as part of the appraisal system, they may not be done at all since, in most organizations, there are no other systems to accomplish them. In addition, my research indicates that despite some ambivalence, most people expect and want to have their performance appraised. They value the feedback and recognition it offers. In many cases, it is the one chance they have to discuss their career and personal objectives with their boss.

Despite the many difficulties which can arise during appraisals (e.g., defensiveness and destructive feedback), the event is usually either neutral or positive for most participants. For example, in some recent evaluations of company appraisal systems, I have found that in less than 10 percent of the cases the superior-subordinate relationship has been worsened because of an appraisal. Interestingly, the data quite clearly show that, on the average, appraisers felt the appraisal was a more constructive event than did the appraisee.

The data also suggest that when organizations invest considerable time in developing and supporting the appraisal process, it tends to go better. Appraisal is clearly not something that can be done in fifteen minutes, once a year. It requires hours of preparation and execution time. This leads to the frequent complaint by appraisers that it simply takes too much time. In some respects, this is a strange complaint since appraisal would seem to be the very essence of a manager's job. Management presumably means dealing with people in order to get work done and the key steps in appraisal (e.g., defining performance and providing feedback) are certainly ones that can help the appraisee perform better. In one of my recent studies, 53 percent of supervisors felt their subordinate's performance had improved and none felt it had gotten worse as a result of a recent performance appraisal. This would suggest that appraisal time is time well spent, Why, then, the hesitancy to spend the time? For one thing, appraisal is not a comfortable interpersonal process for most people. In addition, there are many other activities competing for a manager's time. This suggests that in order for appraisal to be done well, organizations need to structure their systems in ways that encourage supervisors to spend the time necessary to do it well. For example, supervisors should be evaluated on how well they do appraisals, and there should be strong leadership support from the top of the organization.

SUMMARY AND CONCLUSIONS

Our discussion so far leads to a number of conclusions about when and how performance appraisal should be done. If the following conditions are present, it probably should not be done:

- The organization (managers) are unwilling to commit the time that is required to do it properly.

- Jobs are changing so rapidly because of a crisis environment that it is impossible to structure clear responsibilities and jobs.

- Supervisors lack the skill to give feedback and deal competently with their subordinates.

- The jobs are so routine that performance on them does not vary appreciably.

- A union contract exists that essentially makes appraisal unnecessary or incapable of influencing any key records or job issues.

In situations that are favorable to doing performance appraisal, the following features seem to lead to favorable results in most situations:

- A concentration on behavior and objectives, not traits

- The use of a predetermined set of goals and/or job functions

- An opportunity for the subordinate to input into the evaluation process

- A regularly scheduled appraisal cycle that fits the nature of the jobs

- Different meetings to discuss performance, pay, and career development

- A due process appeal procedure that allows the subordinate to surface an unfair appraisal

- Evaluation of managers on how well they carry out appraisals

If these general features are built into an appraisal system, then there is good reason to believe it will have a positive effect.

9
GAIN SHARING

The idea of paying a bonus to employees based upon improvements in the operating results of an organization is an old and well-established one. Thousands of different formulas exist for calculating payout results to employees based upon improvements in operating results. In most cases (e.g., the typical profit-sharing plan), these plans are simple economic incentive plans and are not tied into an overall philosophy of management that is consistent with or part of an organization development effort. A notable exception is the Scanlon Plan which is as much an organization development intervention as it is an incentive plan (Frost et al. 1974; White 1979). It dates back to the 1930s and today enjoys increasing acceptance. Another classic plan is the Lincoln Electric Plan. It, too, dates back more than forty years. Other currently popular plans include IMPROSHARE and the Rucker plan. It is beyond the scope of this book to go into a detailed discussion of all of the different gain-sharing plans. What will be done is to (1) review the critical decisions that need to be made in setting up a gain-sharing plan, (2) look in some detail at the Scanlon plan, and (3) look in less detail at some other plans.

MAJOR DECISIONS IN THE DEVELOPMENT AND DESIGN OF GAIN-SHARING PLANS

Process of Design

The first decision that an organization faces in setting up a gain-sharing plan involves the process which will be used to design it. As was indicated earlier, most nonunion organizations do this on a top-down basis. As was also indicated in the previous chapters, this often is not the best way to go about setting up a gain-sharing plan. Evidence is beginning to accumulate in my research program which shows that a design team drawn from a cross section of the organization can effectively develop a plan. R. J. Bullock and myself have successfully used it to design three gain-sharing plans, one in a unionized plant and two in nonunionized plants. This approach is particularly desirable if the ultimate objective is to have a gain-sharing plan which is based on a participative style of management and an economic payout that rewards group- or plant-level results. As will be discussed further in Chapters 11 and 12, this holds true whether the focal unit is a new organization or a relatively old one in which the management is seeking to begin a renewal process.

It is usually necessary to have a participative design approach when the organization is unionized. Gain-sharing plans depend heavily upon employee acceptance, input, and cooperation to make them work. This, in turn, depends heavily on a reasonably high level of trust and understanding on the part of the employees. In a unionized situation this is difficult to achieve when the plan is management owned and management initiated. The only viable alternative to participative design in a unionized situation is the use of a standardized plan and a trusted third party. For example, in Scanlon Plan installations the details of the plan are frequently developed by a third party with the support of the union leadership and management (Lesieur 1958; Lesieur and Puckett 1969; Moore and Ross 1978). It is then voted on by the work force.

In most cases, the task-force approach is the best way to get employee involvement. To be effective, the task force should be made up of a broad cross section of people who are given the charter of developing a plan which is acceptable to both the management and nonmanagement employees. In situations where I have used the task-force approach, a considerable amount of education has been needed. In my research program, we normally spend a few three-hour sessions acquainting people with various approaches to gain sharing and suggesting that they visit several other plants with gain-sharing plans. The latter seems to be particularly important in building enthusiasm for the plan and furthering understanding.

Membership composition of the design task force is a particularly critical issue. Members need to be good communicators to people outside the task force. They also need to be highly credible individuals so that the plan will gain acceptance. In many cases, the best way to ensure the right kind of individuals will be selected is through an election process. This is somewhat risky but guarantees that employees will see the overall design process as a credible one. In situations where a union exists, an election is almost a necessity unless the union leadership is automatically placed on it. In any case, it is important to have the key union officers on the task force. Without their membership, the support of the union for the plan may be difficult to obtain. Depending on the nature of the task force and the organizational conditions, we have found that it takes anywhere from three to twelve months for a cross-sectional task force to design a gain-sharing plan. This may seem like a long time, but there are a large number of critical decisions that need to be made in order for an adequate plan to be developed.

It is easy for the task force to become an isolated group that loses its communication with the rest of the organization. This is particularly disastrous when a gain-sharing plan is being designed because it increases the risk of plan rejection. It is also important to note that attention needs to be paid to group process issues in the design task force. In many cases, the task force brings together people who have never worked in groups before and who are unfamiliar with task-force work. In unionized situations, it often brings together individuals who have previously had an adversary relationship with each other. It is easy, particularly in unionized situations, for the design process to be an adversary one. If this occurs, it can be fatal because it leads to issue-by-issue negotiation of the design rather than to the development of a total design that fits together. The success of a plan depends on a total plan design that makes sense as an integrated whole not as a set of isolated parts. I have found that a team-building session which establishes joint objectives is a good way to prevent an adversary relationship from developing. A team-building session is often best done at an early meeting of the task force. Continuing attention then needs to be given to issues like how decisions are made, what kind of norms are operating, and the process of the group.

Finally, it is also important to remember that in order to gain momentum, task forces need to meet regularly. My own experience has been that a task force needs to meet at least once a week in order to get a sense of its mission and the importance of its task.

Organizational Unit Covered

The size of the organizational unit that is covered by a gain-sharing plan can and does vary widely. Some cover companies with thousands of employees and some cover small plants or departments with less than fifty employees. In many situations, it is obvious what the appropriate unit is for a gain-sharing plan. This is true, for example, in the case of a freestanding plant with good performance measures and an employee population of less than 500. In these cases, a plan that covers the whole plant normally fits nicely since it allows for good performance measurement and is usually small enough for individuals to see the relationship between their behavior and the bonus amount.

The situation is much less clear when several plants exist on the same plot of land or when a single plant exceeds 500 employees. When these conditions exist, there are advantages to installing two or more gain-sharing plans. The primary advantage, of course, lies in having bonus amounts that are closely tied to the performance of individuals. However, there are significant problems with the idea of having multiple plans in the same plant or separate plans in plants on a single plot of land. In both cases, the potential exists for significant conflict between people on different plans. This can be particularly debilitating when the people are technologically interdependent. In the case of the single large plant, there is likely to be a problem with the types of measures that exist. Often in large plants, there simply are not good measures existing for subunits of the plant.

In summary, deciding how many plans to have must take into consideration the measures which exist, the size of the organizational units or subunits, the interdependencies in the workflow, and the potential for conflict. There is no simple answer because so many complexities exist in most actual situations. The closest we can come to a rule of thumb is to suggest that when significant doubts exist about the advisability of having more than one plan, it is usually best to opt for a single plan. This is typically the safest approach since it does not risk conflict, poor payouts because of bad measures, and other dysfunctional consequences. It does, of course, run the risk of the plan failing to motivate—a significant risk; but often this is not the greatest risk.

Determining the Bonus

All gain-sharing plans are based on a formula that generates a bonus pool which is to be divided up among the members of the plan. A few generally applicable rules exist about the nature of the formula that should be used but, to a large extent, formulas need to be custom-designed. One way to think about the issues involved in developing a formula is to use the analogy of par for a golf course. Par is established based on a consensus of what good performance is. When an individual beats this standard of performance, there has been a saving. When an individual performs worse than the standard, there has been a loss of strokes to par. Gain-sharing plans basically work on the same principle. A par or standard is established. When the standard is improved upon, such that fewer costs are incurred, a bonus pool is available for sharing. When performance is worse than par, such that more costs are incurred, no bonus is available and an actual loss in the plan occurs.

Just as is the case with golf, a critical issue in establishing a gain-sharing plan is where to set par. Other issues involve how the bonus pool will be divided up once it is determined, how frequently performance will be measured for bonus purposes, what costs should be included, and how radical changes in the environment and in the organization will be handled. A brief review of each of these follows.

Developing a Standard. The Scanlon Plan and many other plans start with the assumption that the standard should be based on past history. They simply take a period of past performance, be it one, two, or more years, and say that improvements over that period will be shared (Moore and Ross 1978). This approach is taken in the hope of avoiding a long and acrimonious debate over what is a fair standard. It has the obvious advantage over engineered or estimated standards of being more a matter of record and, therefore, more widely acceptable. Unfortunately, it does not always work since technological changes and environmental changes may outdate old operating results. Also, in new organizations, there is not a long history of operating results upon which to base a standard. If an adequate historical standard does not exist, then the only option is to go with an engineered or estimated standard. There is reason to believe this can work if there is a relatively high level of trust and credibility in the standard-setting process and in the standard. In the absence of this, however, it may be best not to consider a gain-sharing plan. In the absence of a good standard, a plan can easily deteriorate into the kind of game playing that goes on in piece rate plans where individuals spend considerable effort beating the time study man.

Costs Covered. What costs will be included? The Scanlon Plan focuses on labor costs as a proportion of sales dollars. This is based on the view that labor costs are the most controllable costs in an organization. Since the idea is to motivate people and reward them for their performance, it makes sense to focus on costs that can be controlled. The problem with labor costs is that they are a small part of the total cost of products in some manufacturing situations, and they are not the only costs that employees can influence. Employees can often influence material costs, for example, and even utility costs. Not surprisingly, some organizations which have started with a pure Scanlon Plan type labor cost formula have over the years added more and more costs to their bonus calculations. A good example of this is Donnelly Mirrors, which has become a profit-sharing plan that includes all of its costs in the bonus formula. This is not to say, however, that a plan should necessarily start with all costs included. A strong argument can be made for starting with a simple plan and adding more and more costs as employees understand what they can do to reduce costs and begin to understand and trust the plan. This is precisely what Donnelly did. Most profit-sharing plans do not start this way. They start by covering all costs and often suffer from employees not understanding them and not knowing how to influence them.

The best overall conclusion is that each situation needs to be carefully analyzed. In some situations, it probably makes sense to initially focus only on labor costs. In others, because of technology, cost factors, and worker knowledge, it may make sense to include a much wider range of costs and to share gains when those costs are reduced.

Sharing Gains. When gains are realized, plans differ in how these gains are shared. First, there is the issue of how much goes to the company or the ownership and how much goes to employees. There is no easy answer to the question of what is the best percentage split between the organization and the employees. This can only be determined once the issues surrounding what kind of costs are going to be included in the plan have been determined. In short, you need to know what is going to be in the pool before a logical decision can be made about how this pool is going to be split up. In the case of existing plans, the number varies all the way from 0 percent for the company and 100 percent for employees to 30 percent for employees and 70 percent for the company. Neither approach is necessarily right or wrong. In situations where a number of costs are included, it generally makes sense to have the organization's share be larger, while in those situations where few costs are included, minimizing the organization's share is important in order to have the program generate enough bonus to provide a real incentive for the employees.

The second decision that has to be made about dividing the bonus pool concerns who will share in the bonus. There is no simple prescription here. Most plans cover all employees in the organizational unit which is measured. The case for doing this is strong since it emphasizes that everyone has a common fate and that traditional differences like office/factory and management/nonmanagement need to be transcended if a bonus is to be earned. In some plans, however, top management has been left out, as have staff and office employees. Special circumstances (e.g., existing management bonus systems) sometimes justify this but it is usually not advisable since it can set up a conflict between those who are on the plan and those who are not.

The third decision that has to be made concerning sharing has to do with how the money that is given to the employees will be divided among them. In most plans, this is done on the basis of a straight percentage of total salary payments. In other words, no effort is made to reach individual decisions about how much each employee should get. An exception to this is the Lincoln Electric Plan (see Lincoln 1951; Zager 1978). In it, individual payment decisions are made. The result is that some individuals do much better than others in a given performance period. From a motivational point of view, this is a highly effective approach *if* the performance appraisal process can be done in a credible and valid way. This is a big if since, as has already been emphasized, it is often difficult to measure performance effectively and credibly, particularly when substantial bonus amounts are on the line.

Individual bonus plans seem to be particularly difficult to make work in situations where the technology makes people highly interdependent and where it is difficult to recognize individual contributions. This leads to the general recommendation that in participative gain-sharing plans the payout be based on a straight percentage of the person's take-home pay. One modification of this that has worked well in some situations, is to cap the total amount of pay which is subject to bonus payment. This prevents a few highly paid individuals from taking home a disproportionate dollar amount of the total bonus pool.

Paying everyone an equal size bonus has some appeal since it eliminates any "inequality" in the distribution of bonuses, but it is illegal in the United States when overtime is worked by employees who are considered nonexempt by the Fair Labor Standards Act. According to the Act, individuals must be paid time and a half and bonus pay for all overtime hours. This means that the plan must take into account the need to pay a bonus on overtime hours. The easiest way to do this is to simply make the overtime pay part of the same percentage calculations as is the regular pay, and to make the bonus a percentage of total cash compensation.

Frequency of Bonus

The most frequently used period for bonus calculation is one month. This is an attractive time period because it often fits organizational recording needs and it is frequent enough to attract the attention of individuals with respect to motivating their performance. Conditions which might favor a longer payout period include a highly seasonal business and a long production or billing cycle for a product. In these cases, month-to-month performance measures might prove to be erratic and an unreasonable basis for bonus payout. This could result in windfalls and dramatic shortfalls, causing the bonus to lose credibility and creating difficulty from an accounting and cashflow basis. In one plan I installed, an effort was made to offset these problems by a general strategy to educate the employees about the nature of the busines so they could learn to accept the fluctuations as natural. The general recommendation, however, is that a monthly payout be considered and if it does not seem to offer a relatively stable possibility, then a longer payout should be considered.

Managing Change

Changes within and outside organizations that affect the viability of gain-sharing plans are constantly taking place. For example, new equipment is bought so that labor costs can be reduced, products are changed, markets change, and so on. Many of these changes may require modifications to take place in the formula. Such obvious potential changes, such as new capital equipment and changes in product mix, should be anticipated in advance so they can be handled relatively automatically by established rules and procedures. The need for more serious change should also be anticipated, and a formal process for altering the formula and changing the plan should be built in at the beginning. This can be done by establishing a group which is responsible for the management and fine tuning of the plan. In practice, this group often evolves from the group that put the plan together. It is important that this group have the same credibility as the design group and that it represents a good cross section of the organization. If it does not, the changes are likely to be seen as efforts on the part of management to subvert the plan or stop payouts from occurring. The recommendation, then, is that a *steering committee* be appointed to handle unanticipated changes and be responsible for regularly updating the plan.

The steering committee, or some other group, should also be given a charter to study the effectiveness of the plan. A good procedure is to have an annual review of the plan so that a mechanism is established for making sure the plan continues to fit the organization. In many of the projects that are part of my research program, this annual assessment has included an attitude survey, as well as an economic analysis. By comparing survey data from several points in time, it is possible to get a good sense of what effects the plan is having and to take corrective action where needed (see Appendix C).

The Participative System

An essential part of any participative gain-sharing plan is the participative system that is built to support it. Not all gain-sharing plans include participative systems. In many cases, however, they are needed in order for the plan to work, and in most cases, they are needed in order for the potential of the plan to be realized. In the absence of a change in employee behavior, there is no reason to expect a payout from the kind of formula which is typically developed in gain-sharing plans. A payout requires an improvement in performance, and that improvement requires more effective behavior on the part of employees.

Some improvement may be gained simply from the motivation that is tapped through tying pay to performance. This is particularly true in situations where the work is not highly skilled or interdependent and, as a result, effort is directly related to performance. In other situations, however, there are several reasons why a gain-sharing plan without a participative system should not be expected to produce an appreciable improvement in performance or an appreciable bonus. First of all, the motivational impact of the plan may not be large because most gain-sharing plans aggregate a number of people together; as a result, there is only a small increment in the perceived relationship between individual performance and individual pay. In addition, simple effort and good intentions are not enough to improve the operating results of many organizations. What is needed is a combination of people working harder, working more effectively together, sharing their ideas, and working smarter. In order for this to happen, it often takes a formal participative system that captures the willingness of people to offer their ideas and to participate, and turns this willingness into actual changes in the operating procedures of an organization. In the absence of some procedures or systems to accomplish these changes, they rarely seem to occur.

In many participative gain-sharing plans, the key to the participative system is a formal suggestion system with written suggestions and shop floor committees to review the suggestions. Often, there is also a higher-level review committee that looks over those recommendations that involve several parts of the organization. This system of committees is one way of trying to assure that new ideas will be seriously considered and, where appropriate, implemented.

It is not easy to get participative committees operating in most organizations. Many individuals do not have the skills to operate effectively in this kind of participative environment. In addition, managers are sometimes resistant to the idea of having committees of workers participate more actively in workplace decision making because they see their roles being undermined. There are no easy solutions to these problems. The best approach seems to be to use some process training for both the lower levels of supervision and for the shop floor committees. Committees need to be taught to make decisions, process information, communicate, and organize themselves. Lower-level managers need to be trained in their new work roles and supported in that learning (Walton and Schlesinger 1979).

Often the participative system only begins to function effectively after the bonus plan has been in operation for a few months. It takes time to learn how to operate in this manner. Groups need time to learn how to make decisions, and individuals need time to learn what kind of suggestions are useful and what kind of inputs can help the organization function more effectively. A common problem in many plans is that many of the initial suggestions are working conditions and hygiene improvement suggestions, rather than productivity and performance improvement suggestions. This is usually caused by a backlog of previously unheard worker suggestions and complaints about working conditions. In any case, it is important to work through these and see that they are dealt with; only then will employees move on to develop performance improvement suggestions. It is also important to pursue them because they can directly improve the quality of the employee's work life and demonstrate the credibility and sincerity of management in pursuing a participative gain-sharing plan. At the beginning of a plan, it is also important to make a special effort to let people know what has happened to their suggestions and ideas. When plans begin, it takes a while to deal with all the suggestions since there is often a rush of ideas and the organization is usually inexperienced in dealing with them. If the employees are not told why their idea is being delayed, they can easily become discouraged and turned off by the system. It is crucial that the first few interactions that individuals have with the participative system be successful; otherwise, the system may lose the work force's interest before it ever has a chance.

Conditions Favoring Gain Sharing

At several points in our discussion, we pointed out that certain conditions favor the installation of a gain-sharing plan. Table 9.1 summarizes these and adds a number of additional ones. The reason why most of these conditions favor a plan is self-evident. However, some cases may not be clear; they require a brief review.

Table 9.1
Conditions Favoring Gain-Sharing Plans

Organizational Characteristic	Favorable Condition
Size	Small unit, usually less than 500 employees
Age	Old enough so that learning curve has flattened and standards can be set based on performance history
Financial measures	Simple, with a good history
Market for output	Good, can absorb additional production
Product costs	Controllable by employees
Organizational climate	Open, high level of trust
Style of management	Participative
Union status	No union, or one that is favorable to a cooperative effort
Overtime history	Limited to no use of overtime in past
Seasonal nature of business	Relatively stable across time
Work floor interdependence	High to moderate interdependence
Capital investment plans	Little investment planned
Product stability	Few product changes
Comptroller/Chief financial officer	Trusted, able to explain financial measures
Communication policy	Open, willing to share financial results
Plant manager	Trusted, committed to plan, able to articulate goals and ideals of plan
Management	Technically competent, supportive of participative management style, good communications skills, able to deal with suggestions and new ideas
Corporate position (if part of larger organization)	Favorable to plan
Work force	Technically knowledgeable, interested in participation and higher pay, financially knowledgeable and/or interested
Plant support services	Maintenance and engineering groups competent, willing, and able to respond to increased demands

Market.   The plan may lead to increased productivity. If the market cannot absorb this, it can lead to a need for layoffs and can undermine the plan.

Overtime History.   A history of high amounts of overtime hours can cause problems if individuals have become dependent on overtime pay. The plan can cause increased productivity and, as a result, less overtime and less total pay. This can cause employees to set quotas and to restrict their productivity.

Seasonal Nature.   Organizations that have a seasonal business often have to hire and layoff people on a month-by-month basis. This can undermine the plan's sense of group and lead to restrictions of production during slow seasons.

Financial Officer.   Most plans require a spokesperson who is articulate and trusted in order for individuals to see the pay-performance relationship. The financial officer is in an ideal position to do this.

Capital Investment and Product Stability.   It is easier to compute a bonus when there are no changes in equipment or product.

Support Service Group.   The installation of a plan often brings requests from employees for changes that will help them do their work more effectively. These must be responded to effectively or discouragement is likely to set in.

In no situation are all of the favorable conditions listed in Table 9.1 likely to be present. As a result, most plans start with suboptimal conditions existing. As will be discussed in Chapter 12, because conditions can often be changed once the plan has been installed, a plan may work in a situation that might not have been a favorable one at first glance. The task in deciding whether or not to install a plan is to analyze the situation in terms of what conditions are favorable, what conditions are unfavorable and unchangeable, and what conditions are unfavorable but changeable. The challenge, then, is to decide whether or not it is worth trying a plan. Unfortunately for the decision maker, no formulas of decision rules exist to indicate how these conditions should be combined to make a decision. It does seem, however, that if a majority of the existing conditions are not favorable, it is probably not worth going ahead with a plan installation. Finally, it is clear that if the union is not favorable and the measures are not adequate, there is no sense in pursuing a plan, regardless of whether or not the other conditions are favorable.

ILLUSTRATIVE GAIN-SHARING PLANS

The Scanlon Plan

The Scanlon Plan is undoubtedly the best-known company or plant gain-sharing plan. It was developed by Joe Scanlon, a union leader, in the middle 1930s. In this plan, bonuses based on a measure of company or plant performance are given to all employees. Proponents of the plan argue it should not be regarded as just another incentive plan.

> Scanlon deeply believed that the typical company organization did not elicit the full potential from employees, either as individuals or as a group. He did not feel that the commonly held concept that "the boss is the boss and a worker works" was a proper basis for stimulating the interest of employees in company problems; rather, he felt such a concept reinforced employees' beliefs that there was an "enemy" somewhere above them in the hierarchy and that a cautious suspicion should be maintained at all times. He felt that employee interest and contribution could best be stimulated by providing the employee with a maximum amount of information and data concerning company problems and successes, and by soliciting his contribution as to how he felt the problem might best be solved and the job best done. Thus, the Scanlon Plan is a common sharing between management and employees of problems, goals, and ideas (Lesieur and Puckett 1969, p. 112).

Scanlon realized that if his management philosophy was to be implemented, some structural changes were needed in organizations. He pointed out that most wage systems fail to reward individuals for cooperative behavior and fail to produce a convergence between the goals of employees and the goals of the organization. His solution to this problem was a company bonus plan. Scanlon also believed that the opinions and ideas of people lower down in organizations are

are ignored, even though they are of value. To correct this situation, he suggested that organizations use a suggestion system that involves an elaborate committee structure. The Scanlon Plan, then, is a philosophy of management that is basically participatory and involves using a pay incentive system and a suggestion system.

The genius of the Scanlon Plan, and of Joe Scanlon, is the recognition that a commitment to participation and joint problem solving is not enough. Effective use of participatory management requires a congruence between the pay system of an organization and its style of management. This point will be discussed in greater detail in the next chapter. It is mentioned here to stress that it is an integral part of the Scanlon Plan, and because Joe Scanlon was one of the first to articulate the important influence that the fit between the pay system and the management philosophy can have on an organization.

Companies following the Scanlon Plan use widely varying methods of calculating the amount of bonuses employees receive (all members of the organization receive bonuses, usually a percentage of their salaries). Some plans, particularly the early ones, used a straight profit-sharing approach. In recent years, the most common approach has been to base the bonus on a ratio measure that compares total sales volume to total payroll expenses. This is, in effect, a measure of labor cost efficiency (if wages and sale prices are corrected for inflation or move together based on inflation). A base rate is established at the beginning of the plan, and money savings resulting from improvements over the base are shared (often equally by the company and the employees). The ratio measure is used, instead of a profit-based measure, in order to have a measure that is more responsive to the behavior of the employees.

In concept, the pay system is an important part of the overall Scanlon approach to management because it ties the goals of individuals to the goals of the organization. When it is operating properly, the better the organization functions, the better off the employees are. It is to the advantage of employees to produce more, to work faster and more effectively, to cooperate with other employees, to adopt new technologies, and to make suggestions that improve organizational effectiveness. As McGregor (1960), Frost et al. (1974), and many others have pointed out, when it operates properly, the Scanlon Plan can contribute to both organizational effectiveness and a high quality of work life.

The Scanlon Plan has been around long enough to allow some conclusions to be drawn about its effectiveness. The conclusions must be tentative, however, because little actual research has been done on the plan, and most of what has been done is of low quality. Estimates vary on how many firms have tried the plan; before 1970 the figure was thought to be less than 500 (Howell 1967). Interest in the plan has increased tremendously since 1970 and, as a result, there are many more Scanlon Plans. Traditionally, most Scanlon Plans have covered total companies and have tended to be limited to small, often privately owned, companies. Recently, some large organizations have successfully implemented the plan on a plant-by-plant basis. This has resulted in their having as many as twenty different plans. If this approach is adopted by other companies, it could dramatically increase the number of plans which are in existence.

One review of the literature on Scanlon Plans found studies covering fifty-three situations where the plan was tried (Moore and Goodman 1973). This is a rather large number of cases. Unfortunately, the data on most of these cases are poor, and it is therefore difficult to determine just what impact the plan has had in most situations. It is possible, however, to code forty-four of the cases in terms of whether the plan was successful in contributing to organizational effectiveness (Moore and Goodman 1973). The apparent successes outnumber the failures by thirty to fourteen. This is an impressive success rate but it may be inflated, because it seems probable that organizations that are successful in introducing the plan are more likely to write about their experiences than are those who fail. Similarly, researchers are more likely to report positive results than negative ones. However, even if we discount the two-to-one success-to-failure ratio because of selection bias, the success ratio is still impressive and probably indicates that Scanlon Plans are successful at least half the time. The following are outcomes which Moore and Goodman suggest often occur when the plan is successful:

1. The plan enhances coordination, teamwork, and sharing of knowledge at lower levels (Lesieur 1958; McKersie 1963; Scanlon 1949).

2. Social needs are recognized via participation and mutually reinforcing group behavior (Frost, Wakley, and Ruh 1974; Whyte 1955).

3. Attention is focused on cost savings, not just quantity of production (McKersie 1963).

4. Acceptance of change due to technology, market, and new methods is greater because higher efficiency leads to bonuses (McKersie 1963; Schultz 1958).

5. Attitudinal change occurs among workers, and they demand more efficient management and better planning (Lesieur 1958).

6. Workers try to reduce overtime; to work smarter, not harder or faster (Lesieur 1958; Scanlon 1949).

7. Workers produce ideas as well as effort (Shultz 1958).

8. More flexible administration of union-management relations occurs (Helfgott 1962).

9. The union is strengthened because it is responsible for a better work situation and higher pay.

It is interesting to note that higher employee satisfaction and a better quality of work life are not among the outcomes listed. There is a reason for this. Few studies have looked at the impact of the Scanlon Plan on the quality of work life. There is some evidence, however, that it does have a positive impact. First of all, it leads to higher pay because of the bonus and this increases satisfaction. Further, the kinds of outcomes listed often do contribute to employee satisfaction. Finally, several studies, including one by myself at Donnelly Mirrors, have found high satisfaction and commitment levels in Scanlon companies (Frost et al. 1974; Moore and Goodman 1973).

There are a number of reasons why Scanlon Plans may fail. Some of these can best be regarded simply as poor implementation of a potentially good plan. Others reflect more basic flaws in the approach that limit its effectiveness in a number of situations. The following are areas where poor implementation often leads to plan failures.

1. *Formula construction.* The formula needs to accurately measure what is going on in the organization and must be adjustable to changing conditions. Often, rigid formulas that do not reflect employee behavior are developed and lead to failure.

2. *Payout level.* It is important that some bonuses be paid, particularly at the beginning. Sometimes this does not happen because the performance level that must be achieved before a bonus is paid is set too high.

3. *Management attitudes.* Unless managers are favorable to the idea of participation, the plan will not fit the management style of the organization. In some organizations, the plan has been tried simply as a pay incentive plan without regard to the management style, and it has failed because of a poor fit.

4. *Plan focus.* Many plans focus only on labor savings. This presents problems in organizations where other costs are great and are under the control of the employees. It can lead to the other costs being ignored or even increased in order to reduce labor costs.

5. *Communication.* For the plan to work, employees must understand and trust it enough to believe that their pay will increase if they perform better. For this belief to occur, a great deal of open communication and education is needed. Often this is ignored and, as a result, plans fail.

6. *Union cooperation.* For the Scanlon Plan to succeed, the local union must be supportive. In most of the places where it has been tried, the local union has supported it. However, some failures have occurred in situations where unions have not supported it sufficiently.

7. *Threat to supervisor.* The plan changes the roles of supervisors. They are forced to deal with many suggestions, and their competence is tested and questioned in new ways. Unless supervisors are prepared for and accept these changes, the plan can fail. This point goes along with the general point that management must be prepared to manage in a different way.

The following are attributes of the Scanlon Plan that limit its applicability and cause it to fail in some situations.

1. *Organization size.* The plan is based on employees seeing a relationship between what they do and their pay. As organizations get larger, this is harder to accomplish. Most successful Scanlon Plan companies or plants have less than 500 employees.

2. *Performance measurement.* In some organizations, good performance measures and a reasonable performance history simply do not exist and cannot be established. This is often true in organizations where rapid technological and market changes occur. When this is true, the Scanlon Plan is not appropriate.

3. *Measurement complexity.* Often performance can be measured only in very complex ways. The truer this is, the more difficult it is to make the plan work, because there is no clear, easily understood connection between an individual's behavior and rewards.

4. *Administrative costs.* It costs money to administer a Scanlon Plan. Substantial bookkeeping and clerical costs are involved, as well as meeting and administrative time. In some organizations, these can be so large as to discourage use of the plan.

5. *Worker characteristics.* The plan depends on workers wanting to participate and wanting to earn more money. Admittedly, most workers have these goals, but certainly not all do. Unless a substantial majority of the employees wants the benefits the plan offers, there is no way it can succeed.

In summary, there is evidence that the introduction of a Scanlon Plan can lead to a higher quality of work life, greater organizational effectiveness, and stronger unions. However, the evidence clearly shows that these benefits have not always been obtained when Scanlon Plans have been introduced. The following conditions which are adapted from Table 9.1 seem to be crucial for a successful implementation of the Scanlon Plan:

1. Management commitment—from top to bottom—to participative management

2. Union support and the feeling that the Scanlon Plan will strengthen the union

3. Small organization size

4. An organization whose performance can be measured by a simple formula

5. Good communication program about the plan

6. High level of trust in the organization

7. Employees who value money and want to participate and offer suggestions

8. Competent, confident supervisors

9. An organization history of stable, measurable performance that can be used as a baseline for the payout

10. An organization where cooperation among employees is important to the success of the organization

11. Base salaries that are perceived to be equitable

Profit Sharing

Many employees are covered by profit-sharing plans. According to one study, over 350,000 firms in the United States have some form of profit sharing (Metzger 1975, 1978). Most of the profit-sharing plans (75 percent according to Metzger (1978)) defer the payments until retirement and, as such, are not true incentive plans. Many others combine a partial payout with deferment. Thus, in only a few cases (often in smaller companies) is profit sharing used as an incentive. This is probably for the best for a number of reasons. In most organizations, profits are so far beyond the direct influence of most employees that profit-based bonuses are simply not likely to be effective motivators. The exception would seem to be the smaller organization in which labor costs are very high. In this situation, a bonus based on labor costs may act as a motivator.

Finally, although some organizations combine their profit-sharing plan with a participative style of management, most do not. The best way to view profit sharing is as an alternative approach to computing a bonus that has limited applicability as an important organization development intervention. The exception is very small organizations and, occasionally, a larger one that wishes to make it an important part of its overall philosophy of management. Sears, for example, has done this by constantly communicating to workers that they influence profits and that they share in them on a deferred basis. Incidently, even in the case of Sears, there is no published evidence that profit sharing has had a positive influence, and at the present time it is causing problems because the money is used to buy stock which has fallen.

The Rucker Plan

The Rucker Plan was developed by Allen Rucker of the Eddy-Rucker-Nichols Consulting Firm, which has specialized in this plan for over thirty-five years. Under the Rucker Plan, a historical relationship is established between the total earnings of hourly employees and the production value created by the company or plant. According to one proponent of the plan, this relationship will be stable in ninety-five out of one hundred manufacturing firms and can be used as a basis for sharing production gains (Scott 1977, 1978). According to Scott (1977), production value is essentially equivalent to value added by the manufacturer; that is, sales income less material and supply costs. As in the Scanlon Plan, a historical base period and ratio are used when improvements take place, a bonus pool is generated and it is split between the employees and the company.

There is very little evidence available on the effectiveness of the Rucker Plan, making it impossible to make any statement about its usual success rate. In many ways, it is similar to the Scanlon Plan and, as such, might be expected to have a similar success rate. However, it does differ in some important aspects. It takes a different approach to measurement in that it includes materials in a way that assures changes in their cost will affect the bonus. It also places much less emphasis on building a participative management system. A description of it sometimes mentions problem-solving groups, but there is no evidence that these are as central to the Rucker Plan as they are to the Scanlon Plan. There is, however, no reason why an organization who wants to install the plan could not place a strong emphasis on participation. The best way to view the plan is as adding an alternative computational formula which, in some situations, may be better than the one typically used in the Scanlon Plan. As such, it could be used as a good basis for a participative gain-sharing plan. It is most likely to be a preferred plan where it is important to include material costs in the plan, but its applicability to a particular situation can only be determined after a careful analysis of the financial history of the organization.

IMPROSHARE

An industrial engineer, Mitchell Fein (in press), has developed a gain-sharing plan which is based on many of the same principles as are individual incentive plans. The plan, IMPROSHARE, can be applied at either the plant or group level. Unlike the Scanlon Plan, it is based on an engineered performance standard and includes a buyout provision which allows management to change the standard in return for a one-time bonus payment. The buyout is intended to be used in cases of technological or organizational change.

IMPROSHARE was first installed in organizations during the late 1970s. It is not particularly associated with a participative approach to management; rather, it is associated with a more traditional approach. At this point, little has been written about it. There are claims that it is widely used, but there is no evidence of its effectiveness. It is therefore impossible to conclude anything about its effectiveness. One note of caution is in order, however. To the degree that it follows the kind of thinking and practices which are characteristic of individual incentive plans, it runs the risk of producing the same level of dysfunctional consequences. For example, it could lead to an adversary relationship between management and the employees over rates, goldbricking, and false data.

SUMMARY AND CONCLUSIONS

Unproven but promising sums up the situation with respect to gain-sharing plans and their role in improving organization effectiveness. There is certainly enough experience with them to clearly establish that they can be a powerful intervention in an organization. In the remaining chapters, considerable attention will thus be given to how they can be fit into an overall organization development strategy. It is striking, however, how little is known about them. They are not a new phenomenon, yet many potentially answerable questions remain unexplored. As one recent review has noted, the existing research is so poor that it is difficult to reach any conclusion (Bullock and Lawler 1980). Thus, discussion about when, where, and how to install such plans must be based more on careful analysis and theory, rather than on hard data. In some cases, this is not an overwhelming problem; but, in others, it presents serious difficulties. It would be very helpful if more were known about how to choose a design strategy and how to choose among the many possible bonus formulas. In the absence of solid evidence about what can be done, the choice is to simply choose an "off-the-shelf" approach (e.g., Scanlon or Rucker) or engage in a lengthy participative design approach. The latter is obviously more costly and not guaranteed to provide a better answer. Nevertheless, I often find it preferable because it helps assure that the many complexities of specific situations are taken into account and it helps build acceptance for whatever plan is developed. As we shall see in the next chapter, these are key factors in the success of any pay plan intervention.

10
PAY IN COMPLEX ORGANIZATIONS: THE FIT PROBLEM

Organizations consist of multiple systems that interact with and affect each other. Organizational effectiveness depends upon achieving a fit between the multiple systems that exist (Nadler, Hackman, Lawler 1979; Katz and Kahn 1966, 1978; Leavitt 1965). When incongruence exists a conflict situation is set up. Different systems in the organization suggest different behaviors and needed coordination is not present because employees receive conflicting messages about what behavior is expected of them and how the organization regards them. Although employees are capable of exercising some degree of compartmentalization, it is difficult and uncomfortable for them to undergo conflict for a long period of time in an area as important as rewards (Kahn et al. 1964; Kahn and Quinn 1970).

Because the pay system is just one of the many systems that are operational in an organization, its effectiveness is partially determined by how it fits with the rest of the systems in the organization. A pay system which, in the abstract, seems well designed, well thought out, and well administered can turn out to be a disaster for all concerned if it does not fit the organizational context in which it operates. This raises the key question: What determines whether a pay system fits a particular organizational setting? Unfortunately, little research has been done on the relationship between pay systems and organizational environments. Nevertheless, there are a number of points which are suggested by the literature on reward systems and organizational design. This chapter will explore these points. First, an approach to thinking about congruence in organizations will be presented. Then we will review the features of an organization which seem to be the strongest determinants of the type of pay systems that will be effective and, where possible, we will identify those pay systems likely to be effective in each situation.

A CONGRUENCE APPROACH

Open systems theory is a general framework for conceptualizing organizational behavior. It stresses that organizations take inputs from their environment, work on these inputs through some sort of transformation process, and send them back out into the environment. This input-transformation-output approach stresses that to be effective, organizations need to do two things:

1. Deal appropriately with their external environment

2. Have internally congruent and effective transformation processes

Dealing effectively with the external environment requires that an organization have a strategy or set of action plans which position it favorably in the marketplace. Since others have dealt extensively with this issue (Lawrence and Lorsch 1969; Galbraith and Nathanson 1978) our major concern in this chapter will be with the transformation process which an organization goes through. Its effectiveness is determined by the interaction of the major components of organizations. These components are: (1) the task or job, (2) the individuals, (3) the formal organizational arrangements, and (4) the informal organizational arrangements. Figure 10.1 summarizes what has been discussed so far. It identifies the key elements in the congruence approach as well as their relationships to each other.

Table 10.1 takes the congruence approach one step further by identifying, in more detail, the nature of the four organizational components (Nadler and Tushman 1977). Each of the four is made up of a number of key components or dimensions. The pay system is listed as an element of the formal organizational structure because it is usually designed through an explicit process to direct, structure, and control the behavior of individuals in the organization. As is indicated in the table, it is just one of several formal mechanisms designed to do this. It is at this point that the concept of *fit* becomes a key.

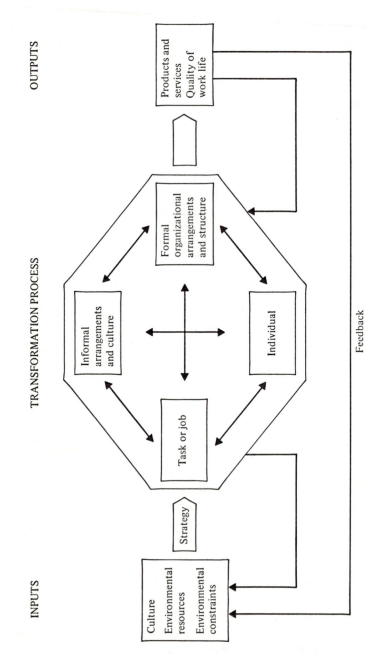

Figure 10.1 Congruence approach

Table 10.1
Key Characteristics of Systems

Task or Job	Individuals	Formal Organizational Arrangements and Structure	Informal Arrangements and Culture
• Complexity • Predictability • Required interdependence • Skill demands • Degree of structure • Feedback • Autonomy • Task identity	*Response Capabilities* • Intelligence • Skills and abilities • Experience • Training *Psychological Characteristics* • Needs • Attitudes • Expectancies • Values	• Organizational design and structure • Methods and procedures • Work resources and technology • Physical working conditions • Information and control system • Reward system	• Small group functioning • Intergroup relations • Communication patterns • Emergent leadership and power • Informal methods and procedures • History of organization • Organizational climate

Between each pair of characteristics, there exists a degree of congruence or *fit*. This has been defined as: the degree to which the needs, demands, goals, objectives, and/or structures of one component are consistent with the needs, demands, goals, objectives, and/or structures of another component (Nadler and Tushman 1977). The importance of fit is not limited to just the relationship between the four key characteristics of an organizational system. Each of these characteristics has additional key fit issues within them. Hackman and Oldham (1980), for example, have addressed this with respect to task. Particularly crucial for our discussion are the fit issues within the area of formal organizational structure. In many respects, if these do not fit together to make a congruent structure, then it does not matter how they interface with jobs, individuals, and informal arrangements. Without fit among the characteristics of the structures, the organization simply cannot perform effectively. Let us now turn to a consideration of how the pay system fits with other parts of an organization.

ORGANIZATIONAL STRUCTURE

The structure and design of complex organizations can be described along a number of dimensions. All of these have some implications for the type of pay system that is needed. A few that seem to stand out as being particularly critical will be focused on in this section. They include: maturity, the number of strategic business units, the number of management levels, the degree of centralization and decentralization, the technology, the information and control systems, the presence of a matrix structure, and the decision-making style of an organization. These dimensions of the structure of an organization have particular importance for the kind of pay systems which are appropriate.

Maturity

There is little doubt that as organizations grow and mature, they require very different pay systems. In the next chapter we give detailed attention to one example of this, focusing on new plants and how the compensation needs of a plant change as it moves from a green field to a fully operating stable system. In the present discussion, we will consider some general points about how the compensation needs of organizations change as they grow and mature.

There seems to be general agreement among people who have written about the topic that the compensation needs and compensation practices of organizations change as they mature (Galbraith and Nathanson 1978; Greiner 1972). Small, simple organizations can operate with highly discretionary and arbitrary systems that, in practice, represent a set of individual contracts between the employees and the owner of the organization. With growth, this approach to compensation clearly becomes inappropriate.

As organizations grow in size, they need to pay considerably more attention to issues of internal equity and formalizing the pay system. In a small organization, a single individual can know all the jobs and, by exercising good judgment, the organization can create a pay system that is reasonably equitable. This is usually not true in large organizations and, as a result, those large organizations that do not have formalized systems often end up with problems of internal and external equity. The problems of internal equity often become particularly obvious when the organization wants to transfer an individual from one part of the organization to another. Unless the organization has a structured pay system, it often finds that even though the jobs that are involved in the transfer may be "similar," the pay levels are not. As a result, movement is difficult—sometimes because the new job pays too little, and sometimes because it pays too much.

More important than equity is the problem of motivation. As organizations grow, performance-based pay becomes more necessary and more difficult to manage. It becomes more necessary because the connection between individual performance and organizational success often becomes remote and organizations tend to lose this as a motivator. Ironically, organizations tend to relate pay to performance less and less as they mature. They typically move from low base-pay systems with profit sharing and bonuses to bureaucratic systems in which most of an individual's pay comes in the form of benefits and base salaries. This seems to be an almost inevitable consequence of the generation of more people who are in support positions with jobs in which performance is difficult to measure and with the bureaucracy that size brings. In many ways, this is probably dysfunctional for the organization. It is even more important that pay be related to performance as organizations grow because the motivation provided by the struggle to keep the organization alive is gone. It is true that as organizations grow, certain kinds of performance-based pay plans become difficult to operate. For example, profit sharing, which is highly appropriate in a small organization where individuals can see and influence profit directly, often becomes very difficult to operate in a large organization (from a motivational point of view). As was mentioned earlier, gain-sharing plans seem to work best in relatively small organizations (500 or less). This implies that organizations should not give up pay as a motivator once they grow in size; indeed, it may be more important to use pay as a motivator as they get larger. They do, however, need to think of pay plans which relate pay to performance in smaller units than that of the total system. For example, the approaches taken by Dana Corporation, Midland-Ross, DeSoto Chemical, and TRW (with the Scanlon Plan) follow this model.

Overall, it is difficult to make general statements about what type of compensation systems are needed as an organization grows. It depends very much upon the type of growth that an organization enjoys. For example, growth due to multi-products has very different implications from growth around a single product (Galbraith and Nathanson 1978). As will be discussed next, growth in a decentralized manner has radically different implications for compensation from growth through centralization. This "contingency view of compensation" is consistent with the general argument that organizations need to be designed in ways that fit with the environment in which they operate, and that the pay system in an organization needs to fit with the other parts of the organization.

Number of Business Units

Many organizations in the United States are engaged in more than one business. Very large corporations, such as General Electric, are engaged in as many as one hundred different businesses, while many smaller and a few larger organizations are essentially one-product organizations. This has important implications for the structure of their pay systems. An organization that is in a single business often faces a similar environment on a company-wide basis, regardless of the number of locations it has. As a result, it can effectively use an identical plan in each of its locations. This is not true for organizations that are in multiple businesses. In fact, quite the contrary is true. Because they often face many different environments and many different competitive situations, it is critical that they have plans which are different in both their mechanics and processes from one business to another, so that they can meet the needs of the businesses in which they are competing. This approach can present problems when it comes time to transfer people from one business to another since comparable compensation levels and packages are not present. This problem, however, is not as severe as the ones which occur when an inappropriate pay system is used in a business area (e.g., too-high pay levels or low or inappropriate motivation).

A number of large, single-industry organizations have gotten into trouble when they have tried to diversify into new businesses. They have imposed the same pay plans in the new businesses that proved successful in their established business areas. In the new businesses, however, they simply did not fit. The pay plans were therefore not able to operate effectively in the new business area. A good example of this is the efforts on the part of some energy companies to diversify. I have worked with several pipeline companies who have gone into gas and oil exploration. Their standard pay systems did not work in the new areas because they were designed for a regulated public utilities type business, not for an entrepreneurial and highly competitive business. Only after they designed new performance-based pay systems were they able to operate successfully in their new business area.

It also seems particularly important in a multi-business organization for incentive pay to be based on divisional results. Failure to do this almost inevitably means that people working in particular businesses will see little relationship between their personal performance results and the incentive pay they receive. Having multiple business units argues strongly for multiple performance-based pay plans.

Number of Management Levels

The number of management levels in an organization can vary all the way from two upward. Large organizations may have as many as thirty different management levels. Of course, the number of levels in an organization is often related to the two structural variables that have been discussed already—size and number of business units. The more business units and the larger the organization, the more management levels there are. In any case, a large number of management levels can produce some rather tricky issues in the mechanics of pay. First, it increases the importance of having a solidly developed and administered base-pay plan that will allow for carefully managed pay differences. Employees' demands for internal equity almost always require that supervisors be paid more than subordinates. For this to happen, large multi-level corporations require a fairly formalized pay system based on a good job evaluation system.

The existence of a large number of management levels in an organization also has important implications for what type of performance-based pay system is appropriate. The more levels there are in an organization, the more it becomes important to create multiple bonus pay plans that are related to hierarchical levels. When many levels exist, it is hard for people at the bottom to relate to overall performance results. Nevertheless, it is important that they have a pay system that is motivating because it is difficult to create intrinsically motivating jobs. The most effective answer is often bonus pools that operate at the top corporate level, divisional level, plant level and so on down the organization. This assures that people at different levels are on bonus plans which are keyed into an appropriate aggregation level in the organization. This approach to creating a series of mini-enterprises in the organization seems to be a good way to offset the lost incentive that often occurs with organizational growth.

Centralization and Decentralization

The degree of centralization and decentralization is relevant to pay administration primarily because it affects the kind of performance criteria data that are available. It also affects the degree to which an operating unit has the people and the skills to administer its own pay system. In a centralized organization, the performance of its parts is often difficult to measure because a decentralized, responsibility-based accounting system is not used. Even if it is possible to measure an individual plant or operating group's performance, this is often not a fair criterion upon which to base pay because the employees in the group often do not make many of the important decisions that affect operating results. If substantial decision-making power is vested in the central office, local plant management can hardly be evaluated on the basis of how the plant performs. The management may in fact resent being evaluated on this basis. In addition, the unit often does not have the people skilled in compensation procedures that are needed to administer a performance-based pay system because the compensation staff is concentrated at the corporate level, rather than the plant level.

When decision making is decentralized and accounting data are gathered on operating units of the organization, the situation is quite different. Under *these* conditions, it is reasonable to base bonus systems on local operating results. When decisions are made at the local level and not the corporate level, the expertise to manage and design organization systems needs to be more broadly spread throughout the organization. If these conditions do not hold, the organization has a more serious problem, and the issue of administering pay at the local level and tying pay to local operating results becomes a moot one. In any case, decentralization raises the possibility of bonus plans to be based on local results and opens up the possibility of total compensation plans that are tied to the needs of the local operation. Centralized management makes both of these difficult to implement and make operational.

Technology

The type of product an organization produces determines the type of technology and production approach which the organization takes. A technological imperative seems to operate which limits the technology options for organizations that are engaged in producing a particular type of product. Production methods, in turn, differ in the degree to which: (1) individual performance is identifiable and measurable, (2) cooperation among the members is necessary and desirable, and (3) whether individuals with multiple skills are advantageous from an organizational point of view. Because of this, organizations that differ in the kinds of products they produce need different pay systems even though they may be similar in other ways.

A number of different authors have developed classification systems for the types of technologies that exist in work organizations. At a general level, most of them can be helpful in thinking through the appropriateness of different approaches to pay. For the purposes of illustration, we will consider the one developed by Woodward (1965). She distinguished among organizations engaged in mass production, unit production, and process production. Although she did not include professional and service organizations in her typology, this seems to be a necessary addition if we are to cover most types of work organizations.

The four different types of technology—mass, unit, process, and service—differ on a number of dimensions. Probably the primary one as far as compensation policy and practices is concerned is interdependence. Process production technologies, such as oil refineries and chemical plants, are highly interdependent. In order to work effectively, they require high levels of cooperation. Because unit production operations usually produce one or a small number of products, they do not tend to be highly automated and repetitive in the tasks that individuals perform. This distinguishes them from mass production technologies that produce large volumes of the same or similar products. Unit and mass production situations may or may not be highly interdependent, but are much less likely to be interdependent than process production technologies. In mass production, for example, it is often possible for a single person to build a small product in its entirety. Where this is not done, and an assembly line exists, the interdependence is of a serial or sequential nature and much less constraining than the type of interdependence which exists in process production facilities.

When interdependence is less, piece rate incentives often can be used. They therefore may make sense in unit and mass production plants. On the other hand, piece rate plans do not fit a process production plant because they reward behavior at the individual level when, in fact, plant- or group-level behavior is the appropriate level at which to reward performance. Similarly, plant-wide bonuses seem to be well suited to many process production plants but may not fit in many large unit and mass production plants.

Skill-based pay plans seem to be particularly appropriate for process production situations but do not always fit well in unit and mass production situations. In mass production there often are advantages to the organization that employs multi-skilled individuals. Particularly in situations where absenteeism and turnover are high, it is desirable to have people who can do a number of jobs. In the case of unit production, the skill mix and task demands are often changing so much it is difficult to even set up a formal skill-based pay plan. Nevertheless, it is still desirable to have individuals who have multiple skills.

Different technologies also vary in the degree to which individual performance is identifiable and measurable. Usually, it is much easier to measure performance in unit and mass production situations than it is in service and process production situations. Because of this, in many process and service situations, piece rate and merit pay plans are particularly inappropriate. Examples of the negative consequences of trying them are plentiful. They include production workers speeding up production at their station while ignoring a pile-up in production further downstream, and a sales person spending time competing with another for sales instead of stocking shelves and serving customers.

In summary, in process production plants where cooperation is important and individual performance is difficult to measure, a group plan or organizational performance-based pay plan often makes sense, as does a skill-based pay plan. In a unit production situation, piece rate plans generally do not make sense because of a lack of repetition in performance of tasks, while plant-level plans or merit pay based on individual objectives may make sense. Skill-based plans often do not fit well either because it is hard to identify the requisite skills. When it *is* possible, a plan which rewards people for mastering different technical specialties is often desirable. In mass production situations, individual piece rate plans and the more traditional approaches to pay often make sense because individual performance is measurable and is relatively independent of other people's performance. When there is interdependence, the attractiveness of group- and plant-level plans is high. Finally, service industry situations are particularly hard to generalize about. In many cases, cooperation is required but it is difficult to measure performance at any level except, perhaps, at the total organizational level. This means that it is often difficult to pay for individual performance or even to identify key individual skills. There are, of course, exceptions to this, such as individual sales people, lawyers, accountants, etc., who have clearly identifiable performance levels. In these situations individual bonus plans are appropriate.

Information and Control Systems

A key element in any organization is its information and control system (Lawler and Rhode 1976). It is a key determinant of behavior and it has a direct effect on what type of pay system is appropriate. This is most noticeable in the area of performance-based pay. As has already been stressed, performance-based pay requires a good performance measurement system. The information and control system can provide this. If the information system does not, then the possibility of having an effective performance-based pay system may be close to zero. The key to the relationship between the information system and the pay system is in the concept of aggregation level. Information systems generally measure performance at one or more levels of aggregation (e.g., plant, work group, or divisional). If a performance-based pay system is used, it needs to base its measurements of performance at these same levels of aggregation.

Finally, it is important to stress that unless the information system provides high quality, valid, and inclusive measures of performance, pay should not be based on them. As was stressed in the chapters on performance-based pay, major problems can occur when pay is based on poor measures of performance.

Matrix Structures

Matrix organizational structures grew out of the management problems associated with the American space effort during the 1960s. A complete treatment of matrix organizations is beyond this book, but it is important to note some ways in which they are different from traditional structures (see Davis and Lawrence (1977) for a more complete treatment). Matrix structures abandon the "one-boss" command structure that is so common in organizations. They depend heavily on temporary groups to do much of the productive work. Because of this, some people are in two or more project groups simultaneously, and thus have several bosses. In addition, there is a need for people who can effectively head these project groups, which is no easy task since these groups are temporary, do not even own the full-time effort of their members, yet are supposed to do the major work of the organization.

It is not hard to see from this brief description of a matrix structure that traditional pay system approaches do not fit. As Davis and Lawrence (1977) point out, it makes job evaluation difficult. In addition, it makes traditional one-on-one performance appraisal inappropriate. The systems group of TRW, which has had a matrix structure since the 1960s, has dealt with these problems in some interesting ways. Performance appraisal can be and often is done on a group basis, so that input is gathered for all the superiors who have seen an individual's performance. In a limited number of situations, peers are also included because they see critical parts of an individual's behavior that are not visible to others. They use a job evaluation system which takes into account the critical role that project leaders play. Finally, they use a management bonus system which is tied into the results of the total organization. This is done to help "hold the matrix together" from a performance point of view. One of the major pathologies that matrices develop is the tendency for overall performance to be lost among all the multiple relationships that have to be managed. A bonus plan can help focus attention on overall performance.

Overall, it seems likely that in most matrix organizations a pay approach which emphasizes bonuses, multiple person input to performance evaluations, and a job evaluation system that is keyed to the importance of project managers is needed. Whatever is done, it is clear that it must recognize the existence of multiple bosses and of the need for pay to help motivate project group performance.

Decision-Making Style

Just as organizational structure and technology have a crucial impact on the mechanical side of pay system appropriateness, the decision-making style of the organization has direct relevance for the process side of pay administration. Congruence seems to be a particularly important determinant of how effective particular process approaches to pay administration will be. Decision-making style also has some implications for which mechanical systems are appropriate, but the primary relevance is to the process side of pay administration.

Consider the suggestion that salaries be made public. In the kind of organization that generally adopts a democratic participative approach to decision making, this practice should develop naturally. As employees begin to participate more in evaluating themselves and others, they will gradually come to know what other people's salaries are, as well as the general pay structure of the organization. In essence, pay will become public as a consequence of management style, not as a result of a specific program. As was mentioned earlier, this is precisely what happened at the top management level in one company which entered into team building and participative management (Dowling 1977). On the other hand, in an autocratically run organization, the policy of openness does not fit. Salary openness demands trust, open discussion of performance, and justification of salaries. None of these are likely to occur as a matter of course in a top-down organization. A good example of this is provided by the experience of a company with team building. As a result of a "successful" team-building session, a group of managers decided to share salary data. Not surprisingly, they found some unexplainable differences in their pay levels. They decided to ask top management for an explanation. The results were nearly disastrous. Top management considered this completely inappropriate and nearly ended the team-building work.

Participative performance appraisal is another practice which can flourish in a participative organization, but not in a more autocratic one. Widespread employee participation in job evaluation programs also fits well with the participative approach to management. Again, it does not fit well with a more top-down autocratic approach to management because it is built on power sharing, openness, trust, and the kind of communication that is typically not present in a top-down organization.

Another way to look at the issue of fit between decision style and the process side of pay administration is to imagine a situation where a traditional top-down approach to decision making is used in the area of pay, but not in the other areas. Imagine, for example, a plant designed around autonomous work groups in which pay is secret and decided on in an autocratic, top-down manner by the plant manager. In this situation, the pay systems would be seriously out of touch with the process used to make other decisions in the plant. Indeed, the pay system would be as seriously out of place as would be open pay and participative pay decision making in a traditional organization. In both cases, the pay system is likely to be a source of major complaint, and pressure is likely to be generated to change it or to change the rest of the organization (this intriguing possibility is discussed in Chapter 12).

Table 10.2 suggests some interesting conclusions about what constitutes a good fit between pay systems and management style. It shows what types of reward system practices are most congruent with a more traditional and authoritarian approach to decision making and what are most consistent with a participative or human resources approach. It is put together based on four major principles:

1. Pay design and administration decisions should be made using the same decision process as is used for other important decisions in the organization.

2. Information about pay should be treated in the same manner as other important information is treated in the organization.

3. In management systems that depend heavily on the growth and development of individual skills and abilities, the growth of skills and abilities should be rewarded by the pay system.

4. In situations where the emphasis is on group and system performance, rewards should be given out based on group and system performance.

Table 10.2
Appropriate Reward System Practices

Reward System	Traditional	Participative or Human Resources
Fringe benefits	Vary according to organizational level	Cafeteria; same options for all levels
Type of pay system	Hourly and salary	All-salary
Base rate pay	Based on nature of the job held; high enough to attract job applicants	Based on skills; high enough to provide security and attract applicants
Performance-based pay plan	Piece rate	Group- and organization-wide bonus; lump sum increase
Communication policy	Very restricted distribution of information	Individual rates; salary survey data; all other information made public
Decision-making-plan design	Top management	Close to location of person whose pay is involved
Decision-making-plan administration	Top management	Close to location of person whose pay is being set

As can be seen in Table 10.2, this leads to a number of interesting points about how pay systems should be designed to fit different approaches in management style. With the participative management style, it is suggested that pay be open, participatively determined, and, where possible, individualized to fit the needs of each person. The autocratic management style leads to an entirely different approach to pay—one that emphasizes careful measurement of performance and tying pay to performance in a top-down manner.

Congruence of Organizational Structure: Integration and Overview

Our discussion of the fit between the pay system and the rest of the formal organization has stressed that congruence must exist between the elements of the formal organizational structure. As far as the decision-making process is concerned, it was emphasized that decisions about such things as rate of production, product quality, new employee selection, and purchasing must use the same decision style as is used for decisions about rewards.

As far as design or structure is concerned, congruence means that the type of base-pay plan (e.g., skill-based versus point method) and performance-based pay plan (e.g., group or individual) used must be supportive, in a measurement and reward sense, of the way jobs and organizations are designed. Specifically, the reward system needs to measure and reward those things that are critical, such as cooperation and skill acquisition, in making the job and the organizational design work. It also needs to measure behavior at the level (individual, group, or department) that the structure emphasizes. Congruence also requires that the reward system emphasize only those differences among people that are supportive of the basic structure and decision-making approach in the organization.

Figure 10.2 summarizes what has been said so far. It emphasizes the point that organizational structure and technology need to interface very closely with the pay system technology, and that the management style of the organization needs to interface very closely with the process used in making pay decisions. It also indicates that, to a lesser degree, management style needs to fit the structure and technology of the organization and that the pay process needs to fit the pay technology. If any of these are not congruent with each other, then the prediction would be that the organization's effectiveness will be severely limited because of the conflicting forces and pressures that will exist within the organization. The figure also shows that the organization interfaces with an external environment. Although it has not been stressed here, for the organization to be effective, it must be structured and managed appropriately with relation to this outside environment (see Katz and Kahn (1978) and Lawrence and Lorsch (1969) for further discussion of this issue).

INDIVIDUALS AND FIT

Throughout this book it has been stressed that the pay system must fit the nature of the individuals who populate the organization. Figure 10.1 makes this point and goes on to point out that the tasks, formal

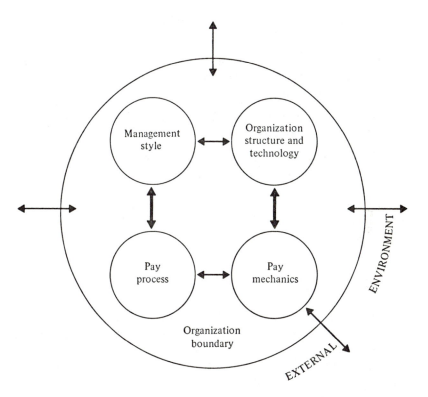

Figure 10.2   A consistency model

structures, and informal structures also need to fit the nature of the individuals. Because so much has already been said about the issue of individual pay system fit, at this point we will just summarize some of the key points in order to highlight the importance of individual differences.

1. When pay is not important to individuals, performance-based pay systems will be ineffective.

2. Skill-based pay systems depend on individuals wanting to and being able to learn multiple skills.

3. Differences in family and personal situations lead to different preferences for benefits.

4. Participative pay design and administration require individuals who favor participative management.

5. It is much easier to establish the belief that pay is based on performance when individuals have a history of seeing their pay based on performance and when they trust the organization.

6. Unionized employees are often opposed to individual performance-based pay systems.

The best way to summarize what has been said about individuals is to conclude with the dictum that no pay system should be put into practice unless it is congruent with the capabilities, needs, and values of the people it will affect. There are a number of ways to determine individual/pay system fit, including surveys and the use of participative design approaches.

TASKS AND CONGRUENCE

Our earlier discussion of technology identified interdependence as a key fit issue with respect to tasks and pay. Highly interdependent tasks suggest such things as skill-based pay, group incentives, and team-based performance appraisal. On the other hand, independent tasks suggest individual performance-based pay and a more traditional approach to job evaluation.

The skill demands of a task can also play a key role in pay policy. When few skills are needed, turnover may not be particularly costly and, as a result, a below average market position for total compensation may be acceptable. On the other hand, if skill demands are high and turnover is likely and costly (e.g., aerospace engineers), an entirely different market strategy is called for. In this situation, it seems wise to be a market leader and, where possible, an innovator in the area of pay. TRW, for example, takes an innovator position with their aerospace division.

It is important to again emphasize that many of the characteristics of jobs which are associated with high internal motivation are also desirable from a pay administration perspective (Hackman and Lawler 1971; Hackman and Oldham 1980). Tasks which are high on feedback, autonomy, task significance, and task identity lend themselves to good pay administration. When these characteristics are present, there tends to be an identifiable piece of work that results in output—the responsibility for which is assignable to an individual or group. When this set of conditions exists, both job evaluation and performance appraisal are much easier to do because objective measures of performance and meaningful job descriptions are usually available. When these conditions are not present, the one alternative is often to go to a civil service type system in which pay is not based on performance and a small number of salary grades is used.

Our discussion has clearly pointed out that pay systems must be fit to the design of the jobs in an organization if they are to be effective. Unsaid so far, but very important, is the point that some job designs simply do not lend themselves to effective pay administration. Stated directly: good pay administration starts, but does not end, with well-designed jobs. This point has some clear implications for how pay administration problems should be diagnosed and solved. Job design problems should always be considered as possible causes for pay administration problems. If it turns out that they are at the root of the pay problems, then the change effort needs to start there.

INFORMAL ARRANGEMENTS, CULTURE, AND CONGRUENCE

So far, little attention has been paid to the important impact that informal and cultural factors can have on the appropriateness of different pay system practices. This neglect needs to be corrected because such factors as communications history, small group behavior, and organizational climate have clear and important implications for pay system practice. They, too, need to be congruent with the pay system.

Earlier, we discussed the importance of communication in determining the effectiveness of many pay practices. For example, it was stressed in our discussion of gain-sharing plans that their success is very much dependent on effective communication because they require trust and understanding to be effective. The same can certainly be said for most approaches to job evaluation, most benefit programs, and for the policy of open pay. This raises the interesting question of whether a good communication system needs to be in place before such pay innovations as gain-sharing plans are tried. Clearly, it is preferable, but it may not be necessary. As will be discussed in Chapter 12, one possibility is to use the pay system changes as a vehicle for improving the communication practices in the organization. This is risky because if it does not happen, the pay system change can fail; but, as was pointed out in the discussion of gain-sharing plans, it can also succeed quite handsomely.

A good example of the strong impact that communications can have on pay systems is provided by some work I did recently with a large multi-division company. Many of the company's operations were located in one city and this, among other things, led to a high level of communications between people in the different divisions. Partly because of this, similar pay practices and pay levels also existed in all divisions. This high level of similarity caused problems for the company, however, because the division operated in different businesses and faced competitors with different pay systems. An analysis revealed that the best approach to pay seemed to be a decentralized one. Major opposition to this appeared in the company because of the feeling that "everyone will know what everyone else is paid and we will have to justify any differences." Despite the opposition, the company decided to move to a decentralized approach. It is too early to tell if it will work—but it clearly will be harder to make it work in this company than it would be in a company with less informal communications. Interestingly, the company sees decentralization in the area of pay as a way to lead to decentralization in other areas.

Many of the participative approaches to pay administration that have been mentioned so far depend on reasonable group process for their effectiveness. A clear example of this is group decision making about skill-based evaluation plans and the participative design of gain-sharing plans. In both cases, poor group process is disastrous. In the former case, it can lead to either perfunctory approval of all increases or the destructive critique of individuals. In the latter case, it can lead to a bargaining process from which a poor design could emerge.

There is no clear statement of what constitutes good group process, nor is there any formula for how to obtain it. It is worth noting a few points, however. In the case of pay decision making, it is crucial that the process be characterized by openness, due process, constructive feedback, consensus-type decision making, and a willingness on the part of group members to go beyond their narrow self-interest. This type of group process is difficult to establish, particularly in organizations where it is not common or in a group which has been operating in other ways. This leads to an important point: group process issues need to be dealt with early in the life of a group if they are going to make pay decisions. This point was illustrated earlier by the example of Graphic Controls, which moved easily to group decision making about pay because they had worked hard on group process issues. It may not always be necessary to start with as much process work as was done in Graphic Controls, but some is almost always needed. For example, when I establish groups to design pay plans, much of the time in the first few meetings is spent on process.

Much of what can and should be done in the area of pay administration is determined by the climate of the organization. Climates that are characterized by trust, openness, and a concern for people simply call for different pay practices than do those that are characterized by a low level of trust, secrecy, and little concern for people. When openness, trust, and concern for individuals exist, many of the more innovative practices that have been reviewed already are appropriate. For example, open pay systems, gain-sharing plans, cafeteria benefits, and skill-based pay all fit well with this type of climate. In the absence of this type of climate, they are not likely to be successful. This raises an interesting point which will be considered extensively in the next two chapters—must the right climate precede these practices? Anticipating the discussion in these chapters somewhat, the answer seems to be that although it need not precede them, it needs to follow relatively quickly, which is likely to happen only if there is careful planning and action.

A good example of the difficulties in putting a pay system that is not congruent with the climate into practice is provided by the pay changes which are mandated by the Civil Service Reform Act. This act calls for many top-level federal government managers to be put on a merit pay system complete with bonuses and performance appraisal. This is so counter to the existing nonevaluative rewards culture that it has encountered major resistance from a number of individuals. It is too early to tell what degree of success it will have, but it is not too early to conclude that unless the culture changes, the merit pay plan will be managed in ways that will make it ineffective.

SUMMARY AND CONCLUSIONS

The most important point made in this chapter is that pay systems exist in the context of complex organizations and that the characteristics of organizations must be taken into account when pay systems are developed. No one pay system will fit all organizations; there are too many factors that must be considered. We have considered some of the most salient ones, but not all of those may be important in a particular situation. The overriding principle is that no one system fits everywhere and that the key to pay system effectiveness is in finding, or creating, a correct fit between the pay system and the rest of the organization.

In most cases, a good fit can be obtained by developing a pay system that fits the existing organization. It is important, however, under certain conditions, to consider changing the rest of the organization so that pay can be effectively administered. This may sound like an argument for "the tail to wag the dog," but it is not. Organizations should not be designed for the purpose of making pay administration easy. On the other hand, when organizations are designed and managed in ways that make it difficult or impossible to administer pay, it may be symptomatic of a fundamentally flawed approach to organizational design and management. Most of the conditions that are needed for effective pay administration (e.g., well-developed jobs and measures of performance) are also characteristic of a good organizational design. It is therefore likely that when it is hard to find an effective pay system, the problem is in the design of the organization. When a design is flawed, the only way to have an effective pay system is to change the rest of the organization. As will be discussed in the next two chapters, accomplishing a fit between the pay system and the rest of the organization—new or old—requires a well-developed strategy.

11
PAY IN NEW PLANTS[1]

The last decade has seen a number of major U.S. corporations design and build new plants that have adopted many innovative management practices (Lawler 1978). They have adopted so many new practices that they seem to employ a new approach to management which is characterized by high employee involvement, participative decision making, and high performance. General Foods, Proctor and Gamble, General Motors, Mead, Cummins Engine, and TRW are among the better-known companies which have built one or more of these new plants.

New plants which are built by large corporations are an unusual kind of new organization. They usually have adequate financial resources, good technological expertise, and a well-developed growth plan. Because of these advantages, they certainly are not typical new organizations; nevertheless, they are important. First, the building of new plants is common in large organizations and, as a result, it is crucial that we learn all we can about how to design them effectively. Second, and perhaps most important, they represent a good test arena for new thinking about organizations. I have suggested elsewhere that some of the new plant's changes may represent an important new

---

1. Based upon Edward Lawler and Ray Olsen, "Designing Reward Systems for New Organizations," *Personnel* 5 (1977): 48–60.

model for how effective organizations can be designed and managed (Lawler 1982).

Because resistance to change is reduced, and because total system change is possible, new plants allow new ideas and systems to be quickly tried and tested. The opportunity for innovation, unburdened by "tradition," is particularly pertinent with respect to pay. Some pay innovations have been tried in new plants that have been very difficult to test in existing plants because of the resistance they have met.

The importance of total system change cannot be overstated. New plants offer the chance to experiment with pay in a very different setting because they allow things to be tested that cannot be adequately tested elsewhere since they do not "fit" elsewhere. Indeed, some of the pay innovations that seem to be successful in new plants probably would not work in traditional organizations.

Because of their importance, we will focus only on the role of pay in these new high-involvement plants. Much of what is said is applicable to any new organization, but the reader is cautioned that it is presented with a high-involvement plant type of organization in mind.

Before we discuss the role of pay in detail, we need to briefly review the key characteristics of the new plants which have been successfully designed to produce a high-involvement work climate. Then, we will focus on how pay can be handled during the different maturity periods which characterize these new plants.

CHARACTERISTICS OF THE NEW PLANTS

One of the most interesting aspects of the new plants is the number of innovations common to all or almost all of them. These innovations are most interesting because they appear to have a high potential for diffusion to other settings. A review of the innovations will indicate just how specific areas of management have been affected and how the plants differ from traditional plants.

Egalitarian Layout

A strong egalitarian emphasis exists in how the work and nonwork areas in the new plants are laid out. Rather than having separate areas in which managers eat and spend their nonwork time, everyone uses the same eating room, rest rooms, and recreational facilities. In many plants, the entrances and parking areas are common to all employees. The intent is to give all employees the clear message that, at least in terms of the physical facilities and typical perquisites of office, a relatively egalitarian system exists in the plant.

Employee Selection

The traditional approach to employee selection has largely gone by the board in the new plants. Instead of the personnel department carefully screening, testing, and selecting applicants, a process is used that includes helping the job applicant make a valid decision about taking the job and getting employees more involved in selection decisions.

The selection process begins with an emphasis on acquainting people with the nature of the jobs they are expected to fill and the nature of the managerial style that will be used in the plant. Ads are run that stress the management style of the plant, and as soon as they arrive for an interview, employees are informed of the different nature of the plant. In most plants, a group interview is held by the managers and workers who will interact with new employees so they can decide together whether the job applicants will fit the management approach in the organization. After the plant becomes operational this approach to selection continues and work-team members are given the responsibility of selecting new members of their teams.

Job Design

In all the new plants, an attempt is made to see that employees have jobs that are challenging, motivating, and satisfying. In some cases, this is done through individually based job-enrichment approaches that emphasize personal responsibility for a whole piece of meaningful work (Hackman and Oldham 1980). In most cases, however, it is accomplished through the creation of autonomous work groups or teams.

Teams are given the responsibility for the production of a whole product. They are self-managing in the sense that they make decisions about who performs which tasks on a given day. They set their own production goals and are often responsible for quality control, purchasing, and the control of absenteeism. Most teams emphasize job rotation for their members, and team members are expected to learn all the jobs that fall within the purview of the group.

In some plants, an effort has even been made to mix interesting tasks with routine jobs. For example, one plant made the maintenance jobs part of the same team as warehousing, so that no one would spend all of his or her time on the relatively boring aspects of warehousing. The end result of using work teams is usually that the people participating feel responsible for a large work area, experience a sense of control, and develop an understanding for most or all of the production process (Lawler 1978).

Pay System

Most of the new plants have taken a skills approach to establishing base-pay levels for employees. Typically, everyone starts at the same salary. As he or she learns new skills, the salary goes up. With this system, a person doing a relatively low-level job may be quite highly paid because he or she is capable of performing a large number of other, more skilled tasks. In most instances, skill appraisal is a simple yes or no decision. Individual, one-on-one performance appraisal is not done in most plants that operate on a team approach. It is seen as inconsistent with the team idea. Career planning and skill appraisal are thus done by the work team. This means that everyone in the group has a say and, as a result, appraisals are usually based on large amounts of information. Interestingly, what evidence there is suggests that peer appraisals can be more valid than supervisor appraisals (Kane and Lawler 1978).

In about half of the new plants, decisions about whether or not an individual has mastered a new job well enough to deserve a salary increase are left to the members of his or her team. In one plant that has a merit pay increase plan, they also evaluate the person's performance. This approach to pay decisions reinforces the participative management style that is used to make most operating decisions.

A few of the new plants have moved toward plant-wide gain-sharing or cost-savings-sharing plans. As the rest of them mature and establish stable base periods for the measurement of productivity gains, it is likely that more of them will adopt these plans. As was stressed earlier, organization-wide sharing of performance gains is highly congruent with the team concept of management and the general participative, egalitarian principles that underlie the design of these plants. Because of this, gain sharing fits better than individual salary increases. As will be discussed later, performance-based pay typically becomes an issue in new plants after they have established a stable operating base. There are many reasons to believe that, at this point, gain-sharing plans can have a very positive impact.

Organizational Structure

One of the important innovations in most of the new plants is in the structural hierarchy. All the plants have located the plant manager only a few levels above the production workers. In some cases, the foreman's role has been eliminated completely. In others, the foremen report directly to the plant manager, and such traditional intermediate levels as general foreman and superintendent have been eliminated.

Where there are no foremen, several teams usually report to a single supervisor, and the teams are self-managed. Most of the time, they elect a team leader who is then responsible for communicating with the rest of the organization. This person undertakes the kinds of lateral relations with other functional and line departments that consume so much time and constitute such an important responsibility for the typical first-line supervisor (Walton and Schlesinger 1979).

The new plants also deemphasize functional/area responsibility. Rather than being organized on a functional basis (maintenance, production, and so on), they tend to be organized on a product or an area basis. Individuals therefore have the responsibility for the production of something, rather than for general maintenance or engineering. This system provides more meaningful job structures and creates a feeling of commitment to the product rather than to a function.

Approach to Training

The new plants place a heavy emphasis on training, career planning, and the personal growth and development of employees. This is usually backed up with extensive in-plant training programs and strong encouragement for employees to take off-the-job training, usually paid for by the organization.

There have been some interesting innovations in in-company training. In some plants, for example, employees take courses in the economics of the plant's business and are rewarded with higher pay when they complete such courses. On-the-job training is also very common and is necessary to implement the concept of multi-skilled employees. Regular career-planning sessions are also scheduled. In some plants, employees present a personal career development plan to their team members; in others, the process is handled by someone in management. As a result of the strong emphasis on training, employees develop the feeling that personal development and growth are important goals.

Management Style

Most of the innovations discussed so far form an integral part of what it means to practice participative management. Operationally, this translates into pushing decisions as far down in the organization as possible. In the new plants, production line employees make purchasing decisions, quality control decisions, and even such personnel decisions as who will be hired and who will get pay increases. When decisions cannot be pushed down, it is typical for inputs to be gathered from everyone in the organization before the final decision is made. In a number of plants, the establishment of personnel policies have been delayed until the workforce has been hired, so that everyone can have a chance to have his or her say about what these policies should be.

Characteristics of High-Involvement Plants: Summary and Conclusion

Despite the many common practices which exist, it is important to note that all the new plants are not simple carbon copies of each other. Although common practices are used in most new plants, each plant has adapted them in ways that make their management style and overall design unique. Part of their success seems to be due to the participative design work which has been done. Participation in design is a key to a high level of commitment to many of the practices and to being sure that a correct design exists.

One final point needs to be stressed. Those new plants which have been successful (the vast majority have been very successful) have developed an integrated set of management policies, practices, and behavior which go together to deliver a clear, consistent message to employees. That message, quite simply stated, says that employees are adults who can be trusted to make important decisions when they are given the information and training they need to make these decisions. The effect of consistently delivering this message seems to be to produce a climate which is characterized by high employee involvement, trust, mutual respect, and a desire for personal growth and development.

There is little doubt that the pay system needs to be consistent with the other systems in a new plant if the proper type of climate is to be built. It is such an important manifestation of management's feeling toward employees that to have it be otherwise risks having contradictory messages sent. In one case study where the pay was traditional in nature, this and some out-of-step factors combined to contribute to the failure of a new organization in developing a high-involvement work culture (Nieva, Perkins, and Lawler 1978). In this plant, the pay practices were like the ones which were shown in Table 10.1 as being typical of a traditional management style, despite the fact that the organization emphasized enriched jobs, participation, and an open climate.

PHASES IN THE DEVELOPMENT OF NEW PLANTS

Undoubtedly, part of the success of the new plants stems from their ability to build from the ground up. In many respects, creation is easier than resurrection. Still, creation is not easy; it takes careful attention to the stages that new plants go through. Each stage requires different management actions and different pay system practices. Failure to recognize this can lead to the inappropriate installation of pay system policies, and serious harm can be done to the work culture.

Any description of the phases that new plants go through is somewhat arbitrary since there are no clear cuts or breaks between them. Nevertheless, it is possible to identify five phases that occur in the development of most organizations. It is also possible, based on what has happened in some of the new plants which have been studied, to specify how the critical compensation issues should be dealt with during these stages. The speed with which a new organization moves through them is a function of its technology and individual circumstances and is therefore difficult to specify. However, an intelligent guess would be that most organizations take as long as five years to reach the fifth phase—although the first three phases may only last two years.

Phase 1: Prestart-Up

The period that immediately precedes the hiring of the majority of the work force is one of the most crucial in the development of an organization's pay system. During this period, a small group of planners and administrators meets to plan the technological aspects of the organization, as well as its basic management practices and policies. It is crucial that compensation system issues be considered. Some of the activities that should take place during this time period are as follows.

Development of Management Philosophy.   One of the first activities during any organization start-up should be the development of a management philosophy. This should predate decision making about pay systems since it is needed in order to test pay system decisions for consistency and congruence. An organization's statement of management philosophy should cover decision-making processes, communication, reward levels, and performance goals for the organization. Once this statement has been developed, preliminary design work on the reward system can follow.

Development of Goals for Compensation System.   Organizations should give explicit attention to the effects that compensation systems are supposed to have. Unless these are made clear and stated in a way that allows objective assessment of the reward system, the effectiveness of the pay system will be impossible to determine later on. In addition, a clear statement of goals is needed as the basis for determining which reward system practices are right for the organization. A statement of goals should consider such issues as whether or not pay will be used to motivate performance and how the reward system will affect the organization's climate.

Development of Decision-Making Approach for the Compensation System.   To the extent possible, management should decide which reward system decisions will be made on a participative basis and what kind of participation will be used. Decisions should also be made about what pay practices are and are not acceptable. Although this may be difficult to do, in many cases, these decisions must be made early in the history of an organization. Otherwise, employees may believe they have been tricked and misled by promises of high levels of participation that do not materialize because management ends up making pay decisions without asking them.

A crucial strategy issue—whether or not the compensation system is going to be a focal point of the organization's management system—is involved here. In all start-up situations, there is only limited time for employees to participate in design decisions. Some decisions have to therefore be made on a more top-down basis because the organization cannot afford the time and effort needed to have everyone participate in all decisions. New organizations have to become productive; otherwise, they cannot justify the large costs that are involved in building one. However, the long-term effectiveness of the system can be damaged if too much pressure is put on it for a fast start-up. A case can be made for having reward system decisions be a high-participation area in most new organizations, although it probably should not be in all. Whatever the decision, the extent of employee participation in reward system design and maintenance must be decided and made public.

Analysis of Potential Work Force.   Before any detailed compensation planning can begin, a good idea of the nature of the potential work force is needed. This analysis should include a study of the demographics of the expected work force, the nature of the jobs and job levels within the organization, and the expected markets from which employees will be drawn.

Survey of Compensation in Market Area.   After determining the nature of its potential work force, a salary survey, focusing on total compensation in the markets from which future employees are expected to be drawn, should be conducted by the organization. This survey should include a detailed analysis of the kinds of benefits that people in the market are receiving, as well as an analysis of their pay levels. Pay rates should then be set which reflect the market. Normally, starting salaries must be set at the market level or slightly above it to attract the types of people who will function well in a high-involvement climate. If a skill-based plan is used, the expectation should be that eventually some employees will be paid considerably higher than the market for single-skilled employees.

Determination of Limitations on Pay and Benefits Decisions.   Most corporations have certain fundamental policies that limit the pay and benefits options available to new plants. Management must therefore assess the restrictions that the rest of the organization may impose on the new plant. This assessment should include both total cost restrictions and any restrictions affecting the mixture of benefits and cash.

Furthermore, this assessment should be made before consideration is given to alternative models. Considering options that will eventually be ruled out by the parent organization can only cause frustration and discouragement.

Development of Reward Systems to Cover Initial Operation of the Plant. Some reward system decisions must be made before the bulk of the employees begin their jobs, including some decisions about pay, fringe benefits (such as life and health insurance), and perquisites affecting where employees will work, park, and eat. Most other reward system issues, such as promotion, can be left for later attention. Nevertheless, the decisions that are made in these areas are particularly crucial, and a number of options should be thoroughly considered.

Pay System Design. Skill-based pay plans and all-salaried work forces are two approaches to pay systems that should be considered by all new organizations. In some ways, these approaches complement each other, but either can be adopted by itself. Also, neither has to be implemented during the start-up of an organization. All an organization has to decide prior to hiring employees is what amount of money it is going to pay individuals when they first start work. All other decisions can be postponed until a later time, which may be particularly desirable in situations where employee participation in the design of the pay system is strongly emphasized.

Skill-based pay has several advantages in new plant situations: (1) it rewards the kind of behavior that is needed early in the life of an organization—acquiring new skills; (2) it helps create a climate of personal growth and development; and (3) it can be combined with a participative approach to reward system decision making if employees in a work group are allowed to decide whether one of their peers has acquired a desired skill. As was stressed earlier, if a participative approach to appraisal is to be used, then clear criteria for testing whether skills have been acquired must be developed in advance of any evaluation.

The all-salary work force approach can help to communicate to employees that everyone who works for the organization is on equal footing in terms of rights and privileges. Although the decision to adopt this kind of system can be delayed until after the work force has been hired, it is probably best made at the beginning. It clearly communicates to new employees that the organization is different, and it is a move that most people favor. Participation in making this decision, therefore, is probably not crucial.

Benefits. Only a minimum number of core benefits need be provided at the start-up of an organization. At the beginning, it is almost impossible to know exactly what kind of benefits package will fit the organization's work force, even though a fairly careful demographic study of potential employees may have been conducted. In addition, any predesigned package makes a number of decisions about what employees will want that can best be made by them after they have joined the organization.

It is important that, at the beginning, only one fringe benefits plan be created for all employees. All too often, multiple benefits plans are developed for people at different levels in the organization and, once in place, they are very difficult to dislodge. This latter approach to benefits is consistent with a more traditional, top-down management philosophy; it is not consistent with a more participative management approach that emphasizes the full partnership of everyone in the enterprise.

Phase 2: Induction and Orientation

The second identifiable phase in the start-up of an organization involves the initial hiring and training of the majority of the work force. Several crucial activities, with respect to the reward system, need to take place during this time period. Most of them involve the pay system and the fringe benefits program.

Communication to Prospective Employees. A thorough description of the pay plan and philosophy should be given to all prospective employees to enable them to make an informed decision about whether to join the organization. This also provides a good opportunity to begin educating the future work force about the compensation system.

In communicating with prospective employees about the compensation package, the stress should be on how much the package is subject to change and how actively involved employees will be in designing the final reward system. A good example of what can be presented is provided by the following section from the employee handbook of a new plant:

> The initial levels in the pay system have been defined to allow employees promotion possibilities based on meeting their production and team goals.
>
> Since we strongly believe that employees want to participate in developing practices and systems that affect their work life, we will develop the higher levels of pay with employees once they have become familiar with our operating philosophy and business requirements. We expect to do this by the end of our first year of operation.
>
> After individuals have completed an initial training period, they will become salaried employees and will remain in a salaried pay system thereafter.

If the development and administration of pay involves participation, it may discourage some employees from joining the organization, but it may also attract some who prefer a more participative and flexible approach to reward systems. In addition, it is quite possible that those who are turned off by the idea of the pay system not being fully developed at start up are just the employees that the organization does not want to hire. If they do not trust the organization enough to accept a more participative approach, or if they are uncomfortable with the ambiguity of an evolving pay system, then they probably should not be in an organization that will be following a more participative management philosophy. In fact, a discussion of the reward system would seem to be one of the best ways to communicate to prospective employees just how the organization, as a whole, will be managed.

Development of Training Module.   If participation in pay decisions is going to be a major feature of the organization, a module on compensation should be developed and implemented for the initial training of newly hired employees. This module should not be limited to just the details of the particular compensation plan that is being used. It should also include broader issues of compensation, such as labor markets, salary surveys, job evaluation plans, and gain-sharing plans. This training is crucial since it forms a basis for later employee participation in pay decisions. Without some training, it is unrealistic to expect employees to make informed decisions about how their compensation system should be structured.

Phase 3: Start-Up

Once employees are hired, trained, and initially introduced to their job, a third identifiable phase begins. During this phase, the organization is usually heavily involved in problem solving and getting systems on line. Depending upon the complexity of the technology being employed and the sophistication of employees, this phase may last from a few weeks to many months. Because it is a very active time for all employees, it is not a time when many decisions can be made about the organization's pay system. However, a few activities can be accomplished that will help prepare for later pay system activities.

Vehicle for Employee Involvement.   Toward the end of the start-up period, it is often appropriate to put into place the vehicles that will allow employees to make decisions. In most cases, this means forming a committee of managers and employees to discuss reward system issues. The number and kinds of committees that are formed will depend on how much and what kind of participation in reward system decisions was decided on during phase 1. If a great deal of participation is desired, then a multi-level model might be used that would include one overall committee responsible for all reward system decisions and a number of subcommittees that would look into such issues as perquisites, benefits, and compensation practices. In any case, in creating these committees, employees who are in communication with other people in the organization and who appear to be opinion leaders should be selected.

Phase 4: Steady State

The fourth phase—best described as the *steady state*—begins once some degree of predictability and regularity emerges in the organization. In terms of organizational effectiveness, the results of the organization should have stabilized, to some extent, and the organization should be at what is considered "normal" performance levels. At this point, a number of important decisions can be made about changes and evolutions in the reward system. Specifically, the following actions should be taken.

Implementation of Compensation Programs.   If they have not already been put into place, all employee-recommended compensation systems should be implemented, including policies concerning promotions, vacations, holidays, pay increases, and additions to the benefit and perquisite packages.

Organization-wide Gain-Sharing Plan Study.   Once a steady state of operating results has been achieved, some kind of organization-wide gain-sharing plan should be explored, using the already established vehicles for employee participation. This kind of plan, undoubtedly, will not be applicable to all organizations. As was detailed in Chapter 9, among factors that should be considered are organization size, the interdependence of the different operating parts of the organization, and, of course, the degree to which employees believe it is a desirable compensation system to have.

One important reason for delaying the consideration of such a plan until the steady-state period is that these plans usually are meaningful only if they can be based on some significant history of operating results. The alternative is to base them on an engineered or estimated standard which is constantly changed as the plant comes on line and people learn their jobs. This has been done, but it is difficult to make credible and, thus, is not usually desirable. In addition, there is reason to believe that a performance bonus is not crucial to the successful start of a new plant. My experience is that during start-up, plenty of intrinsic motivation to get things operating is present. What is needed is not so much more motivation but more skills; hence, the appropriateness of a skill-based pay system.

A second important reason for delaying is that gain-sharing plans can best be understood and developed by employees after they have had some experience with how the organization operates, what cost data mean, and what they can contribute to greater organizational effectiveness. At about this time, employees begin to become concerned about how they can earn more money. For the initial operating period, in most new plants, the skill-based pay system satisfies peoples' desire for economic growth by allowing them to earn more by acquiring more skills. However, individuals eventually top out because there are no more skills to learn. When a significant number (e.g., 20 percent) top out, the issue of some sort of performance-based pay plan can become a "hot" issue in the organization. In a very real sense, gain sharing represents an answer to the question: What can you do to sustain new organizations once the novelty of all the new practices wears out?

There are a number of reasons for believing that a gain-sharing plan can be quite easily and successfully installed in most new plants. The primary reason for this is that many of the conditions necessary for plan success already exist in new plants. If the approach that has been discussed so far has been followed, the participation system will be in place; employees will understand how the organization works and what they must do in order for it to be effective; employees will understand the kind of financial measures that will be used; and a climate of trust will exist, so that employees will believe that if performance is improved they will actually receive a bonus. In one new plant where a gain-sharing plan was installed by R. J. Bullock and myself, it was, as predicted, easy to install and quite effective. Unfortunately, few other cases of a gain-sharing plan being put into a new plant exist at this point. To a large extent, the view that it should be easy and effective therefore remains unproven.

Educational Programs.   Once the compensation systems have been developed, educational opportunities should be provided for employees so they will have a chance to understand how the systems operate. Open administration of rewards involves not only making compensation information available, but also ensuring that employees understand the company's policies and practices and that employees are sufficiently well informed to ask pertinent questions. On the surface, this kind of education may not appear relevant to administering pay, but it is highly relevant. In order to make informed recommendations and decisions regarding such things as pay systems and fringe benefits, employees need information on the cost structure of the organization, the competition it faces, and how the organization operates on a day-to-day basis.

Establish Feedback and Evaluation Systems.   Once the fundamental pieces of the pay system are in place, it is time to put into practice measures that will assess how effectively it is operating. These should include attitude surveys of how employees perceive the reward system and data on such things as absenteeism, turnover, and tardiness. A base-line measurement should be made fairly early so that comparisons can be made later to see how well the reward systems are meeting the goals that were established during phase 1.

Phase 5: Evolution and Renewal of Reward System Programs

Reward systems, like organizations, require growth, change, adaptation, and development. Because organizations change, as do their environments, reward systems must also change. Changes in reward systems, then, should not stop with phase 4. There are a number of change-oriented activities that need to regularly occur in organizations.

Regular Assessment.   Approximately once a year, the effectiveness of the pay system should be reassessed. This should include conducting an attitude survey, as well as reviewing the organization's data on absenteeism, turnover, and tardiness. If these data show any problems developing, corrective action should be taken before serious problems develop. This can be combined with the normal market survey work that is done and with an overall assessment of how the organization is doing. At this point, the goals of the reward system should also be assessed to determine if they are still meaningful and appropriate. In addition, the salary survey data should be checked to be sure that the now highly skilled work force is being paid accordingly.

Advanced Individualized Compensation System.   As an organization matures, the diversity of individuals in the organization will probably increase and, as a result, the kind of rewards that people desire will become more and more diverse. This may come about, for example, because longer-term, highly skilled employees are nearing retirement at the same time as many new, inexperienced employees are joining the organization. In any organization where there is a great diversity of employees, it is important to think about individualizing the reward system. Cafeteria compensation programs that will allow individuals to choose among major fringe benefits are an approach to individualized reward systems that should be considered in efforts to provide attractive options for employees. Special benefits such as sabbaticals, training opportunities outside the organization, unique retirement programs, and flexible work schedules and time periods should also be considered.

SUMMARY AND CONCLUSIONS

New organizations present some unique challenges and opportunities. They provide the opportunity to do it "right" from the beginning and, as a result, to create a system which encourages high levels of employee involvement and is characterized by high levels of effectiveness. In a number of respects, they appear to provide an informative model of how more effective organizations can be created.

With respect to pay, two issues emerge as being crucial: consistency and timing. Consistency can be achieved by making the compensation system decision process similar to that used in other areas and structuring the reward system to fit those behaviors which are consistent with the chosen style of management. Timing requires an evolutionary approach. Although it takes longer for this reward system approach to produce a "complete" reward system, it should produce an effective reward system much faster than any other approach.

12
CHANGING ORGANIZATIONS

Surprisingly little has been written about the role of pay system change in organizational change efforts. With a few exceptions (e.g., Lawler and Bullock 1978; Patten 1977, Patten and Fraser 1975), the issue has been ignored in both the organization development literature and the pay literature. Despite this, a considerable amount can and needs to be said about the important role that pay system change should play in change efforts. The pay system issues involved in changing established organizations are very different from those involved in starting new organizations. The differences stem primarily from two features of existing organizations: (1) the creation of timing issues due to the difficulty in changing all systems in an organization at the same time, and (2) the existence of resistance to change. These factors will be examined in this chapter in order to point out how the many approaches to pay discussed so far can fit into organization development efforts in established organizations.

SEQUENCING SYSTEM CHANGE

The key issue in initiating a change effort is where to start. In most organizations, a number of systems offer potential leverage points for initiating change (e.g., jobs or organizational structure). In order for most change efforts to be successful, a number of systems must be changed; otherwise, congruence will not exist and the changes will not be institutionalized. One strategy is simply to try to change all systems simultaneously. In most cases, however, this strategy is not practical because of the chaos it produces and because the resources to work on all systems simultaneously are usually not available in organizations. What typically happens is that one or more systems become lead systems in the change effort and others become lag systems. The pay system can be either a lag or a lead system. Let us first consider how it can operate as a lead system, then as a lag system. By doing this, we will be in a position to consider what determines which is the best strategy in a particular change effort.

PAY AS A LEAD SYSTEM

There are a number of reasons why starting a change program with the pay system may be both meaningful and strategically desirable:

1. The pay system is important to employees and it impacts on all organization members. Many times, change programs are limited to an issue that is not important to most individuals or that does not affect everyone (e.g., the creation of several self-managing teams). As a result, change is slow and often not very significant in the eyes of many. Pay is an issue that can provide a firm base upon which to begin organizational change.

2. Beginning with the pay system can be an indication of an organization's commitment to meaningful change. A belief that serious commitment exists can lead to attacking serious problems. Many change programs have been stymied and discredited because they started with such insignificant changes as cafeteria painting or fixing the parking lot. The pay system provides a direct route to the core organizational systems and is substantial evidence of deep-seated commitment to improvement.

3. Most organizations have problems with their pay system. Perceptions of inequity, inadequate administration, and nonperformance-contingent rewards are all indicators of maladies in compensation that are common to most organizations. They lead to a felt need for pay system change, a basic precondition for change.

4. Dealing successfully with the pay system can lead to measurable differences in individual performance and organizational effectiveness. This, in turn, can produce a feeling of success and positive feedback. Successful interventions in pay systems can demonstrate clearly the possibility of obtaining improvements through planned changes and, as a result, can encourage further planned change.

5. Beginning with pay can provide a model for how other problems can be dealt with. Usually, organizations have little or no experience in using a systematic process for solving system-wide problems that affect the quality of work life and organizational effectiveness. These mechanisms and processes can be developed and made explicit through changing the compensation system, and organizational learning can thus take place. A good example of this can be found in some of my work in which task forces and surveys have been used to diagnose and solve pay system problems. Later these same approaches were then used to solve other important problems.

6. Beyond providing a specific model of change, beginning with the pay system can lead directly to identifying other problems in the organization since the pay system is so closely connected to the other systems (Patten and Fraser 1975). Performance appraisal problems, dysfunctional management practices, poor supervision, control system errors, poor job designs, accounting inadequacies, and awkward communication networks are all examples of issues that may be highlighted by attempts to change the pay system because they are so closely tied to compensation issues. Commonly, the need for these other changes is made apparent by the initial diagnosis, but effort is only put into problem solving once the pay system change is made. Sometimes, the need for other changes is not even apparent until the pay system changes are in place because the pay change is needed to put them clearly out of tune with the other systems in the organization.

Despite the reasons for believing pay system changes can be a good place to start an organizational change effort, little research exists on how effective this approach is, and little is known about how to design and implement a change program that starts with the pay system. During the last five years, I have been involved in a number of studies which were designed to determine what happens when the pay system is used as the starting point for a change project. Included are studies of management and executive compensation, as well as studies of plant-wide gain sharing and base-pay systems. Most of these studies are still underway since they are attempting to look at the long-term effects of the change efforts. Thus definitive overall conclusions cannot be reached for several years. It is not too early, however, to report some of what has been learned.

Where to Begin?

The first strategic question to be addressed is: What aspect of the pay system represents the best place to begin? The choice is usually between starting with the base-pay system, a special performance-based bonus system, or the total pay system. The choice should be based on a careful diagnosis of the current state of the present pay system. As Patten and Fraser (1975) point out, an attitude survey can be very useful in this diagnosis, particularly when it is combined with an effective feedback process. (See Nadler (1977) for a discussion of survey feedback.) If the base-pay system is in reasonably good shape and improved performance is desired, it is advisable to start with consideration of a performance-based pay system. Consideration of performance-based pay seems to lead more quickly to consideration of such systemic issues as superior-subordinate communication, the trust level in the organization, and the overall effectiveness of the organization. Overall, it leads more quickly to widespread organizational change.

However, if the base-pay system is seriously out of line with people's perceptions of equity, there really is no choice but to begin with it. To do otherwise is to compromise the credibility of the entire effort. When the base-pay plan is the beginning point, it leads naturally to a consideration of performance-based pay. For example, in one plant where Jenkins and I did a change project, we were "forced" to deal with the base-pay system first, even though we had intended to start out with a participative gain-sharing plan (Lawler and Jenkins 1976). The base-pay system was so out of line that the employees were unwilling to talk about a gain-sharing plan until the base pay was fair in their eyes. After a new base-pay plan was put into practice, a gain-sharing plan was developed and implemented.

Finally, it is worth noting that, in many unionized workplaces, there is no choice about where to start. The contract often prevents changes in base-pay. As a result, the program must begin with consideration of a plant-wide or organization-wide gain-sharing plan, an approach that many unions will agree to consider outside of the contract.

Who Should Be Involved?

Once decisions have been made about where the change effort will start, the next question is: Who should be involved? Most approaches to changing pay systems are top-down—they assume that people above those on the pay plan should make the change decisions. However, as was discussed in Chapters 4 and 7, there is evidence that people can design their own systems and that, in some cases, this has produced very positive results. Since there are risks involved in having lower-level employees involved in making pay system changes, a participative effort should only be undertaken when it is part of an overall change program designed to increase the communication and participation levels in the organization. An isolated attempt at participation may just raise expectations which are promptly disconfirmed. Participation also should only be undertaken after a careful mapping has been done of what decisions have to be made and a *clear* decision is made about who is going to study, recommend, and reach a final decision on each.

In most of my change effort projects, small task forces (five to nine people) have been created, consisting of members who represent the groups that will be affected by the changes. Their first task is to diagnose the current situation. Because this diagnosis is a critical informational and educational base for future decisions, it must be accomplished effectively. The diagnosis consists of two questions: What is the objective situation? and What are the perceptions of the pay system in the eyes of the employees?

The objective diagnosis should be designed to firmly establish what compensation practices are currently in place in the organization. Once the objective definition of the compensation system has been established, it is important to determine the individuals' perceptions of the system. A well-designed survey can be instrumental in isolating various perceptions of the pay system and in educating task-force members on the issues involved in pay administration. In addition, a well-designed questionnaire can be instrumental in spreading participation throughout the organization by giving everyone a say in how the new plan will be structured. The results of the survey can also serve as a stimulus for change and as a base-line measure for monitoring improvement resulting from the pay system changes. The survey needs to look at such pay issues as internal equity (How fair is the distribution of pay within the organization?); external equity (How does pay in the organization compare to pay in the community?); the pay-performance relationship and personal equity (Is the pay fair considering the individual's investment of effort and responsibility?). (See Appendix C for some typical questions.) The survey should also consider such nonpay issues as the climate of the organization, the nature of jobs, and superior-subordinate relationships. These nonpay issues are included for two reasons: (1) the pay system must take into account the characteristics of the organization of which it will be a part, and (2) exploring these issues may prepare the way for later changes in other systems.

Mediating Factors

Once the current situation and perceptions have been established, there is one last step that needs to be taken before recommendations for change are made. This step is the analysis of the organizational and situational factors which determine which type of pay system is appropriate. Because many of these factors have already been considered, only five of the more important ones will be reviewed here.

Organization Size. As was stressed in Chapter 9, most approaches to paying for performance vary in their effectiveness as a function of organization size. There are many levels at which performance can be assessed. Performance can be measured and rewarded at the individual, work-group, or organizational level. Organization size needs to be a major determinant of the level at which performance is measured. Size is also a major determinant in the complexity of the administration of the compensation system. As size increases, so does the difficulty of adequately explaining the system and any changes to it.

Interdependence. The extent of interdependence among tasks and individuals within the organization is another critical mediating component of changes to the pay system. High levels of interdependence require systems which reflect that interdependence. There must be a

congruence between the pay system and the individual and group behaviors which are necessary for organizational effectiveness. As was
stressed in Chapter 10, this has some particularly important implications for the design of a performance-based pay plan. It means that
when interdependence is high, it is crucial to use plans that reward
overall group or plant performance, rather than individual performance. For example, in process production facilities (such as food
processing plants, chemical plants, and many complex assembly
plants), it does not make sense to try to measure and reward individual
performance. It simply is not separable enough from the performance
of others to be validly measurable for pay reward purposes.

Degree of interdependence also has some implications for base-
pay programs. High interdependence increases the attractiveness of
skill-based pay plans that reward individuals for having a broad
knowledge of the work setting. With interdependence, this knowledge
can have a very definite payoff. Skill-based pay systems are a good example of an approach which fits well in an interdependent situation,
but may not in an independent one.

Quality and Type of Information.   For a pay system to be effective,
employees must receive information about the things for which they
are compensated, and the organization must produce reliable and
face-valid measures to back up the system. This means that the information system has to provide appropriate information—both the type
of information and the quality of information that is required to make
pay decisions. This point has very important implications for the design of performance-based pay systems and base-pay systems. It
means that if a type of performance, a job characteristic, or any other
factor cannot be measured in a publicly discussible and defensible
manner, it should not be considered as a basis for paying individuals.
This rules out highly subjective and secret measures as a basis for pay
and means that, in some situations, individuals should not be paid for
their performance because individual performance is not and cannot
be measured in a satisfactory manner. Not surprisingly, improvements
in the information systems are often required if pay is to be based on
performance at any level in the organization. This can lead to improvements in the information system that both solve the pay problem
and give managers information that improves their ability to manage.

Value System of the Members.   There are differences in the values
and beliefs of organizational members that must be considered in designing changes in the pay system. For example, organizations often
differ in the degree to which employees feel they should equally share
in a company-wide or plant-wide bonus pool. In one situation I
studied, the employees felt strongly that everyone should be treated
equally; in another, they felt it would be unfair to treat good and poor
performers the same. In another case mentioned earlier, I tried to install a base-pay system which tied the base-pay rate to the number of
jobs a person could do (Lawler and Jenkins 1976). It ended up being
rejected by the employees because they wanted to concentrate on
learning how to do their job better, not on learning other jobs.

Technological Change.   The rate of technological change is important because of the limitations it places on the measurement and evaluation of performance and individual jobs. Stable technologies often
permit relatively complex, sophisticated measures to be developed.
Often, these same measures are not cost effective in rapidly changing
technologies. Rapidly changing technologies often require excessive
administration costs to properly measure and evaluate individual tasks
and individual performance. In situations where change is rapid, it is
therefore desirable to have a base-pay system that has very loose job
descriptions and does not measure individual performance.

Design, Implementation, and Change

Once the important mediating factors have been assessed, it is time to
design the new pay system. Rarely is this a simple process. Occasionally everything seems to fall into place, so that one particular pay
approach is the clear, logical choice. Most situations, however, simply
are not that straightforward. The state of the mediating factors is often such that no one approach is clearly indicated. Although this can
cause frustration, it also can motivate a broad look at the condition of
the organization, which may reveal that changes in other areas are
needed if pay is to be administered in a way that will make the organization more effective and the quality of work life better. Eventually, if
no pay system change can be agreed upon or other changes seem to
have higher priority, then it may be necessary to reexamine the decision to begin with a pay system change.

Regardless of what new approach to pay is chosen, it is crucial that a good change process be used in implementing it. As will be discussed later in this chapter, pay system change can be particularly difficult to manage. Since it is a highly important factor, it is particularly likely to produce distortion and resistance. This makes it extremely important that pay system change include those features which are known to reduce resistance: participation and open communication.

Systemic Effects

In most cases, pay system changes lead to an expressed need for other changes. A physicist once remarked that, "Every time we try to separate something to study it, we find it hitched to everything else in the universe." The same is true for organizations. The compensation system affects and is affected by virtually every other subsystem of the organization. The most important links are to performance appraisal, the information system, the design of jobs, and the managerial style. Not surprisingly, one or more of these usually needs to be changed when pay systems are changed. It is crucial that this be anticipated and prepared for before the pay system changes are made. If it is not, the pay system changes may only increase the frustration level in the organization. This point is clearly illustrated by what often happens when a gain-sharing plan is installed.

The motivation for changing other systems is often very high when a gain-sharing plan is installed. People want it to pay out and they realize that for it to pay a bonus, other changes are needed. At this point, the success of the plan depends on whether or not these other changes can be made. The following is a list of some of the things that often are asked for:

1. Better scheduling systems
2. Better tools and equipment
3. Supervisory training in technical skills
4. Supervisory training in listening and dealing with suggestions
5. Technical training for employees
6. More information on the financial condition of the organization
7. Fair base-pay rates

As the reader can see, these issues cover a wide range of things. Not every one has to be or can be responded to immediately, but some of them must be. Otherwise, the gain-sharing plan is likely to fail because people develop the perception that "no one cares" and that "it is hopeless."

Conclusion

Although a great deal can be accomplished by using pay system change as a lead system in producing meaningful organizational change, it is important to conclude with two cautionary points.

First, it takes time. If an organization is serious about making meaningful changes, it will have to make a strong commitment of time and energy to understanding the current situation and developing successful changes. In my projects, it has usually taken at least six months for the new pay system to be designed and implemented. Change in other systems has taken much longer. Pay system change is no panacea. Typically it is only the beginning of a multiple system change effort.

Second, it is important to take a formative view of compensation system changes. It is not necessary to always be fiddling with the system, but it is vital to respond to problems and situational changes when they occur, as they occur. Because conditions change inside of and outside of organizations, pay systems need to change. This means that even the best conceived and implemented pay change program is not likely to be a permanent "fix" for either the pay problems or any other problems in the organization. The most that can be hoped for is that it will help the organization become more effective in adapting to changes in its environment and will make later changes in the pay system both possible and effective.

PAY AS A LAG SYSTEM

When organizational change efforts do not use the pay system as a lead system, the role of pay in the change may still be a crucial one. Often, it needs to be rapidly changed to be congruent with the changes made in other systems. When the pay system is not changed in a timely fashion, it can prevent the institutionalization of the other changes in several ways. It may not reward the behavior which is needed to make the changed systems work. Worse yet, it may even reward behavior that is the antithesis of what is needed to make the changes work. The implications of this point are clear—change efforts need to anticipate the need for pay system changes and incorporate them into the long-term change strategy.

How soon pay system changes will be needed in a change effort is a function of a number of factors and may be difficult to specify in advance. A good guess, however, is that if the lead system changes involve changes in job design, organizational structure, and/or information and control systems, the desire for pay system changes will appear almost immediately. Similarly, change efforts using survey feedback approaches often raise the compensation issue. Unfortunately, it is impossible to provide a detailed model of when and how pay systems should be changed as part of an organization development effort. There simply are too many possible changes to consider. A brief review of a few cases, however, may help to illustrate the issues that are involved.

There are a number of cases where work redesign was tried and nothing was done to change the structure of the reward system. In several instances, job enrichment and job rotation were implemented, but a traditional job evaluation plan was left in place. As a result, employees demanded higher pay because they had taken on more responsibility. In one plant, for example, a woman who was asked to take notes at team meetings asked for a raise because she had taken on secretarial duties. Management had trouble answering this demand because the job evaluation plan was designed for situations where employees did not rotate and acquire new skills. It is interesting to note that in the new plants where both work teams and a skill-based evaluation plan have been installed, these problems are not present because the evaluation approach is supportive of people changing jobs and acquiring new skills; in fact, it rewards them for doing so.

In another case, a large airline tried an autonomous work-group experiment with its maintenance employees. The experiment failed because the pay system was not changed. The employees were not on an incentive plan, but they had come, over the years, to expect large amounts of overtime. In effect, because harder work did not get them more money and slower work did (it got them overtime), they had decided to work overtime to earn more money. The establishment of the autonomous work group failed to increase performance not because the concept was defective, but because good performance was against the best economic interests of the employees.

Lindholm (1974) has reported on a Swedish case that emphasizes what can happen when a pay system does not fit the way jobs and organizations are structured. In this situation, a piecework system was abandoned in favor of an hourly nonperformance-based wage plan, and the jobs of the employees were enriched. The result was a failure—performance went down and turnover went up—apparently because both the financial incentive to perform well and the positive effect the pay system had on scheduling were gone. The lost extrinsic motivation was not replaced by enough intrinsic motivation to keep intrinsic motivation up, and the better performers were dissatisfied because they could not earn extra income. The effect on scheduling is a particularly interesting one. A common side effect of good performance-based pay systems is their impact on the production support systems in an organization. When people care about their performance they demand good scheduling, parts, and maintenance in order to be productive. This puts pressure on these groups to be effective. When people do not care about their performance, the pressure on these groups is reduced accordingly. Two years later, a plant-wide incentive system was added. Suddenly, productivity went up 45 percent, and turnover dropped to a lower level than before the piecework was dropped. This pay plan seemed to fit perfectly with the new organization design. It provided motivation by tying pay to performance. Because it rewarded plant performance, it encouraged the cooperation and teamwork needed to make the new approach to job and organization design work effectively.

This experiment seems to point to the same conclusion as the research mentioned earlier on the Scanlon Plan: Pay incentive plans can be very effective in an organization that uses participative management, autonomous work groups, and job enrichment. In some ways, this is an ironic conclusion because the proponents of these approaches often argue that participative management, autonomous work groups, and job enrichment are powerful motivators and make pay incentives unnecessary. It is also ironic that traditionally-run organizations are usually in a poor position to use pay as an incentive because the trust level is low—yet these are just the organizations that most need to use pay as a motivator.

Conclusion

The clear message that should be heard from this discussion of pay systems as a lag factor in change efforts is that, in change efforts, it is vital to be prepared to deal with compensation issues. It should be expected that compensation system issues will arise and will have to be dealt with. It should also be determined what types of changes are possible. Figure 12.1 suggests some that are commonly stimulated by nonpay system changes. If compensation system changes are not possible, this should be stated at the beginning and consideration given to not undertaking the project if the lead system changes are ones that will lead to a desire for pay system changes. If only certain kinds of changes are possible, this too should be made clear early in the change process. Expertise should be acquired in the possible options so that informed decisions can be made about what fits the change effort.

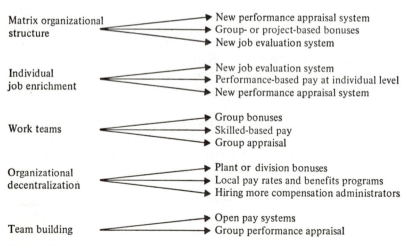

Figure 12.1 Pay system changes likely to be stimulated by other changes

PAY AS A LEAD OR LAG SYSTEM

The strategic decision of whether to use pay as a lag or lead system in an organizational change effort should be made based on a diagnosis of the situation. The key diagnostic data concerns where the energy for change in the organization rests. In most cases, the change effort should begin with whatever system or systems can be identified as ones where an openness to change exists. Usually, as shown in Figure 12.2, openness to change exists because there is a high level of dissatisfaction with the existing state of affairs.

In the case of pay, there are some conditions under which it probably should not be chosen as a lead system, even though there is a high level of dissatisfaction with it. In unionized situations, for example, there often is little that can be done with pay except through collective bargaining, even though dissatisfaction exists. In these situations, it is often wise to avoid it and leave it to the collective bargaining process unless, as was noted earlier, there is an openness to a noncontracted gain-sharing plan. Sometimes, problems of low pay cannot be solved simply because the organization does not have the money (e.g., in government agencies and failing companies). In these cases, little can be gained from focusing on pay.

Finally, in situations where there are a number of serious areas of dissatisfaction, it may not be wise to start with pay. It can take a long time to improve the pay situation, and what is often needed is quick improvement in at least one area. Furthermore, better pay administration, in many cases, can only take place after other key systems (e.g., information systems, job design, or organizational structure) have been improved. If it is recognized that these need improvement, starting with them makes sense since they often have to be improved before the pay system can be improved. Of course, if it is not recognized that they need to be improved, then work on the pay system can be used to create a felt need to improve them.

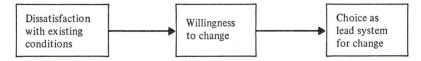

Figure 12.2 Determinants of willingness to change

RESISTANCE TO CHANGE

Why are organizations and individuals resistant to change? Let us first consider individuals. An individual faced with a major change in the organization for which he or she works may be resistant for a variety of different reasons. First, individuals need a certain degree of stability or security. Change presents unknowns which cause anxiety. Second, to the extent that a change is imposed on an individual, it reduces his or her sense of autonomy or self-control. Third, individuals typically have developed patterns for coping with or managing the current structure and situation. Change means that they will have to find new ways of managing their own environments, ways that might not be as successful. Fourth, those who have power in the current situations may resist change because it threatens that power. They have a vested interest in the status quo. Fifth, change may mean a loss in rewards. This is particularly likely in situations where traditional job evaluation techniques are used and a major structural reorganization is involved. Finally, individuals may resist change for ideological reasons; they may truly believe that the way things are currently done is better than the proposed change.

Organizations as systems are also resistant to change. The forces of equilibrium tend to work to cancel out many changes, as was stressed earlier. To the extent that changing one component of an organizational system reduces its congruence or fit with other components, energy will develop to limit, encapsulate, or reverse the change. This is why institutionalization of change may be difficult (Goodman 1979). Pressure toward achieving and maintaining organizational effectiveness can also serve to generate pressures against change. To the extent that an organization needs to give time and attention to dealing with resistance to change and coping with the problems created by change, it may become diverted from being effective.

Two key tasks must be accomplished if change is to be brought about. The first task is to motivate change, or to overcome the natural resistance to change that emerges. This involves getting individuals motivated to behave in ways that are consistent with the immediate change goals and with long range organizational effectiveness as well. The second major task is managing change. We can think of organizational changes in terms of transitions (Beckhard and Harris 1977). The organization exists in a current state (C). An image is developed of a future state of the organization (F). The period between C and F can be thought of as the transition period (T). A key issue in any change effort is how to manage the transition.

Frequently, the transition state is overlooked. People become fixated with the future state and assume that all that is needed is to design the best possible future. They think of change as simply a mechanical or procedural detail. The problems created by the lack of concern for the transition state are compounded by the uniqueness of it. In most situations, the management systems and structures developed to manage either C or F are simply not appropriate or adequate for the management of T. They are steady-state management systems, designed to run organizations already in place, rather than transitional management systems. Management during a transition period is difficult for most managers because they are not familiar with managing change. There are a number of things that can be done to help this process go well. Such things as developing a clear image of the desired future state and using multiple levers for change can facilitate the change effort. The pay system is a good lever that may need to be managed differently during the transition period.

Compensation and Transition Management

The pay system can play a major role in making the transition process a successful one. One reason many change efforts are resisted by individuals is that they are often perceived to be a threat to their pay level. Particularly when the present system is highly standardized and tied to objective measures, such as the number of subordinates, the vagaries of a reorganization or other type of change may lead people to resist the change because of its unclear and potentially negative impact on their pay rate. There is no magical formula for overcoming this resistance, but two approaches can help.

1. Until the change period is complete, there should be a floor put under individual pay rates. That is, no one should have to fear losing pay during the change process. This point is critical where major reorganizations are planned because, in order for the change to go well, some people might have to give up some subordinates and responsibilities. As a result, if the job were reevaluated, it might be evaluated lower. If this problem is likely to be severe the organization may want to assure individuals that their pay will not be cut, even after the change is in place.

2. Assign a group of key individuals the responsibility for the development of an approach to compensation that will fit the new organization. The charge is to develop a corporate rewards philosophy that includes the following:
   a. The goals of the pay system
   b. How the pay system will fit the new organizational structure
   c. The fit between the management style of the organization and the process used to administer the pay system
   d. How the pay system will be managed once it is developed.

The purpose of assigning this task to a group of key individuals is four-fold. First, the creation of a pay philosophy is a necessity if the new organization is going to have an effective pay system. More and more evidence is accumulating that without some sort of widely subscribed-to philosophy in a corporation, pay administration ends up being haphazard and a source of internal conflict. A philosophy cannot answer all the problems associated with rewards, but it can at least provide a touchstone against which new practices, policies, and decisions can be tested. Second, it will give the key individuals a chance to influence how they will be paid in the future and it can very dramatically reduce their fears about what their pay will look like after the restructuring is complete. In essence, they are being offered a chance to develop a reward approach that will fit the new organization that they will be a part of. A big potential unknown in the new organization thus becomes a factor that is under their control and becomes a much less fearful and potentially threatening factor about the reorganized structure. Third, it can assure that serious attention will be given to how the pay system will have to change to fit other changes. This can prevent "surprise" pay system problems from occurring once the other changes have been implemented. Fourth, it can aid institutionalization by helping to assure that an acceptable and appropriate pay system will exist to support and reinforce the new state when it is obtained. More about this point later.

Implementing Change

Putting a floor under existing salaries is important in reducing resistance, but it does nothing to encourage good implementation of change. The reward system can be used to encourage and support successful implementation of the reorganization as well. In most reorganizations, financial rewards are not used to motivate a speedy and successful implementation process. This is an unfortunate oversight. If careful thought is given to rewards and the process of change, often pay can be used to help assure that changes, which are keyed to other systems, are implemented effectively. Specifically, the following points are relevant:

1. In many change efforts, the key question is how to get people to act in ways that are consistent with an effective transition. The organization needs to make it clear that the jobs and associated rewards given to managers after the transition will be dependent upon their contribution to an effective transition process.

2. At some organizational levels, the transition situation may call for the use of one-time bonuses and payments. In most cases, it makes sense for these to be paid on a group basis rather than on an individual basis. There may be a few instances where individuals have particular goals to accomplish that are individual in nature, but, in most cases, one-time financial payments should be based at the group level and tied to transition goals.

3. It is important that transition goals be set with respect to both the rate at which change is introduced and the process that is used to introduce it. Both should be as explicit and quantitatively precise as possible. They are a critical ingredient in the effective motivation of change and should be tied directly to the reception of the one-time payments just mentioned. The goals should include specific dates, what should be accomplished by these dates, and measures of the process that was used in implementing change. These process measures are harder to define than are implementation events, such as having a new unit operating or having people relocated, but they can be measured. Typical of the measures that can be used here are people's understanding of the new system, the degree to which it was explained to them, the level of turnover among people that the organization wished to retain, signs of stress among people involved in the transition, and the willingness of managers to give up people to other parts of the organization where they can make a greater contribution.

The best way to summarize this discussion is to say that the transition process can be managed and that rewards, goals, and performance measures are critical tools in managing this process. They can be used to assure that a rapid implementation of the change strategy takes place and that it does so in a way that minimizes the dysfunctional consequences for both the organization and the people who work within it.

INSTITUTIONALIZATION OF CHANGE

Just as the pay system can have a strong influence on the transition process, it can also have a strong influence on the institutionalization process. The fact that a desired future state is achieved is no guarantee that it will be maintained. There is evidence that unless careful planning is done to support it with the pay system, it will not be maintained. Informative examples of this point are provided by two joint union-management quality-of-work-life projects: Rushton, a coal mine, and Bolivar, an auto parts plant.

In both these projects, initially successful projects tended to falter. This was particularly true in the case of the coal mine, Rushton (Goodman 1979). In both cases, it was recognized that a gain-sharing plan was needed to support the new state which was achieved, but in neither case was one put into place. There were a number of reasons why plans were not installed in the locations, but one was common to both. No serious consideration was given to what a gain-sharing plan would look like, prior to beginning the change. We can only speculate as to what would have happened if gain-sharing plans had been installed at these sites, but there are reasons to believe that a gain-sharing plan could have aided institutionalization at both Rushton and Bolivar. Individuals could have been rewarded for the performance improvements that were obtained and interest in working together and improving performance could have been maintained.

As was mentioned earlier, having a group of key organization members focus on what the pay system will be like when the future state is achieved is one effective way to assure that the pay system will support the institutionalization of the future state. The key is to put into motion some process which will assure the following:

1. A new pay system will exist to support the future state when it is achieved.

2. The new pay system will reward those behaviors which are critical for the effective functioning of the organization in its new state.

3. The new pay system will be understood by and acceptable to the members of the organization.

4. The new pay system will use a decision process and a structure which is consistent with the overall management philosophy that characterizes the desired state.

SUMMARY AND CONCLUSIONS

If there is one message that sums up this discussion of change, it is that most change efforts have to deal with the pay system sooner or later. Although there is little evidence to prove it, a strong case can be made that change efforts are most likely to be successful when they involve a strategic plan that carefully considers the kind of pay system changes that will be needed during each phase of the change effort. Unlike the new plant situation, it is not possible to specify here just what kind of pay approaches should be taken; there simply are too many ways that an overall change project can unfold in an established organization. What can be specified is the need to give attention to the pay system.

13
PAY IN ORGANIZATIONS: A CHANGING SCENE

Throughout this book it has been emphasized that the pay system in an organization needs to fit the other systems in the organization and that the design of the organization, in turn, needs to fit the external environment in which it operates. When combined with a look at the way the environment is changing, this perspective leads to some interesting predictions about how pay systems will need to change in the future. Most of the pay systems that are in practice today follow design principles and processes that date back several decades. Our present approaches to job evaluation, performance appraisal, and performance-based pay are not radically different from those that were used twenty years ago. Similarly, the same closed, top-down process that has always been typical of pay decision making continues to dominate today.

The last two decades have seen an accelerated rate of societal change. What is more, the rate of change in society shows no signs of abating. Evidence that the pay systems in most organizations have fallen behind the general rate of change in society is accumulating. The increase in lawsuits and the higher levels of pay dissatisfaction are two examples of this evidence. If organizations and their pay systems are to catch up and keep pace with the rate of societal change, they are going to have to change rapidly.

It is one thing to state that change is needed; it is quite another to specify what kind of change is needed. In this chapter, the focus will be on specifying the kind of changes that are likely to be needed, given our best projection of how the environment is going to change. First, we will consider some work-force, organizational, and environmental changes that have implications for pay administration. Then, consideration will be given to the kind of pay system changes that are needed in order to keep pay systems congruent with these changes.

The discussion will be future oriented since the purpose of this chapter is to help clarify and stimulate thinking about what long-term practices and policies are needed in the area of compensation. In a sense, this is not so much a how-to-do-it discussion as a strategic discussion of how compensation and organization development specialists should think about the role of compensation in a changing society and in organizations which are struggling to keep pace with their rapidly changing environment. By necessity, this discussion will be highly speculative in nature.

CHANGING NATURE OF THE WORK FORCE

A critical issue in the design of compensation systems is the nature of the work force. As has been stressed thoughout this book, the primary objective of a compensation system is to influence individual behavior. In order to be effective in influencing individual behavior, the compensation system needs to fit the nature of the individuals who work in the organization. This is true with respect to both base pay and performance-based pay. The task of fitting the pay system to the nature of the work force is getting increasingly complex because of some long-term changes which are taking place in the nature of the work force. A brief review of these changes follows.

1. *The work force is becoming more heterogeneous.* A number of forces have converged to increase the heterogeneity of the work force. Legislation in the areas of equal employment opportunity and age discrimination has led to organizations having more minority group members and more women. In the future, it also appears that organizations will have more older people. The increased presence of women, minority group members, and older people in organizations

means that the values, lifestyles, and family situations of organization members are more heterogeneous and, as a result, so are their preferences for and attitudes about compensation. So far, this change has primarily impacted on the lower levels in organizations, but as women and minorities get promoted, it will be felt throughout.

2. *People are less accepting of traditional authority.* There is increasing evidence that people in the workplace are less willing to accept decisions simply because they are given by someone higher up in the organization. They are more likely to ask why a request is made or an order is given and to accept them based only upon expertise.

3. *There is an increasing desire for more influence in the workplace.* Table 2.1, which was presented in Chapter 2, shows how much influence employees currently perceive they have in a number of areas and how much they would like to have. The reactions to pay are particularly interesting. It is the area where people see the greatest discrepancy between how much influence they currently have and how much they feel they should have. Still, in terms of overall influence, it is not one of the areas where they feel they should have a great deal of influence. The implication of this seems to be that although the demand is present for greater influence in the area of pay, individuals, at the present time and probably for the foreseeable future, will not want to have as much control and influence over it as they will over the way they do their work and how their jobs are designed.

4. *Individuals are becoming more self- and money-oriented.* Tied in with a greater self-orientation by people is a reduced commitment to the organizations they work for and the occupations they currently work in. The best way to describe this emerging attitude is to say that people are asking more and more: What is in this for me? In the area of pay, this, when combined with what other people have called the rising expectations phenomenon, seems to have contributed to people being more dissatisfied with their pay and placing more importance on it. Table 13.1 shows the results of a random national sample of employed people (Quinn and Staines 1979). As can be seen from the table, the percentage of people who report satisfaction with their pay and benefits has decreased substantially from 1973 to 1977. The explanation for this cannot be that compensation went down during this time period. The real income of people actually went up, as did their

Table 13.1
Pay and Benefit Satisfaction

Item	Year	Indicating Very True (%)
The pay is good	1970	40.3
	1973	40.7
	1977	27.2
My fringe benefits are good	1970	41.8
	1973	43.7
	1977	32.5

total income. The most likely explanation for this finding is that the old approaches to compensating people simply are not fitting with the changing nature of the work force. Other data suggest that younger people are placing more importance on pay (Bachman and Johnston 1979).

5. *The education level in the United States is rising.* More and more people are completing high school and more and more people are going to college and getting college degrees. Because education has often been sold as a way to move up in society, this seems to be contributing to peoples' expectations about how well they will be rewarded and to their lack of tolerence for decision making based on traditional authority.

6. *People are becoming more knowledgeable.* The popularity of television and other mass media communication vehicles has increased the knowledge level in our society about such issues as discrimination, social equity, and upward mobility. As a result, many employees are developing a clearer picture of how our society works in the area of rewards. This knowledge could potentially lead to more challenges to the way we distribute financial rewards. Issues such as how jobs should be evaluated and what rate of pay is appropriate for the higher levels of management, seem particularly ripe for extensive debate. It may already have had an impact on motivation. Several recent surveys have suggested that people are less and less likely to feel that working hard will lead to pay and other rewards (Quinn and Staines 1979). In addition, there seems to be a growing debate over the social equity of most approaches to job evaluation. Increasingly, the concept of equal

pay for equal work is being challenged. The concept of equal pay for work of equal value is said to be one alternative that is fair to women and others who work in jobs that have traditionally been performed by groups who have been discriminated against.

7. *Family structures are changing.* Because more and more women are working, divorce is increasingly more common, and many individuals are postponing marriage and childbearing to a later age, the nature of the family structure is changing. This has important implications for the needs and desires that people have. In many cases, it means that age groups that traditionally had a strong need for security do not any more. In other cases, it means that single family incomes have become dual family incomes and this has yielded increased purchasing power, as well as the problems associated with geographic mobility in dual career families. This whole trend is best summarized by saying that family structures dramatically changed during the 1960s and 1970s. As a result, many organizational practices that were developed to fit a traditional family structure have become inappropriate.

8. *The role of leisure is changing.* Leisure is becoming more and more available in the American society, and there is evidence it is becoming more and more important to individuals. A combination of things—a shorter work week, higher wages, and the development of a sophisticated leisure industry—has led to the ready availability of a number of satisfying, affordable alternatives to work. The result is that organizations now find themselves competing with an additional attraction (leisure) when they try to attract employees to come to work and to motivate them to perform and become involved in their work.

9. *Rights consciousness has increased.* A number of forces seem to have converged to make the individual employee increasingly conscious of his or her rights to a fair and just decision process in important areas such as pay, promotion, and dismissal. Identifiable forces here include discrimination legislation, higher education levels, and the ready availability of legal talent to pursue cases. The result is that employees seem to be more and more willing to challenge organizational decisions which affect them in important areas. These challenges take many forms ranging from court actions to grievances.

CHANGING NATURE OF ORGANIZATIONS

Just as the nature of the work force is changing, the nature of organizations is changing in some important ways. A number of these characteristics have implications for the kind of compensation systems that are appropriate.

1. *The number of service organizations in the U.S. economy is growing very rapidly.* Service organizations show signs of becoming the dominant economic force in the U.S. economy. As was stressed earlier, service organizations have some very different characteristics from manufacturing organizations. Among these are the fact that they rely heavily on part-time employees and that the performance of individuals is often very difficult to measure. Thus they do not lend themselves to many of the traditional performance measurement approaches that are used in manufacturing organizations.

2. *The rate of productivity growth in U.S. organizations has declined during the late 1970s.* There is some evidence that this is due to increased numbers of service organizations, but there is also evidence that, in many cases, the traditional manufacturing organizations are not increasing in productivity as they should. This inevitably raises the issue of whether pay is being used as an effective motivator.

3. *Organization size and diversity is increasing.* The larger organizations in the United States are getting bigger and bigger. This is not to say that small organizations are disappearing. Small organizations are constantly being created and surviving. Nevertheless, the Fortune 500 industrial organizations, for example, are much larger than they were ten or fifteen years ago, and their growth shows every sign of continuing as the tendency to merge and acquire continues to be strong among large organizations. In many cases, large organizations have also become more diverse. They have entered new businesses and new industries. As a result, they are more internally heterogeneous and have greater problems of internal control and management. This often means that few individuals can identify with or understand company operating results and, as a consequence, company-wide pay incentive plans have little motivational value. Similarly, pay plans that work well in one part of an organization often do not work well in another because the situations differ so greatly.

CHANGING NATURE OF THE ENVIRONMENT

The external environment in which organizations must operate has changed in a number of important ways. Three of these are particularly important and have critical implications for how compensation should be administered.

1. *International competition has increased.* Because of improved communications and transportation, the trade of goods around the world has increased dramatically. This means that organizations in a particular country have to be concerned not only with competitors in their own country, but also with competitors outside. In many ways, this has increased the importance of having high productivity and high organizational effectiveness. Some industries and companies in the United States that have not been able to meet this competition have gone out of business, and others have been severely damaged (e.g., steel, autos, and tires). Foreign competition promises to be an increasing factor in the United States; thus, there is likely to be increased pressure on organizations to administer pay in a manner that will contribute to organizational effectiveness.

2. *There was an enormous growth during the 1960s and 1970s of government regulation of private business.* A number of these regulations had direct impact on how people should be treated in organizations. There is every reason to believe that continued government intervention in this area will exist. A considerable amount of this intervention has strong implications for compensation administration. Specifically, the existing legislation and court action concerning retirement and discrimination, and the proposed legislation and court action concerning privacy, job evaluation, and performance appraisal, all seem to suggest that organizations are going to have to provide highly defensible internal policies and practices with respect to reward administration.

3. *Slower economic growth and high inflation seem likely during the 1980s.* If these become a continuing reality, they could contribute to a number of developments. First, it could intensify the search for pay systems that are more effective at motivating performance and stimulating growth. Second, it could increase the importance of money to individuals because it will be more difficult for individuals to increase

their standard of living. Finally, it may intensify people's concern with social equity. If, as seems likely, it causes people to switch from viewing the world as one in which they are competing for a share of an ever-increasing pie to one in which they are competing for a share of a relatively fixed pie, attention to social equity is a natural consequence.

IMPLICATIONS FOR COMPENSATION SYSTEMS

What kind of pay system changes are needed to deal with the workforce, organizational, and societal changes that have been identified? To a substantial degree, each organization must find its own answer to the question since the effectiveness of a pay system depends on a good diagnosis of local conditions. Nevertheless, it is possible to give some general guidance as to what is likely to be effective. We will first briefly review four general themes that seem to provide some useful guidance and then look at some compensation system practices to see how well they fit each of these four themes.

Individualization

A number of the trends suggested so far come together to suggest that compensation systems in organizations need to be more individualized. Stated another way, they need to fit the needs and lifestyles of the individuals, as well as the particular conditions in which individuals are working. The increased need for this is brought about by the diverse nature of the work force, the increasing size and diversity of organizations, and the need to get more mileage out of pay in order to increase the cost effectiveness of total compensation packages. Compensation systems that use the same pay system in all parts of large organizations, give everybody the same benefits, use the same base-pay plans, and so on, no longer fit the diverse work force which exists and the diverse businesses that organizations often are in. Given that most organizations maintain a rather homogeneous stance toward compensation plans, it is no wonder that, in many cases, pay plans do not fit the needs of the individual or the needs of the business.

In the future, the ideal compensation system may be an individual contract between an employer and a worker which includes unique benefit plans, work hours, pay-performance relationships, and so on. At the present time, this is occasionally done when top-level managers are recruited from the outside. Of course, this is not practical in most situations, but some middle ground between individual contracts and pay systems which pay every person in the same way needs to be found. One reasonable approach may be to combine flexible benefits with lump sum increases. These two approaches could give individuals a tremendous range of choices.

Open Defensible Decision Processes

The traditional approach to making compensation decisions is a secret top-down approach that lacks a due-process appeal procedure. This is slowly changing. People are being given more opportunity to input into decisions and more information about the nature of the decisions. Nevertheless, in order to meet the rising expectations of the employees and the pressure that government is putting on corporations for defensible reward system decisions, the trend toward different decision processes needs to accelerate. Organizations need to move toward decision-making processes in the compensation area which are open, appropriately participative, and incorporate a due-process safeguard system (Ewing 1978). Only with improved openness, participation, and due-process protection are organizational pay systems likely to fit both the changing nature of the work force and the kind of demands the government is likely to make of organizations in our rights-conscious society.

Performance-Based Pay

Pay systems can play a role in increasing individuals' motivation to perform effectively, improving productivity in organizations, and offsetting the lack of involvement and commitment which is characteristic of today's work force. The key is appropriately tying pay to performance. A good case can be made that it is more important now than it ever has been in the history of modern work organizations that pay be tied to performance in a motivating manner. Pay shows evidence of becoming more important, thereby increasing its ability to motivate performance. Furthermore, the need for better performance is constantly growing.

In addition to the trends that make it more important to tie performance to pay, there are some trends that make it more difficult.

Included among these trends are the increased demand for fair and due process, the growth of service industries, the growth of large, complex organizations, and the increasing dissatisfaction with pay. These trends do not diminish the fact that one possible avenue to organizations remaining effective in the face of increased size, more heterogeneous and diverse work forces, and the growth of service organizations, is through paying for performance. However, it does highlight that the best way to do this in the future may be through plans that are quite different from the individual salary increase plans that dominate today.

More Egalitarian Reward Systems

The typical work organization is definitely not egalitarian in nature. Not only do some people receive much greater levels of total compensation, the pay level of an individual often determines whether or not he or she is eligible for a wide array of special benefits and perquisites. In large organizations, many different, carefully defined levels exist in reward systems. This has the effect of slicing organizations up into horizontal strata that are defined by the kind of rewards which are received. This runs counter to the desire of many for more participative organizations and to the concern for social equity. The answer does not rest in rewarding everyone the same, but it may rest in decreasing some of the differences. A good place to start would seem to be with the difference between hourly and salaried employees and with the multiple benefit plans which often exist. These changes have the dual advantage of increasing the perception of social equity and the perception that everyone is a full member of the enterprise.

Summary and Conclusions

Table 13.2 shows how the four themes fit the major changes which have been identified. A "yes" indicates they are in correspondence, a "?" indicates it is unclear, and a "no" indicates they are not in correspondence. By necessity, the scoring of a particular fit is subjective and open to debate. Nevertheless, a couple of interesting trends do appear. There is strong support for the idea of individualization of pay. The only problem with this concerns the degree to which it leads to unequal benefits which, in turn, runs into issues of social equity.

Table 13.2
Relationship of Pay Practices to Social Trends

Social Trend	Pay Practices			
	Individual-ization	Due Process	Performance-Based Pay	Equality
Work Force				
Heterogeneous	yes	?	?	?
Authority	yes	yes	?	?
Influence	yes	yes	?	?
Self-oriented	yes	yes	yes	no
Education level	yes	yes	?	yes
Knowledgeable	yes	yes	?	yes
Family structure	yes	?	no	?
Leisure	yes	?	yes	?
Rights conscious	?	yes	?	yes
Organizations				
Service	?	?	yes	?
Productivity	yes	?	yes	no
Diversity	yes	?	?	no
Environment				
Competition	yes	?	yes	no
Regulation	yes	yes	no	yes
Inflation	yes	?	yes	?

Good support exists for the ideas of due process and performance-based pay. The latter, in particular, has some strong positives and some strong negatives. This probably reflects the tendency of some organizations to increase their commitment to it while others retreat. Finally, there is only mixed support for greater equality. This suggests that it may be the slowest to take hold and that it probably is not as important as the others.

PAY PRACTICES IN THE FUTURE

A number of specific pay practices can help to contribute to the development of pay systems which are more individualized, defensible, performance-based, and egalitarian. Table 13.3 lists a number of the

Table 13.3
An Assessment of Approaches to Pay

	Individual-ization	Due Process	Performance-Based Pay	Equality
Flexible benefits	yes	yes	yes	yes
Gain sharing	yes	yes	yes	yes
Open pay system	no	yes	no	no
Decentralized administration	yes	no	no	no
Skill-based pay	yes	yes	yes	no
Mini-enterprise	yes	yes	yes	yes
Participative design	yes	yes	?	?
All-salary pay	no	no	no	yes
Lump sum increase	yes	yes	?	no
Flexible work hours and arrangements	yes	no	no	no
New benefits	yes	no	no	no

key practices which have been reviewed in this book. It also shows the extent to which they contribute to each of four characteristics. In the table, a "yes" means the practice contributes, a "?" means it is unclear, and a "no" means the practice does not contribute. Most of the policies are self-explanatory because they have been discussed throughout this book. A few, however, warrant elaboration since they have only been alluded to earlier.

Mini-enterprise refers to the concept of breaking out a business unit or product line of a large organization into a profit center and then tying pay to the performance of that mini-enterprise. Doing this can contribute to increased organizational identification and performance motivation for those people who are part of large, diverse organizations that are in multiple businesses.

Decentralized administration refers to the corporate strategy of giving separate business units the ability to develop and design their own compensation system. This contrasts with a highly centralized approach which legislates the same type of job evaluation, pay, benefits, and so on, for all parts of an organization.

Flexible work hours and arrangements refers to the many different approaches which are possible in setting up work hours. Job sharing by husbands and wives, flextime, and various permanent part-time work arrangements fit here.

New benefits refer to the many innovations which are possible with respect to how people receive pay. Sabbaticals, child care, and financial counseling are just a few examples of the many benefits which may have appeal to some individuals.

As can be seen from the table, although a number of approaches exist that can make a substantial contribution to meeting the future needs of compensation systems, in many respects the list is far too short. Considerable creativity, experimentation, and development work is needed. New developments are needed in the area of both the process and the mechanical side of pay administration. Unless these occur, it is likely that compensation systems will not fit the organizations in which they must operate and, as a result, their cost effectiveness will decrease.

Particularly vulnerable in the future is the ability of pay systems to motivate. It is difficult to administer performance-based pay when a strong requirement exists for openness and due process. It is all too easy under these conditions to simply give up the idea of performance-based pay and to pay entirely on the basis of seniority, job content, and job level. If this happens in the future, and it seems likely that it will, the costs in terms of organizational effectiveness and productivity are likely to be high. Pay remains one potentially effective motivator in a society where work and organizational effectiveness are becoming less central to many individuals. Given this, it seems a shame to abandon one potential aid to increased organizational effectiveness and individual satisfaction.

Not listed in Table 13.3 is the large number of traditional pay practices that do not fit or contribute to any of the four characteristics. For example, the distinction between hourly and salaried employees, subjective performance evaluation for the purpose of giving merit pay increases, and standard benefit programs all receive "no" on these four characteristics. The fact that they and many others do not contribute does not mean they should be stopped. It does, however, raise questions about their desirability, particularly if they are part of a system which contains none of the practices listed in Table 13.3. Those organizations which have completely failed to build elements of individualization, due process, performance-based pay, and equality into their pay systems are, according to this analysis, out of touch with their environments and getting more so all the time. They need to seriously consider change.

In some respects, the list of practices presented in Table 13.3 is an impressive one. Just getting some of them installed and operating in most large organizations would constitute an enormous change effort—one which needs to be managed carefully and well. Otherwise, the result is likely to be chaos. The implications of this point seem clear: pay system changes need to be treated as major interventions in organizations and they need to be managed accordingly. Although organization development experts may not have a great deal to contribute in the pay system design area, they should have a lot to say about the design of the change process.

Finally, a note of caution: In no way should the pay practices listed in Table 13.3 be considered a list of the changes that each organization should try to put into place. They are not intended as an outline for a pay system. They are simply a list of some pay practices which are congruent with what have been identified as four key characteristics that pay systems increasingly should have. The way to treat the list is as a check list of possible changes which should be used as part of a diagnostic change effort that involves looking at what will work in a particular organization and which considers how the different parts of the pay system fit together.

SUMMARY AND CONCLUSIONS

The need for new approaches to pay administration is not a new one, nor will it ever go away. As society changes, so must its organizations; as organizations change, so must their pay systems. This means that there will always be a need for new pay systems, and that today's effective pay system can quickly become tomorrow's ineffective one. What constitutes an effective pay system is therefore a moving target and more likely to be a process than an end state.

APPENDIX A
THE EXPECTANCY THEORY MODEL
IN MORE TECHNICAL TERMS[1]

A person's motivation to exert effort toward a specific level of performance is based on his or her perceptions of associations between actions and outcomes. The critical perceptions which contribute to motivation are graphically presented in Figure A.1. These perceptions can be defined as follows:

1. The effort-to-performance expectancy ($E \rightarrow P$): This refers to the person's subjective probability about the likelihood that he or she can perform at a given level, or that effort on his or her part will lead to successful performance. This term can be thought of as varying from 0 to 1. In general, the less likely a person feels that he or she can perform at a given level, the less likely he or she will be to try to perform at that level. A person's $E \rightarrow P$ probabilities are also strongly influenced by each situation and by previous experience in that and similar situations.

---

1. From D. A. Nadler and E. E. Lawler, "Motivation: A Diagnostic Approach." In *Perspectives on Behavior in Organizations,* edited by J. R. Hackman, E. E. Lawler, and L. W. Porter. New York: McGraw-Hill, 1977.

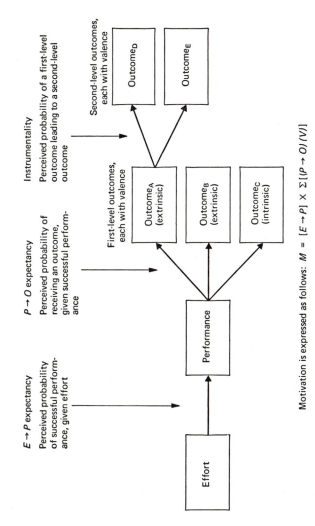

Motivation is expressed as follows: $M = [E \rightarrow P] \times \Sigma [(P \rightarrow O) (V)]$

Figure A.1   Major terms in expectancy theory

2. The performance-to-outcomes expectancy $(P \rightarrow O)$ and valence (V): This refers to a combination of a number of beliefs about what the outcomes of successful performance will be and the value or attractiveness of these outcomes to the individual. Valence is considered to vary from +1 (very desirable) to −1 (very undesirable) and the performance-to-outcomes probabilities to vary from +1 (performance sure to lead to outcome) to 0 (performance not related to outcome). In general, the more likely a person feels that performance will lead to valent outcomes, the more likely he or she will be to try to perform at the required level.

3. Instrumentality: As Figure A.1 indicates, a single level of performance can be associated with a number of different outcomes, each having a certain degree of valence. Some outcomes are valent because they have direct value or attractiveness. Some outcomes, however, have valence because they are seen as leading to (or being "instrumental" for) the attainment of other "second level" outcomes which have direct value or attractiveness.

4. Intrinsic and extrinsic outcomes: Some outcomes are seen as occurring directly as a result of performing the task itself and are outcomes which the individual thus gives to himself (i.e., feelings of accomplishment, creativity, etc.). These are called "intrinsic" outcomes. Other outcomes that are associated with performance are provided or mediated by external factors (the organization, the supervisor, the work group, etc.). These outcomes are called "extrinsic" outcomes.

Along with the graphic representation of these terms presented in Figure A.1, there is a simplified formula for combining these perceptions to arrive at a term expressing the relative level of motivation to exert effort toward performance at a given level. The formula expresses these relationships:

1. The person's motivation to perform is determined by the $P \rightarrow O$ expectancy multiplied by the valence (V) of the outcome. The valence of the first order outcome subsumes the instrumentalities and valences of second order outcomes. The relationship is multiplicative since there is no motivation to perform if either of the terms is zero.

2. Since a level of performance has multiple outcomes associated with it, the products of all probability-times-valence combinations are added together for all the outcomes that are seen as related to the specific performance.

3. This term (the summed $P \rightarrow O$ expectancies times valences) is then multiplied by the $E \rightarrow P$ expectancy. Again the multiplicative relationship indicates that if either term is zero, motivation is zero.

4. In summary, the strength of a person's motivation to perform effectively is influenced by (1) the person's belief that effort can be converted into performance, and (2) the net attractiveness of the events that are perceived to stem from good performance.

So far, all the terms have referred to the individual's perceptions which result in motivation and thus an intention to behave in a certain way. Figure A.2 is a simplified representation of the total model, showing how these intentions get translated into actual behavior.[2] The model envisions the following sequence of events:

1. First, the strength of a person's motivation to perform correctly is most directly reflected in his or her effort—how hard he or she works. This effort expenditure may or may not result in good performance, since at least two factors must be right if effort is to be converted into performance. First, the person must possess the necessary abilities in order to perform the job well. Unless both ability and effort are high, there cannot be good performance. A second factor is the person's perception of how his or her effort can best be converted into performance. It is assumed that this perception is learned by the individual on the basis of previous experience in similar situations. This "how to do it" perception can obviously vary widely in accuracy, and—where erroneous perceptions exist—performance is low even though effort or motivation may be high.

2. Second, when performance occurs, certain amounts of outcomes are obtained by the individual. Intrinsic outcomes, not being mediated by outside forces, tend to occur regularly as a result of performance,

---

2. For a more detailed statement of the model, see Lawler (1973).

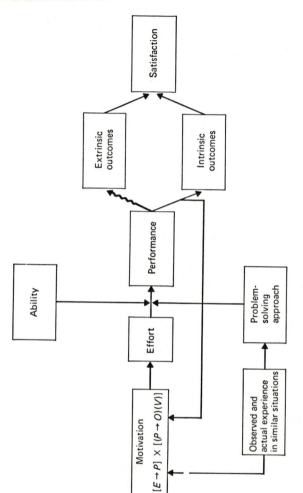

Figure A.2 Simplified expectancy-theory model of behavior

while extrinsic outcomes may or may not accrue to the individual (indicated by the wavy line in the model).

3. Third, as a result of the obtaining of outcomes and the perceptions of the relative value of the outcomes obtained, the individual has a positive or negative affective response (a level of satisfaction or dissatisfaction).

4. Fourth, the model indicates that events which occur influence future behavior by altering the $E{\rightarrow}P$, $P{\rightarrow}O$, and V perceptions. This process is represented by the feedback loops running from actual behavior back to motivation.

APPENDIX B
MEASURING MOTIVATION USING
EXPECTANCY THEORY[1]

Expectancy theory suggests that it is useful to measure the attitudes individuals have in order to diagnose motivational problems. Such measurement helps the manager to understand why employees are motivated or not, what the strength of motivation is in different parts of the organization, and how effective different rewards are for motivating performance. A short version of a questionnaire used to measure motivation in organizations is included here.[2] Basically, three different questions need to be asked (see Tables B.1, B.2, and B.3).

USING THE QUESTIONNAIRE RESULTS

The results from this questionnaire can be used to calculate a *work-motivation score*. A score can be calculated for each individual and scores can be combined for groups of individuals. The procedure for obtaining a work-motivation score is as follows:

1. From D. A. Nadler and E. E. Lawler, "Motivation: A Diagnostic Approach." In *Perspectives on Behavior in Organizations,* edited by J. R. Hackman, E. E. Lawler, and L. W. Porter. New York: McGraw-Hill, 1977.
2. For a complete version of the questionnaire and supporting documentation, see D. A. Nadler, C. Cammann, G. D. Jenkins, and E. E. Lawler, eds. *The Michigan Organizational Assessment Package* (Progress Report II). Ann Arbor, Mich.: Survey Research Center, 1975.

Table B.1

Question 1: Here are some things that could happen to people if they do their jobs *especially well*. How likely is it that each of these things would happen if you performed your job *especially well*?

		Not at all likely		Somewhat likely		Quite likely		Extremely likely
a	You will get a bonus or pay increase	(1)	(2)	(3)	(4)	(5)	(6)	(7)
b	You will feel better about yourself as a person	(1)	(2)	(3)	(4)	(5)	(6)	(7)
c	You will have an opportunity to develop your skills and abilities..	(1)	(2)	(3)	(4)	(5)	(6)	(7)
d	You will have better job security.................	(1)	(2)	(3)	(4)	(5)	(6)	(7)
e	You will be given chances to learn new things	(1)	(2)	(3)	(4)	(5)	(6)	(7)
f	You will be promoted or get a better job	(1)	(2)	(3)	(4)	(5)	(6)	(7)
g	You will get a feeling that you've accomplished something worthwhile...............................	(1)	(2)	(3)	(4)	(5)	(6)	(7)
h	You will have more freedom on your job..........	(1)	(2)	(3)	(4)	(5)	(6)	(7)
i	You will be respected by the people you work with ..	(1)	(2)	(3)	(4)	(5)	(6)	(7)
j	Your supervisor will praise you..................	(1)	(2)	(3)	(4)	(5)	(6)	(7)
k	The people you work with will be friendly with you...	(1)	(2)	(3)	(4)	(5)	(6)	(7)

1. For each of the possible positive outcomes listed in questions 1 and 2, multiply the score for the outcome on question 1 ($P \rightarrow O$ expectancies) by the corresponding score on question 2 (valences of outcomes). Thus, score 1a would be multiplied by score 2a, score 1b by score 2b, etc.

2. All of the 1 times 2 products should be added together to get a total of all expectancies times valences_____.

3. The total should be divided by the number of pairs (in this case, eleven) to get an average expectancy-times-valence score _____.

4. The scores from question 3 ($E \rightarrow P$ expectancies) should be added together and then divided by three to get an average effort-to-performance expectancy score _____.

5. Multiply the score obtained in step 3 (the average expectancy times valence) by the score obtained in step *d* (the average $E \rightarrow P$ expectancy score) to obtain a total work-motivation score _____.

Table B.2

Question 2: Different people want different things from their work. Here is a list of things a person could have on his or her job. How *important* is each of the following to you?

How Important Is . . . ?	Moderately important or less				Quite important		Extremely im...
a The amount of pay you get	(1)	(2)	(3)	(4)	(5)	(6)	(7)
b The chances you have to do something that makes you feel good about yourself as a person	(1)	(2)	(3)	(4)	(5)	(6)	(7)
c The opportunity to develop your skills and abilities . .	(1)	(2)	(3)	(4)	(5)	(6)	(7)
d The amount of job security you have	(1)	(2)	(3)	(4)	(5)	(6)	(7)

How Important Is . . . ?							
e The chances you have to learn new things	(1)	(2)	(3)	(4)	(5)	(6)	(7)
f Your chances for getting a promotion or getting a better job	(1)	(2)	(3)	(4)	(5)	(6)	(7)
g The chances you have to accomplish something worthwhile.	(1)	(2)	(3)	(4)	(5)	(6)	(7)
h The amount of freedom you have on your job.	(1)	(2)	(3)	(4)	(5)	(6)	(7)

How Important Is . . . ?							
i The respect you receive from the people you work with	(1)	(2)	(3)	(4)	(5)	(6)	(7)
j The praise you get from your supervisor.	(1)	(2)	(3)	(4)	(5)	(6)	(7)
k The friendliness of the people you work with	(1)	(2)	(3)	(4)	(5)	(6)	(7)

Table B.3

Question 3: Below you will see a number of pairs of factors that look like this:

Warm weather→sweating   (1) (2) (3) (4) (5) (6) (7)

You are to indicate by checking the appropriate number to the right of each pair how often it is true for **you** personally that the first factor leads to the second on **your job**. Remember, for each pair, indicate how often it is true by checking the box under the response which seems most accurate.

	Never	Sometimes		Often		Almost always
a Working hard → high productivity	(1)	(2)	(3)	(4)	(5)	(6)	(7)
b Working hard → doing my job well	(1)	(2)	(3)	(4)	(5)	(6)	(7)
c Working hard → good job performance	(1)	(2)	(3)	(4)	(5)	(6)	(7)

ADDITIONAL COMMENTS ON THE
WORK-MOTIVATION SCORE

A number of important points should be kept in mind when using the questionnaire to get a work-motivation score. First, the questions presented here are just a short version of a larger and more comprehensive questionnaire. For more detail, the articles and publications referred to here and in the text should be consulted. Second, this is a general questionnaire. Since it is hard to anticipate in a general questionnaire what may be valent outcomes in each situation, the individual manager may want to add additional outcomes to questions 1 and 2. Third, it is important to remember that questionnaire results can be influenced by the feelings people have when they fill out the questionnaire. The use of the questionnaire as outlined above assumes a certain level of trust between manager and subordinates. People filling out questionnaires need to know what is going to be done with their answers and usually need to be assured of the confidentiality of their responses. Finally, the research indicates that, in many cases, the score obtained by simply averaging all the responses to question 1 (the $P \rightarrow O$ expectancies) will be as useful as the fully calculated work-motivation score. In each situation, the manager should experiment and find out whether the additional information in questions 2 and 3 aid in motivational diagnosis.

APPENDIX C
QUESTIONNAIRE ITEMS CONCERNING PAY

Satisfaction/Equity	*Response Alternative*
My fringe benefits are fair.	a
Other companies in this area have better fringe benefits than this one does.	a
Considering what my co-workers make, my fringe benefits are fair.	a
I am very dissatisfied with my fringe benefits.	a
My fringe benefit package here is the best I have ever had.	a
My pay is fair, considering what other people in this organization are paid.	a
This organization pays a fair wage.	a
My pay is fair for the kind of job I do.	a
I am very content with the way management handles pay.	a
My pay is fair.	a
Considering your skills and the effort you put into your work, how satisfied are you with your incentive awards?	e

Satisfaction/Equity	Response Alternative
All in all, how satisfied are you with your total cash compensation?	e
I am very dissatisfied with my pay.	a
Other companies in this area pay better than this one does.	a
I don't make the kind of money I should for the job I do.	a
Considering my skills and effort, I make a fair wage.	a
My pay is fair, given what my co-workers make.	a
My pay is fair, considering what other places in this area pay.	a
My pay is fair.	a
My pay is fair, considering what other people in this organization are paid.	a
I am very happy with the amount of money I make.	a
All in all, my pay is about what it ought to be.	a
This organization pays a fair wage.	a
My pay is fair for the kind of job I do.	a
Considering my skills and the effort I put into my work, I am very satisfied with my pay.	a

Understanding	*Response Alternative*
I understand what the objectives of the pay plan are.	a
I have a real understanding of how the pay system works.	a
Procedures regarding the pay plan are not generally well understood by participants.	a

Understanding	*Response Alternative*
An attempt should be made to increase members' understanding of the pay plan.	a
I understand how my last salary action was determined.	a

Communications	*Response Alternative*
The last time a salary action was made for you, to what extent did you and your supervisor discuss it.	c

Effectiveness/Objectives	*Response Alternative*
The pay plan fulfills its objectives well.	a
The attraction and retention of competent employees is fostered by the pay plan.	a
The pay plan significantly contributes to the motivation of participants.	a
The pay plan helps foster interdependency and collaboration.	a
XYZ does a good job of obtaining salary market data.	a
I feel the pay system should be kept as it is.	a

Performance/Goals	*Response Alternative*
Goal setting is done effectively between me and my supervisor.	a
After goal setting is done, my supervisor reviews them with me during the year.	a
My goals are distinctive and specific.	a
My goals are highly qualitative.	a
My goals are highly quantitative.	a
I am often reluctant to develop definitive goal statements.	a
My annual goals are used to evaluate my performance at the end of the year.	a

Performance/Goals	*Response Alternative*
How much influence do you have in developing your yearly goals?	b
My supervisor meets with me regularly to talk about how well I'm meeting my goals.	a

Performance Measurement/Appraisal

I know the criteria used to judge my performance.	a
My supervisor does a good job of judging my performance.	a

To what extent was the actual evaluation of your performance based on the following?

The results I achieved in my job	c
My job-related behaviors	c
My skills and abilities	c
My personality and personal characteristics	c
Things I can control	c
Predetermined goals	c
Specific incidents	c
General impressions	c
My self-appraisal completed before the interview	c

The next set of questions focuses on the subject matter, or the content of the appraisal interview. How much was each of these areas discussed?

My career and personal development	c
Specific career development goals for me	c
Strengths in my past performance	c
Weaknesses in my past performance	c
Ways to improve my performance	c
Things my supervisor could do to aid me in performing better	c
Setting future performance goals for me	c
My salary	c

Performance Measurement/Appraisal	*Response Alternative*
To what extent did you and your supervisor review your performance before a recommendation for your salary action was made?	c
This organization has measures that show what our productivity is.	a
Performance appraisals are fairly and honestly done in this organization.	a

Pay/Performance

My individual performance actually has little impact on my incentive award.	a
My incentive award should be based on my individual performance.	a
To what extent does your performance have an impact on the size of your incentive award?	c
To what extent is the size of your incentive award based upon the attainment of your preestablished goals?	c
For the purpose of determining your pay, how important is . . .	
Your performance	d
The performance of your division	d
Corporate performance	d
Subjective perceptions of your supervision	d
Your education and experience	d
The amount of responsibility and pressure on your job	d
Increased productivity means higher pay to employees.	a
When our performance measures increase, we get a bonus.	a
My performance actually has little impact on my salary action determination.	a

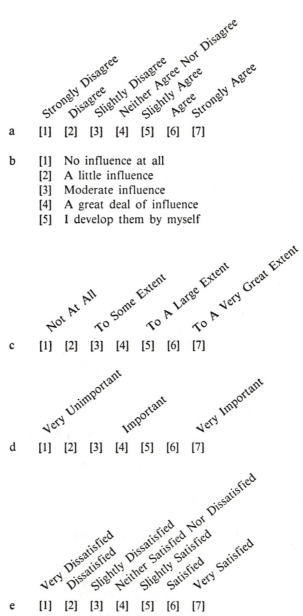

a   [1]   [2]   [3]   [4]   [5]   [6]   [7]
     Strongly Disagree / Disagree / Slightly Disagree / Neither Agree Nor Disagree / Slightly Agree / Agree / Strongly Agree

b   [1]   No influence at all
     [2]   A little influence
     [3]   Moderate influence
     [4]   A great deal of influence
     [5]   I develop them by myself

c   [1]   [2]   [3]   [4]   [5]   [6]   [7]
     Not At All / To Some Extent / To A Large Extent / To A Very Great Extent

d   [1]   [2]   [3]   [4]   [5]   [6]   [7]
     Very Unimportant / Important / Very Important

e   [1]   [2]   [3]   [4]   [5]   [6]   [7]
     Very Dissatisfied / Dissatisfied / Slightly Dissatisfied / Neither Satisfied Nor Dissatisfied / Slightly Satisfied / Satisfied / Very Satisfied

REFERENCES

Adams, J. S. 1965. Injustice in social exchange. In *Advances in experimental social psychology,* vol. 2, ed. L. Berkowitz, pp. 267–299. New York: Academic Press.

Alderfer, C. P. 1969. An empirical test of a new theory of human needs. *Organizational Behavior and Human Performance.* 4: 142–175.

Arthur Friedman's Outrage. Employees decide their own pay. *The Washington Post.* February 23, 1975, pp. C1 and C8.

Bachman, J. G., and Johnston, L. D. 1979. The freshman, 1979. *Psychology Today* 13: 78–87.

Beckhard, R., and Harris, R. 1977. *Organizational transitions.* Reading, Mass.: Addison-Wesley.

Beer, M., and Gery, G. J. 1968. Pay systems preferences and their correlates. Paper presented at APA convention, San Francisco, August 1968.

Belcher, D. W. 1974. *Compensation administration.* Englewood Cliffs, N. J.: Prentice-Hall.

Bullock, R. J., and Lawler, E. E. 1980. Incentives and gainsharing—stimuli for productivity. Paper presented at American Productivity Center, Productivity Research Conference, Houston, April 22, 1980.

Cammann, C., and Lawler, E. E. 1973. Employee reactions to a pay incentive plan. *Journal of Applied Psychology* 58: 163–172.

Campbell, J. P.; Dunnette, M. D.; Lawler, E. E.; and Weick, K. 1970. *Managerial behavior, performances and effectiveness.* New York: McGraw-Hill.

Cofer, C. N., and Appley, M. H. 1964. *Motivation: Theory and research.* New York: Wiley.

Davis, S. M., and Lawrence, P. R. 1977. *Matrix.* Reading, Mass.: Addison-Wesley.

Dowling, W. 1977. Consensus management at graphic controls. *Organizational Dynamics* 5: 22–47.

Dunnette, M. D., and Borman, W. C. 1979. Personnel selection and classification systems. In *Annual review of psychology,* vol. 30, ed. M. R. Rosenzweig and L. W. Porter. Palo Alto, Calif.: Annual Reviews.

Ewing, D. E. 1978. *Freedom inside the organization.* New York: Dutton.

Factory, What the factory worker really thinks about his job, unemployment, and industry's profit. *Factory management and maintenance* 105 (1947): 86–92.

Fein, M. An alternative to traditional managing. In *Handbook of industrial engineering,* ed. G. Salvendy. New York: Wiley, in press.

Fragner, B. N. 1975. Employees' "cafeteria" offers insurance options. *Harvard Business Review* 53: 2–4.

Frost, Carl F.; Wakeley, John H.; and Ruh, Robert A. 1974. *The Scanlon Plan for organization development: Identity, participation, and equity.* East Lansing: Michigan State University Press.

Galbraith, J. R., and Nathanson, D. A. 1978. *Strategy implementation: The role of structure and process.* St. Paul: West.

Gillespie, J. J. 1948. *Free expression in industry.* London: Pilot Press.

Goodman, P. 1979. *Assessing organizational change: The Rushton quality of work experiment.* New York: Wiley Interscience.

Greiner, L. Evolution and revolution as organizations grow. 1972. *Harvard Business Review* 50: 37–46.

Hackman, J. R., and Lawler, E. E. 1971. Employee reactions to job characteristics. *Journal of Applied Psychology* 55: 259–286.

Hackman, J. R., and Oldham, G. R. 1980. *Work redesign.* Reading, Mass.: Addison-Wesley.

Helfgott, R. 1962. *Group wage incentives: Experience with the Scanlon Plan.* New York: Industrial Relation Counselors, Industrial Relations Memo, No. 14.

Henderson, R. I. 1979. *Compensation management: Rewarding performance,* 2nd. ed. Reston, Va.: Reston.

Hinrichs, J. R. 1969. Correlates of employee evaluations of pay increases. *Journal of Applied Psychology* 58: 481–489.

Howell, W. J. 1967. A new look at profit sharing, pension, and productivity plans. *Business Management* (December): 26–42.

Hulme, R. D., and Bevan, R. V. 1975. The blue collar worker goes on salary. *Harvard Business Review* 53: 104–112.

Jaques, E. 1961. *Equitable payment.* New York: John Wiley and Sons, Inc.

Jaques, E. 1979. Taking time seriously in evaluating jobs. *Harvard Business Review* 57: 124–132.

Kahn, R. L., and Quinn, R. P. 1970. Role stress: A framework for analysis. In *Occupational mental health,* ed. A. McLean. 1964. New York: Rand McNally.

Kahn, R. L.; Wolfe, D. M.; Quinn, R. P.; Snoek, J. D. 1964. *Organizational stress: Studies in role conflict and ambiguity.* New York: Wiley.

Kane, J., and Lawler, E. E. 1978. Methods of peer assessment. *Psychological Bulletin* 85: 555–586.

Kane, J., and Lawler, E. E. 1979. Performance appraisal effectiveness. In *Research in organizational behavior,* vol. 1, ed. B. Staw, pp. 425–478. Greenwich, Conn.: JAI Press.

Katz, D., and Kahn, R. L. 1966. *The social psychology of organizations.* New York: Wiley.

Katz, D., and Kahn, R. L. 1978. *The social psychology of organizations,* 2nd ed. New York: Wiley.

Kerr, S. 1976. Overcoming the dysfunctions of MBO. *Management By Objectives* 5: 13–19.

Landy, F. J.; Barnes, J. L.; and Murphy, K. R. 1978. Correlates of perceived fairness and accuracy of performance evaluation. *Journal of Applied Psychology* 62: 751–754.

Landy, F. J., and Farr, J. L. 1980. Performance rating. *Psychological Bulletin* 87: 72–107.

Latham, G. P., and Yukl, G. A. 1975. A review of research on the application of goal setting in organizations. *Academy of Management Journal* 18: 824–845.

Lawler, E. E. 1966. Managers' attitudes toward how their pay is and should be determined. *Journal of Applied Psychology* 50: 273–279.

Lawler, E. E. 1971. *Pay and organizational effectiveness: A psychological view.* New York: McGraw-Hill.

Lawler, E. E. 1972. Secrecy and the need to know. In *Readings in managerial motivation and compensation,* ed. M. Dunnette, R. House, and H. Tosi, pp. 362–371. East Lansing: Michigan State University Press.

Lawler, E. E. 1977. Reward systems. In *Improving life at work,* ed. J. R. Hackman and J. L. Suttle, pp. 163–226. Santa Monica, Calif.: Goodyear.

Lawler, E. E. 1978. The new plant revolution. *Organizational Dynamics* 6: 2–12.

Lawler, E. E. 1982. Creating high involvement work organizations. In *Perspectives on organizational behavior,* 2nd ed., ed. J. R. Hackman, E. E. Lawler, and L. W. Porter. New York: McGraw-Hill.

Lawler, E. E., and Bullock, R. J. 1978. Pay and organizational change. *Personnel Administrator* 23: 32–36.

Lawler, E. E., and Cammann, C. 1972. What makes a work group successful? In *The failure of success,* ed. A. J. Marrow, pp. 122–130. New York: Amacom.

Lawler, E. E., and Hackman, J. R. 1969. The impact of employee participation in the development of pay incentive plans: A field experiment. *Journal of Applied Psychology* 53: 467–471.

Lawler, E. E., and Jenkins, G. D. 1976. *Employee participation in pay plan development.* Unpublished technical report to Department of Labor, Ann Arbor, Mich.

Lawler, E. E., and Levin, E. 1968. Union officers' perceptions of members' pay preferences. *Industrial and Labor Relations Review* 21: 509–517.

Lawler, E. E., and Olsen, R. 1977. Designing reward systems for new organizations. *Personnel* 54 (5): 48–60.

Lawler, E. E., and Rhode, J. G. 1976. *Information and control in organizations.* Santa Monica, Calif.: Goodyear.

Lawrence, P. R., and Lorsch, J. W. 1969. *Developing organizations: Prognosis and action.* Reading, Mass.: Addison-Wesley.

Lazer, R. I., and Wikstron, W. S. 1977. *Appraising managerial performance: Current practices and future directions.* New York: Conference Board, Report 723.

Leavitt, H. J. 1965. Applied organizational change in industry: Structural, technological, and humanistic approaches. In *Handbook of organizations,* ed. J. G. March, pp. 1144–1170. Chicago: Rand McNally.

Lesieur, F. G., ed. 1958. *The Scanlon Plan.* Cambridge: M.I.T Press.

Lesieur, F. G., and Puckett, E. S. 1969. The Scanlon Plan has proved itself. *Harvard Business Review* 47: 109–118.

Levinson, H. 1970. Management by whose objectives? *Harvard Business Review* 48: 125–134.

Lincoln, J. F. 1951. *Incentive management.* Cleveland: Lincoln Electric Company.

Lindholm, R. 1974. Payment by results—Leading system in production development. Paper presented at EFPS-EAPM Conference, Amsterdam, October.

Linestad, H., and Norstedt, J. 1972. *Autonomous groups and payment by results.* Stockholm: Swedish Employers' Confederation.

Locke, E., and Schweiger, D. 1979. Partners in decision making: One more look. In *Research in organizational behavior,* vol. 1, ed. B. Staw. Greenwich, Conn.: JAI Press.

Locke, E. A. 1976. The nature and causes of job satisfaction. 1976. In *Handbook of industrial and organizational psychology,* ed. M. Dunnette, pp. 1297–1349. Chicago: Rand McNally.

Locke, E. A. 1979. How to motivate employees. Paper presented at NATO conference on changes in nature and quality of working life. Thessaloniki, Greece, August 19–24, 1979.

Macy, B., and Mirvis, P. 1976. A methodology for assessment of quality of worklife and organizational effectiveness in behavior-economic terms. *Administrative Science Quarterly* 21: 212–226.

McGregor, D. 1957. An uneasy look at performance appraisal. *Harvard Business Review* 35: 89–94.

McGregor, D. 1960. *The human side of enterprise.* New York: McGraw-Hill.

McKersie, R. B. 1963. Wage payment methods of the future. *British Journal of Industrial Relations* 1: 191–212.

Metzger, B. L. 1975. *Profit sharing in 38 large companies,* vol. I. Evanston: Profit Sharing Research Foundation.

Metzger, B. L. 1978. *Profit sharing in 38 large companies,* vol. II. Evanston, Ill: Profit Sharing Research Foundation.

Meyer, H. H. 1975. The pay-for performance dilemma. *Organizational Dynamics* 3: 39–50.

Meyer, H. H.; Kay, E.; and French, J. R. P., Jr. 1965. Split roles in performance appraisal. *Harvard Business Review* 43: 123–129.

Milkovich, G. T., and Anderson, P. H. 1972. Management compensation and secrecy. *Personnel Psychology* 25: 293–302.

Mobley, W. H.; Hand, H. H.; Meglino, B. M.; and Griffeth, R. W. 1979. Review and conceptual analysis of the employee turnover process. *Psychological Bulletin* 86: 493–522.

Moore, B. E., and Goodman, P. S. 1973. Factor affecting the impact of a company-wide incentive program on productivity. Report submitted to the National Commission on Productivity, January, 1973.

Moore, B. E., and Ross, T. L. 1978. *The Scanlon Way to Improved Productivity.* New York: Wiley-Interscience.

Nadler, D. A. 1977. *Feedback and organization development.* Reading, Mass: Addison-Wesley.

Nadler, D. A., and Lawler, E. E. 1977. Motivation: A diagnostic approach. In *Perspectives on behavior in organizations,* ed. J. R. Hackman, E. E. Lawler, and L. W. Porter, pp. 26–38. New York: McGraw-Hill.

Nadler, D. A., and Tushman, M. L. 1977. A diagnostic model for organizational behavior. In *Perspectives on behavior in organizations,* ed. J. R. Hackman, E. E. Lawler, and L. W. Porter, pp. 83–100. New York: McGraw-Hill.

Nadler, D. A.; Hackman, J. R.; and Lawler, E. E. 1979. *Managing organizational behavior.* Boston: Little, Brown.

Nash, A. N. and Carroll, S. J. 1975. *The management of compensation.* Monterey, Calif.: Brooks/Cole.

Nealey, S. 1963. Pay and benefit preference. *Industrial Relations* 3: 17–28.

Nievea, V.; Perkins, D. N. T.; and Lawler E. E. 1978. Improving the quality of life at work: An evaluation of the Centerton experience. Unpublished technical report to Department of Labor.

Patchen, M. 1961. *The choice of wage companions.* Englewood Cliffs, N. J.: Prentice-Hall.

Patten, T. H. 1977. *Pay: Employee compensation and incentive plans.* New York: Free Press.

Patten, T. H., and Fraser, K. L. 1975. Using the organizational rewards system as an OD lever: Case study of a data-based intervention. *Journal of Applied Behavioral Science* 11: 457–474.

Porter, L. W., and Lawler, E. E. 1968. *Attitudes and performance.* Homewood, Ill.: Irwin-Dorsey.

Porter, L. W.; Lawler, E. E.; and Hackman, J. R. 1975. *Behavior in organizations.* New York: McGraw-Hill.

Porter, L. W., and Steers, R. M. 1973. Organizational, work and personal factors in employee turnover and absenteeism. *Psychological Bulletin* 80: 151–176.

Quinn, R., and Staines, G. 1979. *The 1977 quality of employment survey.* Ann Arbor, Mich.: Institute for Social Research.

Renwick, P. A., and Lawler, E. E. 1978. What you really want from your job. *Psychology Today* 12: 53-66.

Scanlon, J. N. 1949. Talk on union management relations, Industrial Relations Center. *Proceedings of conference on productivity,* University of Wisconsin.

Scheflen, K. C.; Lawler, E. E.; and Hackman, J. R. 1971. Long-term impact of employee participation in the development of pay incentive plans: A field experiment revisited. *Journal of Applied Psychology* 55: 182-186.

Schlachtmeyer, A. S., and Bogart, R. B. 1979. Employee-choice benefits—Can employees handle it? *Compensation Review* 11: 12-19.

Schultz, G. P. 1958. Worker participation on production problems; a discussion of experience with the Scanlon Plan. *Personnel* 28: 201-211.

Schwab, D. P.; Heneman, H. G., and DeCotiis, T. A. 1975. Behaviorally anchored rating scales: A review of the literature. *Personnel Psychology* 28: 549-562.

Scott, R. C. 1977. Productivity sharing incentive programs: Are they for you? *Furniture Design and Manufacturing* (March).

Scott, R. C. 1978. Automatic steps toward reduced costs. *Industry* 43.

Sheridan, J. H. 1975. Should your production workers be salaried? *Industry Week* 184: 28-37.

Smith, C. A. 1979. Lump sum increases—A creditable change strategy. *Personnel* 56: 59-63.

Steele, F. 1975. *The open organization.* Reading, Mass.: Addison-Wesley.

Steers, R. M., and Rhodes, S. R. 1978. Major influences on employee attendance: A process model. *Journal of Applied Psychology* 63: 391-407.

Tannenbaum, R., and Schmidt, W. 1958. How to choose a leadership pattern. *Harvard Business Review* 36: 95-101.

Tosi, H. L.; House, R. J.; and Dunnette, M. D., eds. 1972. *Managerial motivation and compensation.* East Lansing: Michigan State University Business Studies.

Vroom, V. H. 1964. *Work and motivation.* New York: Wiley.

Vroom, V. H., and Yetton, P. W. 1973. *Leadership and decision-making.* Pittsburg: University of Pittsburg Press.

Wahba, M. A, and Birdwell, L. 1976. Maslow reconsidered: A review of research on the need hierarchy theory. *Organizational Behavior and Human Performance* 15: 212-240.

Wall Street Journal. 1979. Vol. C., no. 1, p. 1.

Walton, R. E. 1972. How to counter alienation in the plant. *Harvard Business Review* 50: 70-81.

Walton, R. E. 1975. The diffusion of new work structures: Explaining why success didn't take. *Organizational Dynamics* 3: 3-22.

Walton, R. E., and Schlesinger, L. A. 1979. Do supervisors thrive in participative work systems? *Organizational Dynamics* 8: 25-38.

White, J. K. 1979. The Scanlon Plan: Causes and correlates of success. *Academy of Management Journal* 22: 292-312.

Whyte, W. F., ed. 1955. *Money and motivation: An analysis of incentives in industry.* New York: Harper.

Woodward, J. 1965. *Industrial organization: Theory and practice.* London: Oxford.

Work in America. 1973. Cambridge: M.I.T. Press.

Zager, R. 1978. Managing guaranteed employment. *Harvard Business Review* 56: 103-115.